EVERYBODY SING !!!!

Everybody Sing!

COMMUNITY SINGING IN
THE AMERICAN PICTURE PALACE

ESTHER M. MORGAN-ELLIS

THE UNIVERSITY OF GEORGIA PRESS   ATHENS

Publication of this book was supported by the AMS 75 PAYS
Endowment of the American Musicological Society, funded in
part by the National Endowment for the Humanities and the
Andrew W. Mellon Foundation.

A portion of chapter 5 originally appeared as "Edward Meikel
and Community Singing in a Neighborhood Picture Palace,
1925–1929" in *American Music* and is reproduced here courtesy
of the University of Illinois Press.

© 2018 by the University of Georgia Press
Athens, Georgia 30602
www.ugapress.org
All rights reserved
Designed by Erin Kirk New
Set in 10.5 on 14 Minion Pro
Printed and bound by Thomson-Shore
The paper in this book meets the guidelines for
permanence and durability of the Committee on
Production Guidelines for Book Longevity of the
Council on Library Resources.

Most University of Georgia Press titles are
available from popular e-book vendors.

Printed in the United States of America
21 20 19 18 17 C 5 4 3 2 1

Library of Congress Cataloging-in-Publication Data

Names: Morgan-Ellis, Esther M., 1984– author.
Title: Everybody sing! : community singing in the American
    picture palace / Esther M. Morgan-Ellis.
Description: Athens : The University of Georgia Press, [2018] |
    Includes bibliographical references and index.
Identifiers: LCCN 2017023353 | ISBN 9780820352046 (hardcover :
    alk. paper) | ISBN 9780820352039 (ebook)
Subjects: LCSH: Motion picture audiences—United States—
    History—20th century. | Community music—United States—
    History and criticism. | Motion pictures—Social aspects—
    United States—History—20th century.
Classification: LCC PN1995.9.A8 M67 2018 | DDC 302.23/43—dc23
    LC record available at https://lccn.loc.gov/2017023353

This book is dedicated to my Oma,

Dorothea Ammann Parés Morgan,

who always believed I could do anything.

CONTENTS

ACKNOWLEDGMENTS

My interest in picture palace community singing developed while I was a graduate student at Yale University. This book is based on the dissertation I wrote there, but it cannot be considered a mere revision. It is the completion of a project that as a doctoral candidate I had only begun. During four additional years of research I broadened my understanding of the cultural context for community singing, investigated additional archives and trade press sources, caught up with new scholarship on the subject, and corrected one or two misunderstandings. The story of this book is populated with wonderful people who contributed at all stages and to whom I owe a great debt of thanks.

I discovered the existence of palace-era community singing when I encountered the Fleischer sing-along films while studying for my comprehensive exams. One of my exam topics was cartoon music, for which I must thank the entire Yale Music Department faculty; not every program would allow a student the latitude to pursue such a "frivolous" course of study. I am also grateful to my topic advisor, Michael Veal, for overseeing my exam preparation. As I was groping for a dissertation topic, I encountered the earlier sing-along practice of the illustrated song. I eventually wrote a proposal for a dissertation that was to compare repertoire and imagery in the illustrated song and Fleischer sing-along films—or something like that. Committee members Sarah Weiss and Seth Brodsky were so kind as to approve my prospectus and offer valuable input, while Jim Hepokoski agreed to direct the dissertation.

In this early stage I received assistance from a number of scholars and archivists. In 2009 I visited the MarNan Collection of illustrated songs in Minneapolis, Minnesota, where Margaret Bergh was so very kind as to house me and offer unfettered access to the collection for ten days. She has repeatedly granted me permission to use images from that visit in conference talks, lectures, and recitals, and she worked with Mark Ryan to provide the high-quality scans that appear in this volume. I began to correspond with musicologist Daniel Goldmark, who inaugurated the field of cartoon music studies and is the leading expert. He was very helpful then and has continued to support my work over the years. I also met with film scholar Rick Altman, who gave a talk on campus in 2010. He spoke with me for about an hour, answered some questions I had about his work on illustrated songs, and provided me with additional resources. I obtained digital versions of the existing Fleischer Screen Songs from animation historian Jerry Beck, who also kindly granted permission for me to post some of the films online, while Ray Pointer supplied copies of Song Car-Tunes and provided me with information about where to find extant prints.

As I began to read the trade press, I learned that live theater sing-alongs had not died out with the illustrated song. On the contrary—they had only become more widespread and more interesting. After making this belated discovery, I decided to include a single chapter in my dissertation about organist-led sing-alongs of the 1920s. I presented my preliminary research at the 2010 American Musicological Society conference, where—to the surprise of many—the renowned scholar of ancient and medieval music theory Thomas J. Mathiesen revealed himself to be an expert on all things related to the theater organ. Since our meeting, Tom has been my most valuable resource. He provided resources and feedback as I was writing my dissertation, including the exceptional catalogs he has produced for the slide collections at the Ohio and Embassy Theaters. These reveal his superior knowledge of slide producers, and they are required reading for anyone who wants to pursue further research. Most recently he read and responded in great detail to my book manuscript. We have now been corresponding for six years, and I cannot properly express the enormous impact that he has had on my work.

In my final years of graduate study, it became clear that the topic of picture palace community singing in the 1920s and 1930s had come to eclipse the practices that had first attracted my attention, and I redesigned my dissertation such that illustrated songs and Fleischer films became footnotes to a different story. Jim was so kind as to support my change of plan and to provide extensive commentary on every chapter as it was drafted. At least a dozen of his sentences must live on in this volume, although I have forgotten now which ones they are. I also received excellent feedback from my colleague and writing advisor Lynda Paul, whom I visited obsessively at the Yale Writing Center. I credit her with teaching me how to write, and I still pass on her advice to my students today.

In 2012 I visited the Fox Theatre in Atlanta, where historic collections manager Michele Schuff was very helpful as I spent several days working in the song slide archives. It was my first visit to Georgia, and I never could have guessed that two years later I would be living in Dahlonega, just seventy miles north of Atlanta. In 2016 I visited the American Theatre Organ Society archives in Norman, Oklahoma, in order to peruse their collections of ephemera, scripts, periodicals, and slides. Jeremy Wance, associate director of the American Organ Institute, arranged and guided my visit, and graduate assistant Kaitlynn Eaton was also very helpful both during and after my time there. I would also like to thank my Yale friend and colleague Andrew Schaeffer, who pestered me about visiting the ATOS archives for years, connected me with Jeremy, and gave me a tour of the theater organs housed at the University of Oklahoma.

Several people, including both scholars and enthusiasts, have reached out to me after reading my work and offered valuable assistance. Tom Miller, the grandson of theater organist Bob West, was so kind as to share photographs, correspondence, and personal documents concerning his grandfather. Silent-era film exhibition expert Kathryn Fuller-Seeley provided excellent feedback and recommendations for future research. And film scholar Malcolm Cook generously shared his forthcoming book chapter on singalong films, which had a significant influence on my own discussion of the topic. I also received invaluable assistance from a colleague at the University of North Georgia, Paul Dunlap, who created the color scans of sing-along slides from my collection that appear in the color insert.

I must thank Elizabeth Crowley, formerly of UGA Press, for soliciting the proposal for this book in the summer of 2015. She was very encouraging from the start and helped me through the early stages of the process. When she left UGA, Patrick Allen took over my book and has also been very congenial and supportive. Further thanks are due to Jon Davies and Susan Harris for their persistant helpfulness. I have had a great time working with UGA Press and hope to have another opportunity to do so in the future. I would also like to thank the reviewers who provided feedback on my proposal and manuscript. Their thoughtful insights and suggestions shaped this book.

Finally, I cannot begin to catalog the contributions of my husband, Jura Pintar. He provided feedback on drafts, typeset my dissertation, and prepared all of the grayscale images in this volume. Those things are trivial, however, compared with a decade of unconditional and unceasing support.

INTRODUCTION

During the mid- to late 1920s, millions of Americans participated in sing-alongs every week at their local picture theaters. The theater organist usually led community singing as part of his or her solo presentation, during which lyrics were projected from glass slides onto the screen. The sing-along was one of many short, independent acts that made up a varied program. Audiences might sing well-worn favorites from the previous century or the latest Tin Pan Alley hits; the songs might be sentimental or comical (tongue twisters and parodies were especially popular); the participatory experience might stand alone or be interrupted by solo performances; and the sing-along might be enhanced with stage action, props, a contest, or anything else that the exhibitor and organist could dream up. Indeed, there were nearly as many approaches to community singing as there were picture houses that offered it. Although not all theaters welcomed community singing, it could be found in the towns and cities of every state in the nation. When sound technology began to transform the film industry around 1930, many organists lost their jobs; their primary function in most theaters, after all, had been to accompany the on-screen action. At the same time, the production of sing-along films increased to meet audience demand, while many large urban theaters kept an organist on staff to offer specialized entertainment—in many cases, community singing.

This study, which is the first extended exploration of picture palace community singing, investigates the history and practices of this phenomenon in American film exhibition, with a focus on several important theaters in Chicago and New York City. To provide the reader with both general knowledge about picture palace sing-alongs and an understanding of how community singing varied between organists and theaters, I oscillate between a comprehensive, nationwide perspective and a specific, localized one. Chapter 3 in particular is concerned with the universal practices of organist-led community singing, while chapters 1, 4, and 5 include detailed case studies. In this way, I provide a vivid picture of the community singing experience many moviegoers of the 1920s and 1930s shared.

WHY THE PICTURE PALACE?

Theater historians generally agree that the first picture palace was the Regent, which opened in Harlem in 1913.[1] Thomas W. Lamb—who would become the preeminent architect in the film industry—designed the theater, which was unique in that it was a deluxe house dedicated to motion picture exhibition. The Regent struggled at first to attract a clientele; New Yorkers understood motion picture entertainment to be inherently low class, and they could not make sense of this elaborate new theater with its stage boxes and orchestral musicians. The situation turned around when Samuel L. Rothafel, later known as "Roxy," took over management of the house. Pursuing tactics he had pioneered in Milwaukee, Rothafel upgraded the projection technology, installed a velvet curtain to shield the screen between pictures, improved the ventilation system, dressed the theater staff in smart uniforms, and adorned the stage with backdrops, potted plants, colorful lights, and an electric fountain. He also doubled the size of the orchestra and had it perform a sophisticated repertoire in full view of the audience. Rothafel's idea was to offer a high-class cultural experience to his upwardly mobile patrons—and it worked.[2] Although the 1,800-seat Regent was small by later standards, Rothafel's novel approach to film exhibition set the standard for the picture palaces of the next decade. In *American Showman*, Ross Melnick details Rothafel's increasingly grand successes as an exhibitor in New York City. Over the course of several years, Rothafel developed and popularized a new mode of film exhibition reliant on live acts, carefully synchronized music, large orchestras, and grandiose picture houses. The motion picture theater, previously one of many cheap amusement venues that competed for the pedestrian's nickel, was reclassed as a sumptuous destination for artistic entertainment.

For the next two decades, the picture palace offered affordable entry to a fantasy world. These escapist havens catered to middle-class Americans, for whom the palace experience offered an inviting glimpse of life at the top of the social ladder. At the same time, the picture palace fantasy was cast in racialized terms and was available primarily to white audiences. Most picture palaces were segregated, even in the North, where African American patrons were typically seated in the balcony or side galleries—if they were even admitted.[3] For the most part, these patrons attended black theaters in their own neighborhoods, where community singing was conducted by African American theater organists.[4] The theaters that catered to white patrons also restricted black employees to subservient roles, thereby reinforcing the race-based hierarchy.[5] In this way, black social mobility was actively limited even as white theatergoers were encouraged to imagine their own potential for class attainment. Because this study is confined to the large, urban palaces that received attention from the trade press, the experience of black theatergoers is not represented. While many aspects of the community singing experience discussed in this volume applied to black theaters as well, further study on the topic is necessary.

In the 1920s and 1930s, picture palace entertainment was ubiquitous in white urban culture. Most people still visit movie theaters today, but the motion picture experience of the 1920s and 1930s was unlike anything currently available. While the ninety-year transformation has encompassed innumerable characteristics, two changes in particular are of significance to this study. First, the contents of the theatrical experience were once far more varied, incorporating live entertainment as well as films. And second, patrons were more regular in their attendance, often visiting the same theater at least once a week. Chapter 1 is dedicated to the first of these aspects. It offers a detailed account of an actual picture palace show from 1927, in which the community sing is situated among the other noncinematic elements of the program. This chapter seeks to place the reader in the shoes of a picture show patron by using a descriptive account of both the entertainment and the personal relationships that assured a theater's success. My claim that picture palace entertainment is culturally significant, however, relies on the second of the characteristics. Because a large number of people enjoyed the programming on a regular basis, the picture palace provides a meaningful perspective on early twentieth-century music consumption, marketing, and discourse. A survey of the attendance habits of palace-era patrons is therefore in order.

No general studies of theater attendance were conducted in the 1920s themselves.[6] Instead, industry professionals and nonindustry sociologists surveyed specific segments of the population, usually on a localized scale, to gather data for their own purposes. Those within the film industry were primarily interested in tracking tastes for the purposes of film production and advertising. Their reports tell us a great deal about what theatergoers enjoyed but contain little useful information about their numbers or attendance behaviors. Sociologists of the time were generally interested in the moviegoing habits of young people. Reformers had been fearful of the effects of film consumption on children since the nickelodeon era (1905–ca. 1913), and their concerns, which I discuss in chapter 5, continued to influence film exhibition for decades to come. As a result, sociological commentaries of the time tended to ignore the habits of adult theatergoers and therefore provide only a partial account of attendance habits.[7]

All the same, one can piece these studies together to create a meaningful account of motion picture theater attendance in the 1920s. For example, the *New York Times*, citing various "surveys made by civic associations," reported in 1923 that 40 percent of children in both cities and towns visited the theater about once a week, while 40 percent went twice a week or more often. Only 3 percent of children did not attend the theater at all.[8] Also in 1923, a national poll of thirty-seven thousand high school students, conducted by a consortium of organizations concerned with child welfare, revealed that most young people visited the movie theater at least once a week in the company of either their families or friends.[9] These are high numbers, and they support the conclusion that children in the 1920s attended the picture theater far more often than children today.

The results of these polls were often included in *Film Daily Yearbook of Motion Pictures*, an annual compilation of data concerning the film industry. The *Yearbook* published other statistics as well, although the journal did not always indicate the source of its information. For example, the 1927 edition of the *Yearbook*, issued when picture palace entertainment was at peak popularity, claimed that the weekly picture theater attendance in cities of 25,000 was 14,800—an indication that at least half of all urban Americans were visiting the movie house once a week or more. In 1951, *Film Daily Yearbook* published a retrospective set of attendance figures claiming that weekly paid admissions to movie theaters had hit 65 million (more than half of the total population) in 1928.[10] However reliable or complete these figures might be, it is clear that enormous numbers of urban Americans attended the theater regularly and that most theatergoers patronized the movies every week.

This last conclusion is also supported by the programming practices of picture theaters in the 1920s. At the height of the picture palace era, a large, urban theater—that is, the type of theater with which this study is primarily concerned—typically changed its program on a weekly basis.[11] This means that each week the various components of the experience—overture, organ solo, stage show, short films, and feature—were all new. Palaces worked on this schedule because they expected patrons to return each week to enjoy the new round of offerings. In the extreme case of the serial short film, it was necessary to attend to catch developments in the story. The spectacular nature of palace presentation also encouraged patrons not to miss a show, for each often promised to be grander than the last.

In general, the picture palace tried to become an important part of local life. Theater owners and managers took every opportunity to support community activities and to promote the picture palace as a center for wholesome and neighborly entertainment. Although this strategy was most important in the neighborhood house and where programming for children was concerned (the topic of chapter 5), it proved valuable for theaters of all sizes and characters. The two theater employees who enacted this strategy were the organist and the master of ceremonies. Both of these regular performers strove to develop personal connections with their patrons, who in turn were encouraged to think of the stage personalities as friends and the picture palace as a second home. Since movie theater admission prices were relatively low and competition from home-based leisure activities was limited, it is not surprising that picture palace attendance easily became a weekly habit.

Because of the constant presence of picture palace entertainment in the lives of so many, we can study the offerings of palaces to learn about the tastes and experiences of urban Americans. But how much can we learn? When we study the public for motion picture entertainment, we discover two things: that patrons chose to attend the show because they expected to enjoy it and that the public freely expressed their appreciation or distaste for a given presentation. Excellent public transportation in urban areas meant that a city dweller was free to attend the theater of his or her choice. Because of this freedom, the negotiations between exhibitor and audience were complex. Exhibitors presented entertainment that they thought would appeal to the patrons whom they hoped to attract; at the same time, they policed audience behavior within their individual theaters and worked persistently to influence their patrons' tastes. In turn, patrons would express their approval or disapproval while simultaneously developing a preference for the offerings made available. In the upscale picture palace environment, patrons typically did not boo or harangue live performers, but they did exercise their right to withhold applause; they also wrote letters to the performers and theater managers. Because of the active role taken by consumers, we can determine which entertainment offerings pleased the patrons and met their expectations for appropriate content, even though the theater audience normally had no direct role in the planning of any individual program.

Exhibitors themselves held a variety of opinions concerning their obligation to the public. In 1941, Rothafel, reflecting on his career, had the following to say: "All you hear about these days is the everlasting cry of theatre managers that they are looking for 'what the people want.' That idea is fundamentally and disastrously wrong. The people themselves don't know what they want. They want to be entertained, that's all. Don't 'give the people what they want'—give 'em something better."[12] To be sure, this statement is charged with Rothafel's famously over-the-top showmanship, and we should take his pronouncement with a grain of salt. All the same, his attitude suggests that one cannot learn about the audience by studying the provided entertainment. From his point of view, the theater patron had neither a valid opinion on the subject of entertainment nor any influence on what he or she was offered.

Other entertainers, however, took quite the opposite view. Harold J. Lyon, music supervisor for a theater in Iowa, advised organists to program music that appealed to their patrons. "The applause is the best way to judge how well the audience likes your numbers," he wrote, "so don't kid yourself into believing that your community does not appreciate anything."[13] The celebrated Chicago theater organist Edward Meikel (whose career will be detailed in chapter 5) adhered to this same philosophy and explained that he conducted community singing only because his audience demanded it: "It is my frank opinion that you can't shout down a thing editorially against popular preference. . . . The public seems to want community singing, and there isn't a showman in the world who isn't trying to give the public what it wants."[14] While there was at least one showman who was not trying to give the public only what it wanted—Rothafel—Meikel was an influential and successful entertainer in his own right, and his words represented a popular opinion.

Popular Remarks From Famous Men

A. J. B.—"Who started Community Singing?"

Ed. Meikel—"I don't know who started it, but I do know that my audience demands it, and of course I must please them."

A. R. G.—"You're right Ed, the dear public must always be pleased."

This exchange appeared alongside advertisements in a June 1928 edition of *Exhibitors Herald and Moving Picture World.* "A.J.B." must be the exhibitor A. J. Balaban, while "A.R.G." can only be the trade-press critic A. Raymond Gallo. The inclusion of this whimsical spot illustrates the popular acceptance of Meikel's position (although Gallo's reference to "the dear public" suggests a touch of sarcasm).

By 1924, Emil Breitenfeld, a columnist in the Photoplaying pages of the monthly *American Organist*, had already taken the middle ground with a third opinion: "It is the audience who decides. The theaters must please them and the organist must please them. With this rule it is absurd to quarrel. . . . They are not hard to please. Let us find out what they want and give it to them. And in order to find out what they want let's study them a bit."[15] According to Breitenfeld, the exhibitor had to assume a Rothafelian total control of the entertainment but could not succeed without a careful study of his patrons. The audience was then free to accept or reject whatever the exhibitor devised. If this is an accurate description of film exhibition in the picture palace era—and I believe that it is—then we can indeed learn about the tastes and inclinations of theater patrons by studying the entertainment they consumed.

Community singing provides a powerful example of the give-and-take that existed between exhibitor and customer. Because patrons were actually called upon to participate in the entertainment, they were able to directly determine its character and success; if the audience refused to sing, the turn would be revised or eliminated. Community singing also reflected the exhibitors' desire to actively influence taste. Beginning in the mid-1920s, a great deal of conflict arose over whether it was in the theater's best interest to offer only high-class (that is, cultured and artistic) entertainment or to allow patrons to influence programming choices with their preference for low-class community singing. This debate played out in the pages of the trade press over a number of years; the wide range of opinions expressed by exhibitors and commentators will be surveyed in chapter 4. One side in the conflict claimed that it was the responsibility of the picture palace to educate its patrons with better entertainment, while the other insisted that theaters must provide the entertainment demanded by the audience, no matter how distasteful. In the end, community singing lasted because it was so popular with audiences that no business-minded exhibitor could afford to eliminate it. In this way, patrons once again asserted their control over the picture palace show. They did not decide to bring community singing into the theater, but they embraced it and made it a part of their lives.

Organist-led community singing was only widespread for a handful of years: roughly 1925 to 1933. The course of events that led to the practice of picture palace community singing is intriguing, to say the least. I will introduce the ideologies and players behind the community singing move- ment—a serious effort to promote music appreciation and disseminate white, middle-class cultural values—in chapter 2, where I will also discuss the role of the Great War in keeping the practice alive and bringing it into the theater. The downfall of picture palace community singing was just as surprising to trade professionals as its initial popularity. The collapse of the theater organ profession following the widespread adoption of sound tech- nology and the subsequent replacement of organist-led community singing by short films is the topic of chapter 6.

SOURCES

The scope of this study is determined by its sources. Because this study relies largely on material from the national film trade press, it is limited to the theaters and organists that these journals reported on: that is to say, urban picture palaces with three thousand or more seats and the console artists employed therein. Geographical coverage is also impacted, since the trade journals kept their largest offices in New York City and Chicago, for which reason these cities are overrepresented in the trade discourse. Finally, national trade journals only reviewed the motion picture programs of the- aters that served white populations. While African American patrons were permitted to attend most of the theaters discussed in this study, they were not welcome. Exhibitors did not factor black tastes or preferences into their programming decisions, and African American patronage was not dis- cussed in the trade press. In addition, trade journals did not review stage entertainment or organ solos in African American theaters. Despite significant gaps in the trade press coverage, managers and organists from all walks of life shared their ideas, opinions, and experiences in the pages of trade journals, thereby leaving a significant record of activities in small-town and neighborhood houses. The four journals that most regularly described the practice of community singing, either as directed by organists or by films, were *Variety, Exhibitors Herald, Motion Picture News*, and *Film Daily*. Those sources lie at the heart of this study.

Variety is a well-known source to scholars of popular American music in the twentieth century. The journal, still prominent today, was founded in New York City in 1905 as a weekly. It initially covered the vaudeville trade but quickly expanded to incorporate other forms of popular entertainment. In the 1920s, contributors published on the topics of vaudeville, legitimate theater, films, picture house presentations, radio, cabaret, nightclubs, recorded music, and outdoor performances. The sections dedicated to each of these subjects were regularly reordered according to the level of public interest, and the attention that *Variety* paid to motion picture entertainment in the late 1920s reflected that medium's growing popularity and importance: over the course of several years, the space that *Variety* dedicated to the review of films and picture palace stage shows steadily increased, while the Pictures section moved closer and closer to the front of the journal.

Two columns in the Pictures section of *Variety* are of special importance to this study. The first is House Reviews (later called Film House Reviews and, in the mid-1930s, Variety House Reviews, to reflect the fact that most theaters of that era only offered pictures). This column reviewed all of the live entertainment that took place in nationally important theaters each week, including the organ solo and any community singing contained therein. The second is Presentations (later called New Acts). This column highlighted notable stage acts and described them in greater detail than was allowed in House Reviews. Exceptional organ solos were sometimes selected for this column, such as Jesse Crawford's much-anticipated first appearance in November 1926 at the magnificent New York Paramount. In addition to these weekly review columns, *Variety* published a large number of articles on the topic of organ music in theaters, many of which described the related practice of community singing.

Exhibitors Herald, also based in New York City, plays the most important role in this study. Founded in 1915, the *Herald* published weekly articles, reviews, and commentaries concerning all aspects of film exhibition. It underwent a series of name changes during the period in question. In 1927 it merged with *Moving Picture World*—the most important trade journal of the nickelodeon era—and became *Exhibitors Herald and Moving Picture World* (later shortened to *Exhibitors Herald-World*). In 1931, the *Herald* acquired *Motion Picture News* and was reborn as the *Motion Picture Herald*.[16] This trade journal, in all of its permutations, is referred to as the *Herald* in this study.

Despite these transformations, the format of the *Herald* did not change significantly. Its articles and reviews were contributed by *Herald* staff and by trade professionals, including organists. The journal was read by theater managers, organists, and other members of the film exhibition industry. While the *Herald* addressed all aspects of film exhibition, the regular sections concerned with music—Music in the Theatre, Presentation Acts, and later Music and Talent—are naturally of the greatest relevance here. The weekly column Organ Solos, inaugurated in 1927, provided reviews of organ presentations offered in major theaters across the country. Since it contains almost all of the extant information about the contents and presentation of organ solos, this column is vital to any study of organist-led community singing.

Motion Picture News, founded in 1913 and absorbed by the *Herald* in 1931, published short articles and film reviews on a weekly basis. It included more exhibitor-contributed content than the other journals and emphasized management techniques—many of which concerned the use of music—that were meant to attract crowds.[17] This content was published in a special section known in the mid-1920s as Your Idea and Ours, later replaced by Managers' Round Table Club. These sections contain most of the available information about community singing and other musical entertainment offered during children's shows.

Finally, *Film Daily* (launched as *Wid's Films and Film Folks* in 1915) published short articles and reviews on a daily basis.[18] This journal reviewed many of the sing-along short films, and each Sunday *Film Daily* published reviews of presentation acts at the major theaters in New York City. While the scope of information on community singing is extremely limited, *Film Daily* provides a corroborating source for accounts of several important houses.

One additional source for this study is the *American Organist*, the journal of the American Guild of Organists. This monthly publication offers a striking contrast to the trade journals. The articles are long, jargon free, and targeted at an audience comprising primarily church and concert organists. Perhaps not surprisingly, these articles adopted a generally defensive tone. Authors who published in the Photoplaying section of the *American Organist* regularly sought to legitimize the theater organ in the eyes of their colleagues, and there is only minimal discussion of community singing. The Photoplaying section was discontinued in 1930 with the spread of talking pictures.

This study also engages with the remnants of community singing ephemera, including lantern slides, song pamphlets, and instructional sheets for organist-led sing-alongs. I have learned a great deal about community singing repertoire and practice by examining song slides. I have visited the MarNan Collection in Minneapolis, Minnesota, the Atlanta Fox Theatre Archives in Atlanta, Georgia, and the American Theatre Organ Society Archives in Norman, Oklahoma. Collectively, I have spent about three weeks examining thousands of slides. I have also worked with digital collections of slide images that belong to the George Eastman House in Rochester, New York, the Embassy Theatre in Fort Wayne, Indiana, and the Ohio Theatre in Columbus, Ohio (now housed at the Embassy). These slides enable a variety of insights into the community singing experience. In addition to preserving the repertoire, they also testify to the humorous quality of most picture palace sing-alongs. Alterations made by organists indicate the level of control these musicians exercised in the theater, even when the slides were supplied in complete sets by music publishers or rental exchanges, and singing instructions incorporated into the slides help to re-create the perspective of a 1920s participant.

Chapter 2 was shaped by a visit that I made to the Arthur Friedheim Library of the Peabody Institute in Baltimore, Maryland, to examine the May Garrettson Evans Collection and the Archives of the Peabody Institute. There I learned about one of the founders of the community singing movement, Henrietta Baker Low, and followed the development of community singing activity in Baltimore under the auspices of the Peabody Preparatory Division. This work was vital to understanding how community singing became a popular form of amusement in the 1920s picture palace. It also brought into stark relief the contrast between the serious goals outlined by community music activists in the early to midteens and the lighthearted practices of popular community singing a decade later.

Another source for this study has been the diverse library of community singing books published during the 1910s, 1920s, and 1930s. These volumes range from hardbound keepsakes to cheaply produced promotional giveaways, but they all reflect the enthusiasm for community singing that gripped Americans in these years. Like slides, these songbooks indicate what repertoire was popular. Unlike slides, though, they often indicate who consumed that repertoire. In addition, songbooks sometimes contain prefaces that extol the power and importance of community singing. These texts, which attempt to explain the ideals and beliefs that motivated the community singing movement, have been invaluable for me as I try to understand what community singing meant for Americans in these years.

1 A VISIT TO THE ORIENTAL

The best way to explain picture palace entertainment is to re-create an instance of it. This chapter will walk the reader through a single show at a specific theater in order to reconstruct the moviegoing experience of the palace era. Because Chicago was both the locus of organist-led community singing and the home of the most influential picture palace chain, I examine a program at a major Chicago theater, the Oriental. The date of the show—October 18, 1927—falls at the height of silent-era picture palace culture, just before the introduction of sound and the Great Depression were to effect enormous changes to film exhibition. Before the tour begins, however, some general background information is in order.

In picture palaces of the 1920s and 1930s, community sings were most often led by the theater organist as part of what was called the organ solo. For this portion of the program, the spotlight turned to the console and the organist took charge of the entertainment, usually for about ten minutes. He or she exercised near-total autonomy over the solo: this was the organist's chance to connect with patrons, establish a unique personality and style, and build a loyal following. Some organists focused on light classical fare; some performed the latest popular hits; some staged miniature stage dramas or featured guest soloists; and some, week after week, offered exuberant community singing. The organ solo always reflected the theater's character, however, and an organist carefully gauged his patrons' tastes before programming a new type of solo.

Given that the picture palace program was long and highly varied, an individual theater usually emphasized one of its elements above the others in order to best target a specific segment of the patronage. In some cases the organist and his community sing were the primary draw, but even then the organ solo occupied no more than fifteen minutes of the show. As a result, the organ solo was often a secondary offering, while the emphasis fell on a charismatic master of ceremonies, a lavish stage show, or the feature film. Many theaters combined several strong elements and played down a deficiency. For example, hoping that a weak feature film would go unnoticed, one house might attract the audience with a star organist and big-name visiting performers. Less-dominant items could also draw patrons. The newsreel, for instance, became an important attraction when Fox began issuing their popular sound news shorts in 1927, while the serial short film could also develop a loyal weekly patronage.[1]

Each theater exploited its strengths to bring in the customers, and each patron in turn had her own reason for visiting the picture palace. Few patrons were interested in only a single element of the program, but none were indifferent to the strengths of each theater. Therefore, a patron was likely to seek out a theater that focused on the types of entertainment that she was most interested in. Alternatively, a patron might develop interests based on what the local theater offered. Either way, we can make inferences about the audience that visited each individual palace based on the reputation of the theater and its location in the city, which suggested a theater's class and determined whether the audience was entirely local or populated with visitors. We must examine all of a theater's offerings to understand what attracted the audience and what the audience members expected from their experience. This in turn allows us to determine what role the organ solo played in this or that theater and how the patrons perceived and enjoyed the organ solo.

The role of the organist varied enormously between venues, but we can never isolate the organ solo from the character of the theater and the totality of that theater's offerings. The organ solo was never enjoyed independently of the rest of the program. Even if a patron greatly enjoyed the community sing, he most likely attended the theater to see another live act or the feature film. At the same time, a patron expected a complete and varied program, and he would leave the theater disappointed if the organ solo were missing. We must remember that the audience for the organ solo was also the audience for the orchestral overture, the stage band, the live prologue, and the comedy shorts. Indeed, the picture show experience might be further understood to include the obsequious service, palatial architecture, gaudy decorations, subtle light design, excited crowds, comfortable seats, and long lines.

Ross Melnick has proposed the concept of a "unitary text" as "comprising all of the film, music, and live performance offered by a theater and often bracketed by breaks in the schedule," while he suggests that the broader theatergoing experience might be understood as a "megatext."[2] Both of these frameworks are vital to the task of situating the activity of community singing within the complete picture palace experience. Each element of the program provided patrons with a different flavor of entertainment, but only the complete show—including both unitary text and megatext—could satisfy their desire for fantasy and escape. What follows is an explication of the megatext that informed the experience of countless 1920s' theatergoers.

BALABAN AND KATZ AND THE CHICAGO ORIENTAL

It cannot be claimed that the Oriental was a *typical* picture palace because there never was such a thing. Each theater met the needs of its patrons as best it could, given the specific circumstances of location and ownership. However, the Oriental did represent a highly influential approach to film exhibition. This approach was developed in the 1920s by Barney and A. J. Balaban and Samuel Katz, who founded the exhibition chain Balaban and Katz (B&K), which eventually merged with Paramount to gain nationwide control over exhibition practices.[3] The B&K style was maximally invested in live performance, stage spectacle, and captivating theater personalities. Any show of theirs provides us with an interesting case study for the role of live performance. The Oriental program on October 18, 1927, also featured an influential theater organist who made his name through community singing, Henri A. Keates. While Keates's organ programs are fascinating on their own terms, it is more informative to observe the organist and his community sings within the highly varied and charismatic world of palace-style exhibition. In 1927 the Oriental Theatre represented the pinnacle of palace architecture and programming in Chicago and the apex of an exhibition system that had been developing for the past decade. To properly situate a show at the Oriental in Chicago's moviegoing culture, however, the story must begin with B&K, the Chicago film exhibitors who joined the industry late but eventually set the standard for picture palace operation.[4]

The first innovation that B&K brought to the picture palace industry had to do with location and catered directly to the middle-class audience that they—and all motion picture exhibitors—hoped to entice. The entire palace industry was built on the prospect of making motion picture entertainment palatable to middle-class patrons. Early exhibitors noticed that while members of the middle class were certainly interested in film, these potential customers were loath to admit that they patronized the often-dingy, working-class nickelodeons.[5] The first New York palace was built with the idea that middle-class patrons would be attracted to a luxurious theater that offered a high standard of service. The palace experience was meant to be much more sophisticated on every level than that offered by the nickelodeon.[6]

Before the Balaban brothers and Katz made plans to open their first picture palace, the Central Park, on October 27, 1917, they had observed that, because of the construction of a mass-transit system in Chicago, most of Chicago's middle-class residents had moved away from the city center and into grow-ing suburbs on the outskirts of the city. Instead of building their palace in the downtown entertainment district, therefore, B&K selected a location in the west end, where their target audience lived. The exhibitors wagered that a neighborhood theater designed and intended for the exclusive use of Chicago's middle-class residents would eliminate the stigma of movie-going and attract the crowds. Their experiment was wildly successful, and it laid the foundation for a Chicago picture palace empire that would change the future of the industry. B&K built their next three palaces in middle-class suburbs before finally constructing in Chicago's downtown, the area where the Oriental would eventually open.[7]

Location played an important role in the exhibitors' early success, but over time it was the impeccable service and lavish stage shows that came to char-acterize B&K theaters, and it was these features that had the greatest impact on picture palace culture outside of Chicago. We shall begin by examining an element less central to this study: the service. A B&K palace was heavily staffed with uniformed attendants, from the ticket girl to the doorman to the elevator operator. The head office mandated the qualifications, training, and appearance of their employees (for example, an usher had to be a white, college-aged man of average height and weight, while a page boy had to be a young African American male of small stature). This expertly tailored ser-vice staff was tasked with making the patron feel wealthy and important, as if he were staying in an upscale New York hotel or visiting European royalty. Middle-class Chicagoans were not used to such treatment, and the staff at a picture palace gave them a taste of the service that the wealthy enjoyed every day—at least in the middle-class imagination, if not in reality.[8]

The most important B&K service-staff members were the ushers. The exhibitors detailed the selection and training of these young men in an advertisement featured in the house magazine.[9] This advertisement did not seek to recruit ushers but instead boasted about their sophistication in order to illustrate the high quality of the B&K organization. From the text of the notice we learn three important things. First, ushers always came from good families, had "the advantages of good breeding," and had at least a high school education. (Most were enrolled in college.) Second, ushers were chosen with the same discernment as a member of the armed forces and were trained by a West Point graduate, which explained their military-like precision and loyalty. And third, ushers learned "discipline, service and self-restraint" at the Balaban and Katz School for Ushers before entering service in a theater. The advertisement noted that the ushers were the only members of the theater organization who came into direct contact with patrons on a daily basis. Because of this, they were the public face of B&K and were directly responsible for leaving a good impression on the visitors. All of this led the notice to conclude that the importance of properly training ushers "*cannot be overestimated*" (emphasis in original). The ushers were indispensable to B&K in their effort to create an opulent environment and to secure regular middle-class patronage.

Perhaps the greatest luxury that a B&K palace offered seems surprisingly mundane now: air conditioning. This feature is ubiquitous to most buildings today, but in the 1920s it was a valuable selling point. When B&K installed air conditioning in their theaters, they not only attracted patrons but transformed the role of the picture palace in society. Before B&K, it had been unbearable to attend the movies when the weather was hot, and most theaters simply closed in the summer. Barney Balaban, who had worked for the Western Cold Storage Company before joining his brother as an exhibition entrepreneur, developed an affordable and efficient cooling system for the first theater built by B&K, the Central Park. This enormous system, which occupied an entire room beneath the auditorium, made the Central Park the first air-conditioned theater in the world.

B&K continued to refine and improve the system with each theater that they built, but what they did with the *notion* of air conditioning was much more impressive. First, without any additional effort, they were able to capitalize on the ability to stay open for business twelve months a year. Instead of repelling patrons in the summer, the theater became a destination for anyone who wished to escape the heat. Second, B&K chose to feature air conditioning in their advertisements. Most middle-class Chicagoans did not have regular access to air-conditioned spaces, which meant that air conditioning was more than just a way to cool down: it was an enviable luxury reserved for the well-off. Air conditioning may have been a practical feature in B&K houses, but it also represented the lifestyle of the upper class, along with the gilded décor and uniformed staff. (Whether or not the upper class regularly enjoyed these things is not important; B&K only needed to sell the perception of privilege.) To draw attention to this new luxury, B&K framed advertisements for their theaters with icicles, a striking graphic representation of the pleasures on offer. They also accompanied these images with descriptions of the delightful climate within and advertised their palaces as the number-one destination to escape summer heat. Finally, B&K met with a bit of luck (perhaps engineered, although we cannot know): the Public Health Commissioner of Chicago announced that B&K theaters had the cleanest air one could find and suggested that all those suffering from lung troubles, as well as pregnant women, spend a considerable amount of time in these air-conditioned havens. In the end, what had been a comfort and luxury was transformed into a health imperative, and theater attendance became not an indulgence but an obligation.[10]

While the service and climate at a B&K theater helped to maintain a regular and dedicated patronage, it was the show that ultimately attracted an audience. The B&K formula for stage entertainment eventually influenced the entire industry, but it grew out of necessity. As fledgling exhibitors, B&K needed to offer entertainment that would draw the crowds. They faced a serious problem, however, due to the way in which the motion picture industry was organized until 1948, when the Supreme Court decided in *United States v. Paramount Pictures* that it constituted an illegal trust. Along with the picture palace era came the vertical integration of the motion picture industry, in which a single company produced, distributed, and exhibited films. This allowed each film company to maximize profits by controlling all of the steps in the process and monopolizing the entertainment market wherever possible. Film production companies integrated vertically by acquiring theaters in which to exhibit their pictures, while at the same time powerful theater owners acquired production companies to supply their own demand for films. Warner Brothers followed the former strategy in the late 1920s, when their success with sound films allowed them to expand into exhibition and corner the market in certain regions.[11] Marcus Loew, on the other hand, developed the production company Metro-Goldwyn-Mayer in the 1920s to supply films to his chain of theaters and to avoid costly dependence on other producers.[12] Film production companies of the 1920s granted initial access to films, or first-run privileges, to their own theaters. After the first (and most profitable) run was complete and the film had been shelved for some months, it would be made available to theaters affiliated with other production companies and to independent theaters. Not even the vertically integrated film giants could produce enough material to satisfy the demand for weekly changes, so all of the theaters relied to a certain extent on outside products.[13] Because the B&K chain was not initially affiliated with a production company, however, it never had access to first-run films and could not rely on feature exhibitions to attract patrons. Instead, B&K heavily promoted live entertainment and invested in bringing the best theater talent to Chicago.[14]

Live entertainment, then, was the most important part of a B&K show, and the performers who provided it filled four different roles, each of which was required to make any show complete. Every performance at a B&K house featured a charismatic band leader, who served as master of ceremonies, chatted with the audience, and linked acts together; an organist, who offered a solo in addition to incidental music; visiting "name" performers who were featured in advertising and attracted patrons during a contractual stay of a week or more; and resident performers, both singers and dancers, who often appeared in conjunction with other acts and built up the climactic points in the stage show. While visiting stars were important to picture palace success, the central B&K strategy was to acquire the most promising stage talent for their theaters and then to build that talent to celebrity status through incessant promotion. Their two greatest success stories were organist Jesse Crawford, for whom Chicago mourned in 1926 when he left to take up a prestigious position at the New York Paramount, and Paul Ash, a band leader whose celebrity was so great that his signature stage show style was termed "the Ash policy" and imitated throughout the nation.[15] The Oriental Theatre's opening-night marquee exemplified the B&K attitude toward live entertainment. On it, Paul Ash and organist Henri A. Keates got top billing, while the feature film and its celluloid stars were relegated to second place.[16]

B&K theaters, as well as most other picture palaces, presented their programs of live and filmed offerings using the model of continuous performance, in which shows began in the late morning and repeated until around midnight. A single show might last from two to three hours, 60 to

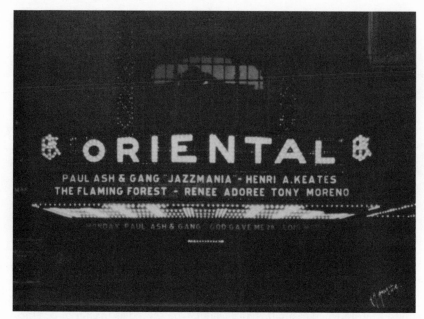

The marquee of the Oriental Theatre, with band leader Paul Ash and organist
Henri A. Keates given top billing. Theatre Historical Society.

105 minutes of which were dedicated to the feature film. Each show was
roughly identical. Certain modules might be absent during slow hours, or a
module might be cut if the show ran long, or the orchestra might be given
a break from accompanying the film, but the key elements (stage show
and feature) remained constant.[17] Because the nickelodeon theaters of the
1900s and 1910s had not offered a unified show with distinct, ordered parts,
patrons were free to arrive and depart whenever they chose—they exercised
total power over the length of their stay.[18] The picture palace, however, did
offer a unified show, and the management of audience behavior changed
accordingly. At the palace, the audience was expected to wait in the lobby
until the previous show was over, stay for the entire show to which they
were admitted, and leave at its conclusion.[19] Some theatergoers retained
the nickelodeon-era habit of coming and going as they pleased, and this
was typical behavior in neighborhood houses, if not in the large downtown
palaces that are the focus of this study.[20] Ideally, however, a palace patron
shared a nearly identical experience with his fellow audience members:
each witnessed the same elements of the show in the same order. This, in

addition to the charisma of the live performers, allowed a sense of community to develop among theatergoers that had not been possible—at least on such a grand scale—in the nickelodeon.

The tactics employed by B&K in their Chicago theaters were designed to achieve the goal shared by every picture palace impresario: to entice middle-class patrons by providing them with fantasy and escape. The motion picture can provide imaginative escape (through exotic images) and emotional release (through storytelling) no matter where it is exhibited, but the picture palace environment was designed to enrich and compound these effects. Each detail of the architecture, decoration, live entertainment, and service was finely tuned to provide the visitors with precisely the brand of escape they desired, and exhibitors realized at once that what the middle-class patrons most wanted was escape from their ordinary lives and social positions. They desired wealth and importance, and they longed to be part of the social elite. To make this fantasy a reality, if only for a few hours, exhibitors often modeled their theaters on European palaces and exclusive New York hotels; they adorned the interiors with fine art and expensive chandeliers; they staged elaborate fantasies of splendor and royalty; and they staffed their palaces with dignified and obsequious servants. The palace was advertised as a second home for the middle class. For a fee, any member of that class was invited to enjoy the accoutrements of wealth and status.[21]

The official B&K policy was to admit any theatergoer who could pay for a ticket. In practice, however, African American patrons were either turned away or seated in the balcony. Black Chicagoans who attempted to purchase admission to downtown houses even faced threats of violence. For this reason, most of the city's African American population attended smaller theaters in their segregated neighborhoods. Even though most of these theaters were owned by white proprietors, they employed African American musicians, stage performers, and ushers, and they catered to black tastes. Most importantly, Chicagoans who patronized these theaters did not face humiliation or assault.[22] Chicago's first African American picture palace—the Regal—opened in 1928 under the auspices of B&K.[23] The 2,798-seat theater featured Sammy Williams at the organ. Like his white counterparts at most other B&K houses, Williams dedicated most of his efforts to community singing.[24]

Where downtown patronage was concerned, the Oriental was a crowning achievement in B&K's mission to provide white, middle-class Chicagoans

The Rapp and Rapp skyscraper that contains the Oriental Theatre.
Chicago Architectural Photographing Co. Collection, Theatre Historical Society.

with an escapist haven. Before the Oriental, the notion of picture palace escape only included the fantasy of living an idealized, upper-class lifestyle. The Oriental, which opened on May 8, 1926, in downtown Chicago, combined class-based escapism with an exotic fantasy world. At the Oriental, patrons might imagine themselves as bejeweled shahs instead of monocled Rockefellers. Other Eastern-themed theaters would appear in the wake of the Oriental, but the B&K behemoth was the first and most prominent.

The Oriental Theatre was designed to have an extraordinary visual impact on all who entered its doors. The theater still stands today, but the contemporary visitor experiences the striking architecture and décor as an echo of the past. When the Oriental opened as a picture palace, it represented the future of motion picture architecture and entertainment. Today we catch a glimpse of the awe that the Oriental inspired when we read contemporary descriptions of the interior and accounts of the effect that the theater had on those who entered. In 1927, the Oriental offered patrons a dazzling vision of an exotic land that, in most cases, they would never visit.

While the Oriental departed from the picture palace standard in several respects, it was still constrained by the norms of construction and outward appearance. Like most downtown palaces, the Oriental was not a freestanding structure. It was necessary for theater financiers to make efficient use of valuable downtown real estate, so a picture palace often occupied the ground floor of a much larger structure. The Oriental was located in the New Masonic Temple Building, designed by the same architects responsible for the theater itself. The facade of the Oriental was much like any other contemporary palace, which perhaps heightened the shocking effect of the aesthetic wonders within. On what was otherwise an unassuming street front, a grand marquee advertised the current offerings, while an enormous vertical sign bearing the name of the theater in bright lights marked it clearly for all to see.[25]

The firm of C. W. and George L. Rapp designed the Oriental. Their architectural firm rose to great prominence in the picture palace field through their work for B&K. Various accounts of the architects' complex relationship with the theater tell a great deal about the aesthetic effect that the Oriental had when it opened. At the same time, these accounts are undoubtedly tinged by modern aesthetic sensibilities, which have often been offended by the "hasheesh-dream decor" of the Oriental.[26] David Balaban, named for his grandfather, reports that Rapp and Rapp were so appalled by the

final result of their design that they refused to visit the Oriental after it had opened, an indication that they were either coerced into working on the theater or that something had gone wrong as their plans were being realized.[27] Theater historian David Naylor, in agreement, contributes a rumor that the annoyed architects tore up their complimentary tickets to the opening performance. He describes the theater as "an embarrassment to the firm."[28] The Theatre Historical Society of America, on the other hand, informs us that the idea for the Oriental came from the architects themselves and that Rapp and Rapp had to work hard to convince B&K that an Eastern-themed theater would be successful. The Theatre Historical Society also points out that Rapp and Rapp had the Oriental photographically documented in great detail, an indication that they were not ashamed of their work.[29] It is likely that late twentieth-century commentators projected their own distaste for the garish theater onto the architects in a misguided attempt to clear the firm's name.

The Oriental's décor set it apart from other Chicago picture palaces, but many of the theater's architectural features would have been familiar to any moviegoer. Rapp and Rapp had long since perfected their picture palace technique, and the architects applied the same time-tested principles to each new assignment. For example, early movie theaters were prone to catastrophic fires, due to the dangers of film exhibition combined with poorly designed exits. In the 1920s, the possibility of a fire breaking out was still a major concern for exhibitors. Additionally, the enormous audiences drawn by the picture palace show presented new difficulties in crowd control. As Rapp and Rapp perfected their picture palace design, they put a great deal of thought into how patrons might be gently directed so as to avoid discomfort and panic. To begin with, the architects provided a large number of exits. They then developed a general floor plan that funneled crowds into and out of the building with maximal efficiency. The center of Rapp and Rapp's crowd-control system was the lobby, and the lobby they designed for the Oriental fulfilled two functions: it facilitated the swift exodus of one audience through the side ambulatories while another took their seats, and it could hold as many patrons as could the auditorium.[30] Therefore, when a visitor—even a first-time visitor—arrived at the Oriental on October 18, 1927, he would have realized that crowds extending "out on the sidewalk as

Opposite: The lobby of the Oriental, designed for optimal crowd control. Chicago Architectural Photographing Co. Collection, Theatre Historical Society.

The main foyer of the Oriental. Chicago Architectural Photographing Co. Collection, Theatre Historical Society.

far as around the corner" indicated a long wait for admittance, for he would have known that an unseen lobby was already full of patrons waiting for the next show.[31]

Upon entering the Oriental, a patron would have been dazzled by the ornate interior. Eastern decorations clung to every corner of the theater. The ceiling was detailed with molded plaster ornamentation, while friezes and relief carvings lined the walls. Imported Eastern art hung where the walls were unornamented, heavy drapes framed the mezzanine overlooks, and Asian antiques dotted the walkways. The furniture, which contributed to the comfort and luxury of every picture palace, was also suited to an Eastern theme.[32] The most striking pieces were the massive "elephant thrones" that lined the walls of the foyer and promenade.[33] This garish scheme of interior decoration appalled some commentators, but a writer for the film trade journal *Exhibitors Herald* came to the Oriental's defense:

> Last Thursday afternoon this writer walked through the then far from completed interior of the Oriental theatre in Chicago. Under the white light of day, amplified by terrific white artificial illumination provided for the hundreds of rushing workmen within, the theatre looked like anything but a beautiful interior. The rich paintings, dominated by red and gold, looked trashy. The heavily ornamented furnishings looked expensively cheap. The organ console, done in red and gold, looked like an overgrown music box. Then this writer saw the theatre on Friday night under the correct illumination and full of people. That's different!
>
> The name applies wholly to the theatre. It is Oriental! No other word describes it so well. The "expensive cheapness" was gone entirely. It had become Oriental splendor. The advance advertising of the theatre had termed it a "jewel casket" and that's the phrase that fits it. A minute after coming in from modern Madison street you're in the India you read about when you were a child.[34]

A theater like the Oriental was fantasy, not reality. That fantasy did not withstand close inspection by the jaded professional, but it did not need to. The picture palace was designed as an exotic home away from home to which patrons could escape on a weekly basis. This home did not need to be livable or genuine—it simply needed to fulfil the fantasy that patrons were already eager to experience. The Oriental was so successful in doing so that it transported this journalist not only to another world, India, but to another time, that of his childhood.

The auditorium of the Oriental. Chicago Architectural Photographing Co. Collection, Theatre Historical Society.

Many picture palaces of the 1920s imitated specific European structures in order to provide patrons with escape. For example, the first picture palace—the New York City Regent, constructed in 1913—was modeled on Venice's Palace of the Doges.[35] With the Oriental, however, Rapp and Rapp took a novel approach. In the theater's official press release, chief of design Arthur Frederick Adams noted that the Oriental was not intended to emulate any "particular monument from the East" or even to incorporate the designs and motifs that one might associate with Eastern temples and palaces. In fact, Rapp and Rapp did not base their theater on Eastern architecture at all. Instead, the architects modeled it on the Indian Durbar, a festival celebrated three times in Delhi (1877, 1903, and 1911) to mark the coronation of British royals. Adams wrote of the architectural vision, "Instead of really copying any Oriental art, [Rapp and Rapp] have introduced the spirit of the gorgeous pageant which is theatrical in every detail."[36] The architects had devised a new mode of expression for the escapist mandate of picture palace entertainment. Rapp and Rapp chose to base their latest theatrical masterpiece on an event instead of a monument—but an event that centered on royalty and fabulous riches and that reflected the lifestyle of the Western nobility who ruled India, not the natural landscape of that country or the daily existence of its inhabitants. The introduction of Eastern elements added a dimension of cultural escape to a theater experience that had traditionally centered only on class escape.

Even though the Oriental was not designed after a preexisting monument, its interior was still clearly that of a palace. The Oriental was luxurious first and Eastern second. Its cavernous waiting areas—like those of all picture palaces—were designed to impress patrons with high ceilings, glamorous furnishings, and gilded ornaments. The Oriental featured a four-level entrance hall, from which a visitor could climb the stairway to the balcony or enter a passageway to the orchestra foyer. Orchestra-level patrons used the main foyer, while balcony patrons used the mezzanine foyer. Balcony patrons could admire the main hall from the mezzanine, from the additional lower-balcony landing, or from the men's lounge near the midbalcony foyer.[37]

While these public spaces were designed to exude glamour and opulence, the additional private spaces within the theater provided the service and convenience central to the class-attainment fantasy. All B&K houses had smoking rooms and luxurious lounges for men and women, complete with attendants and, occasionally, musical entertainment. Additionally, many theaters provided complimentary professional childcare in a space below the auditorium that was equipped with complete playground facil- ities. Moviegoers could leave their children in the care of fully qualified nurses, which meant that women shopping with their families during the day could still attend a B&K show.[38] Despite the glamorous allure of these spaces and amenities, the auditorium itself was the ultimate destination for every patron, and the picture palace show had drawn them in the first place. The Eastern fantasy, if more realistic in the public spaces (which might actually be mistaken for rooms in a palace), naturally continued into the theatrical space.

Perhaps the first sight to strike a patron upon entering the auditorium of the Oriental was the four thousand square foot stage curtain. This monu- mental piece featured a victorious Indian rajah returning from battle and was painted in Japanese metallic pigments on velour in the B&K scenic shops. Because the focus of the audience shifted between films and live per- formers, the curtain played a special role in the picture palace show. For the first portion of an Oriental show, the curtain would remain down so as to draw attention to the musicians. Later, the curtain would rise to reveal an elaborate stage set, and stage performers would share the focus with the orchestra. A screen for film projection would move into place when it was time to exhibit shorts or run the feature. The position of the cur- tain indicated where the patron was to direct her attention, and the strik- ing appearance of the Oriental's curtain contributed an exotic flavor to the show whenever it was in place.[39]

The spaces surrounding the stage and its curtain were primarily dedi- cated to musical concerns. Next to the stage, the organ opening dominated the side wall, as in all picture palaces. It was the custom of Rapp and Rapp to hang draperies from a plaster arch over the opening, which served to reduce the overwhelming power of the instrument.[40] In front of the stage was the orchestra pit. This was a natural attribute for any theater that fea- tured stage entertainment, but picture palaces, because of their varied offer- ings, had unique requirements for their musical facilities. Shortly before the construction of the Oriental, theater designers had developed a special approach to pit design that better suited the needs of motion picture exhi- bition. In the Oriental, the conductor, orchestra, piano, and organ console were each located on separate lifts within the pit. With this system in place, the conductor and orchestra could be elevated for the overture, the pianist could be brought into place to accompany a stage act, the organist could be revealed for the organ solo, and then, when it was time for the feature film, all of the musicians could be easily removed from view.[41] (The organist and orchestra were both expected to accompany the film, but they could not be allowed to distract from it.) In addition, the stage band was situated on a platform that rolled onto the stage from the raised orchestra lift. This meant that the band could move into place quickly for the show and then disappear into the pit without any disturbance.[42] The musicians were a significant draw for the theater, and it was important that they be visible during musical features. The Oriental auditorium was designed with careful consideration for the needs of its performers.

The stage, like the pit, was also highly mechanized—a moving wonder that elicited fascination and comment when the Oriental first opened. The theater featured "flying stages," an improvement on a preexisting modular stage design that provided new options for the presentation of live entertainment and allowed for quicker scene changes.[43] This architectural emphasis on stage presentation illustrates the important role that live acts played at the Oriental; the wonderful new stages could be leveraged as an advertising ploy because the presentation of live entertainment was vital to the show.[44] Additionally, they serve as a reminder that technological advances in the movie theater were not limited to recorded sound and colored films. Film exhibitors worked constantly to improve the show, and their efforts produced innovations that ranged from lifts to spill cards (an ingenious method for counting patrons) to air conditioning.[45] Unfortunately, the flying stages presented one more opportunity for technical malfunction: they broke down on opening night and band leader Paul Ash had to entertain the crowd while the sets were slowly moved into place. Ash's experience and celebrity saved the day, however, and it was reported that his "ready wit supplied his nimble tongue with nifties that got him out of these bunkers with the giggles all on his side of the scorecard."[46]

The auditorium of the Oriental, as in all picture palaces, was carefully designed so that every seat provided a clear view of the stage and screen, without interference from columns. The live entertainment that played a major role in the picture palace show consisted largely of singing, dancing, and production numbers, not acting as one might see in a stage play. This meant that the auditorium could be tailored for film viewing in ways that

Seating in the auditorium of the Oriental. Chicago Architectural Photographing Co. Collection, Theatre Historical Society.

provided an advantage over traditional theaters. In the case of a play, it is vital that each member of the audience hear the spoken dialogue and see the details of the actors' movements and facial expressions. Therefore, no seat can be positioned too far away from the stage if its occupant is to enjoy the show. In the picture palace, however, both of these concerns evaporated: a patron could easily discern facial expressions and movements because they were emphasized by the camera and enlarged on the screen and silent films meant that audibility was not an issue. Film exhibitors soon realized that they could capitalize on the nature of their medium by creating enormous auditoriums with seats fanning out away from the stage instead of stacked up near it. This allowed picture palaces to accommodate the maximum number of patrons without sacrificing comfort—and comfort, of course, was vital to the luxurious escape that a picture palace promised.[47] The seats in the Oriental were organized into an orchestra level, a grand balcony, and a small mezzanine below the balcony that added 366 seats. The Oriental also had rare functional boxes (those in most picture palaces were simply ornamental and could not seat patrons).[48] While admission prices varied with seating levels and shows, almost anyone could afford a ticket to the Oriental fantasy.

PROGRAM AT THE ORIENTAL

Each show staged at the Oriental constituted a unique unitary text—a complete program of live and filmed entertainment—that was consumed by thousands of Chicagoans simultaneously. As we shall see, the unitary text was dependent on the megatext. In other words, the program offered on October 18, 1927, would have had a different significance and reception if it was experienced by another audience in another theater. All the same, the program was in many ways typical of the Oriental, which in turn offered a style of entertainment that was common to picture palaces throughout the country. As such, this case study will serve as an example both of palace-era programming practices and of the interplay between unitary text and megatext.

Because the Oriental was a picture palace, we will start with the movie itself. The feature film that week was MGM's *Spring Fever*, a golf comedy starring William Haines and Joan Crawford that garnered a modest review from *Variety* and decent mentions in *Film Daily* and *Motion Picture News*.[49]

The local *Chicago Daily Tribune* concluded that "there's no doubt but most of you will find 'Spring Fever' mighty satisfactory entertainment."[50] To read a review of a 1920s feature, however, is not to understand its success, reception, or value to the theater. All of these elements were dependent upon the palace in which the film was exhibited. *Spring Fever* might have been a major hit in a theater that depended heavily on the feature to draw patrons, but it might have been largely ignored in a theater with more varied offerings. The significance of a feature also depended on whether it was exhibited as a first- or subsequent-run film (that is, whether it was new or had already been seen in other theaters).

The entire show on October 18 was reviewed for *Variety*, and the reviewer's comments tell us exactly what *Spring Fever* meant to the patrons who saw it there: "The screen feature, 'Spring Fever,' somewhat above the Oriental's usual run, was still a long shot for any other Loop stand. . . . It is now well known that Paul Ash's stamping ground is, for films, a detour off the road to success. So 'Fever' can consider itself sidetracked for obvious reasons."[51] Because the jargon used in trade press reviews can be distracting, a loose translation might be helpful: "*Spring Fever* is of higher quality than Oriental patrons are used to, but it is not a great film. It would probably not have succeeded elsewhere in Chicago. Moreover, being shown at the Oriental will not help this film achieve success. Why? Because patrons come to the Oriental to see stage-band director Paul Ash, not the film, and he dominates the show in a way that prevents any film from really being noticed." Or as another *Variety* writer put it in 1927: "Such places like the Oriental depend on their stages, not their screens."[52] Although

This advertisement appeared in *Variety* in August 1926.

we cannot generalize about why patrons were attracted to the movies, we can explain why patrons visited the *Oriental*. They came to see the super-star band leader Paul Ash and his elaborate stage presentations. While the *Variety* reviewer conceded that Haines might have been a draw in some quarters, the Oriental had developed its reputation not by offering the best feature films but by providing the finest live entertainment available in Chicago.

The order of elements in the *Variety* review for the Oriental program on October 18, 1927, tells a great deal about the kind of show that theater offered. The first paragraph of a *Variety* review always revealed what was important at the theater in question, and this one was no exception: "A standard Paul Ash–Oriental stage band presentation this week, meaning one of those shows in accordance with the plan that has established the house as the flagship of the jazz show fleet."[53] The message is clear: Ash and his stage band presentation were the key to success at the Oriental. Anyone reading this review in 1927 would have been interested primarily in what Ash was up to. The reviewer provided the vital information up front and only then mentioned the feature film (the dismissive nod that I quoted and "translated" above). Additionally, the reviewer equated the quality of the Ash stage show with the quality of the entire program. In short, the show on October 18 was "in accordance" with Oriental standards.

While there is a great deal of information from the trade press about the contents of the stage show at the Oriental, the succession of events within the program is less clear. The Oriental show certainly opened with an instrumental overture, for that was the practice in all picture palaces, but neither of the trade press reviews mention it. The *Variety* review focused on the stage show, the film, and the organ solo, while the *Exhibitors Herald* printed one review for the stage show and another for the organ solo. The *Variety* reviewer ordered his discussion of events in a hierarchy of importance. At the end of the review, he lumped all of the "unimportant" elements into a dismissive closing comment: "News reels, shorts, trailers, etc., not to be forgotten" (although, by failing to describe or even list them, the reviewer ensured that these elements would indeed be forgotten; readers today cannot know which shorts and trailers were exhibited).[54] While the reviewer withheld certain details about film contents and exhibition, we can hazard a guess about the program order based on general information reported in the trade press. A 1926 account of a show at the New York Rialto, for example, provided the following program order: orchestral overture, newsreel, organ solo, stage presentation, and finally the feature film.[55] Any trailers would certainly have followed the feature, while the unmentioned short subjects would have joined the newsreel and trailers in their respective positions.[56] That the organ solo preceded the stage presentation at the center of the show indicates its relative importance compared to the shorts, especially at a theater like the Oriental.

The organ solo at the Oriental on October 18, 1927, was well documented by reviewers at both *Variety* and *Exhibitors Herald*, for its success was vital to the success of the entire show. The *Herald* dedicated a special column each week to the description of organ solos that were performed in important theaters all over the country. The cultivation of a noteworthy organist— one known for his inviting manner and entertaining presentations—was a priority for any picture palace, and the trade press responded to this need by offering positive models and advice for the console artist. Some organists provided a great deal of variety, shifting from serious to comical and from classical to popular—but not Henri A. Keates. He had introduced a "community singing policy" at the Oriental's grand opening and met with such success that there was never a reason to deviate from the practice.[57] The Oriental was known as a "singing house," and its patrons expected the same thing every week: uninterrupted community singing led by their beloved organist. The *Variety* reviewer who witnessed Keates's performance on October 18 portrayed the organist as an unassailable favorite with the Oriental patrons:

> Henri Keates was accorded the usual glad hand and hearty vocal response for his slides and organ solo; the screen stuff, hoked up to kill, but just the kind they eat up. Keates is probably the only theatre organist in the country who invariably can support an encore. At the show caught it was estimated about 75 per cent of the audience responded, a very large number and enough to make plenty of racket. Perhaps 15 of the other 25 per cent had colds, though some of the singing 75 had them, too, but sang, nevertheless.
>
> An exact opinion of Oriental audiences may be gained just by witnessing one of Henri's organ numbers. Repetitional weeks and continued success prove the element.[58]

In reality, Keates was not the only organist who could rely on the demand for an encore. Although he was one of the most successful in engaging his audience, there were very popular performers all over the country. Indeed,

Here's the man who put community singing on the map—Henri A. Keates is his name and he presides at the console of the Oriental theatre, Chicago —Henri has played organ solos in nearly every picture house of note and has always succeeded with his own novelties—before singing became a fad in theatres Keates gave organ concerts and classical recitals proving that a good organist can and should play every class of music—and most of all what the public wants.

This photograph of Henri A. Keates was published in *Exhibitors Herald and Moving Picture World* in July 1928. The caption indicates that Keates was capable of playing "high class" music but chose to provide his patrons with the entertainment they demanded— community singing.

perhaps none was so famed for his unbroken streak of encores as Edward Meikel of Chicago (about whom this reviewer really ought to have been aware). The point that the reviewer was trying to make, however, was valid: the patrons at the Oriental adored Keates, and his solo was a highlight of the program.

While this review certainly captures the atmosphere of Keates's solo, the details come from the *Herald* account. That week at the Oriental, Keates seems to have employed a common gag: he told the audience a fictitious story intended to give cause for singing and inspire hearty participation. In addition, Keates's narrative was designed to further cement the bond between organist and audience:

Henri Keates (Chicago Oriental) worked in that ever popular saying "It Pays to Advertise" in his organ story of this week. All in fun, he informed the audience, he was somewhat addicted to reading advertisements in the magazine and his jocular comment on the thin hair, real estate, get fat, weight reducing and wrinkle and face lifting advertisements went over big. He completely won over his audience when he advised that he told the representative who called in connection with his answering an ad for singing lessons that his audience did not need any such thing.[59]

Like most organists, Keates communicated through the medium of lantern slides projected from the booth by the technician. Such slides could either be purchased or made by hand. As the organist at an important Chicago theater, Keates had the resources to create his own organ novelties; less-prosperous performers often wrote to him and requested to borrow his custom slide sets. As was common practice, the words on Keates's slides—usually composed by his wife—fit a well-known tune and could be read silently in time with the music.[60] Unfortunately, we cannot know the exact phrases printed on the lantern slides he displayed, but we do know that they succeeded marvelously in their aim: to incite the audience into song. The *Variety* reviewer estimated that 75 percent of the audience engaged in community singing and even excused most of those not singing with the remark that they must have had colds. In other words, the reviewer believed that 90 percent of the patrons were delighted with the organ solo and at least had the desire to join in. He could not help but pair his comment about

This advertisement for Keates and his program of community singing appeared in a December 1928 issue of *Exhibitors Herald and Moving Picture World*. It was in this month that Preston Sellers took over as head organist at the Oriental, while Keates began to rotate among several Balaban and Katz houses. Keates, however, maintained a dedicated fan base at the Oriental and continued to perform there on occasion until at least 1931.

the sniffling 15 percent with a snide remark on the quality of the vocalizing, a note that betrays the reviewer's highbrow status; commentators frequently disparaged the quality of audience singing, usually with shades of resignation and disdain.

After getting the participants in the right mood with jokes and compliments, Keates launched into an unconnected set of the hit songs that were popular fodder for picture palace community sings everywhere, including "Underneath the Wabash Moon" (1927), "Bye, Bye Pretty Baby" (1927), and "Side by Side" (1927). He also led the singing of "Just Once Again," a brand-new release ostensibly coauthored by Walter Donaldson and Paul Ash himself. Like most organ solos, Keates's presentation had nothing to do with the subsequent stage show or the feature film. (The Chicago Granada's Albert F. Brown was the only organist to regularly link his solos with the feature film; he pioneered a form of stage presentation accompanied by the organ and offered miniature song-based stage dramas as prologues to the film.[61]) The purpose of Keates's presentation was to get the audience excited and to instill a sense of camaraderie and friendliness, which would in turn prepare the audience to enjoy the stage show.

The *Variety* review omits details of repertoire and presentation technique, but in sum it is the more interesting of the two, for the *Variety* reviewer explains what Keates's audience expected from the organ solo and gives insight into his role at the Oriental. It also reveals something important about the perspective of trade press reviewers who worked in the film exhibition industry. These trade representatives often looked askance at cheap gags and participation stunts, especially when the results were less than artistic. Although this reviewer maintained good humor, he clearly spoke with the air of one who is more refined than his subjects. He derisively described Keates's screen material as "hoked up to kill" and was less than generous in his admission that the patrons liked it that way. In addition, his concluding remark—"an exact opinion of Oriental audiences may be gained just by witnessing one of Henri's organ numbers"—is hardly an endorsement of Keates's work. This statement is significant, however, for it reflects the contrast between ideological assessments and practical concerns that will resurface throughout this study. Critics of theater organists regularly dismissed the preferences of the audience. Instead, they condemned the elements of an organ presentation that had popular appeal (and therefore made the organist into a success) and demanded a higher

THE ORIENTAL
THEATER
4/20 Wurlitzer

The console of the Oriental Theatre's 4/20 Wurlitzer was designed to match the heavily
ornamented interior of the auditorium. American Theatre Organ Society.

standard of artistry in place of lowbrow comedy. Critics also preferred
that audiences exhibit more refined tastes and greater personal restraint,
which led them to deplore the methods employed by showmen to entertain. It seems clear, however, that the audience at the Oriental was out for
a good laugh, not intellectual stimulation, and we can be sure that Keates's
"hoked up" approach to community singing was calculated to appeal to the
maximum number of patrons. Most of those who participated would have
been weekly visitors to the Oriental and were decided fans of Keates's style.
If a theatergoer wanted to hear a serious program of Offenbach, Rossini,
or Victor Herbert, she would have to attend one of Keates's Sunday Noon
Organ Concerts at the more-prestigious Chicago Theatre.[62]

Keates's community sing was followed immediately by the stage show,
the true focal point of the program. Paul Ash was the undisputed star of
the Oriental, and his dazzling career was carefully scripted by the theater
chain that recruited him. The means through which Ash became a celebrity
reveal the innermost workings of the B&K style of picture palace entertainment and are therefore worth detailing. Since B&K based the success

of their theaters on live entertainment, not films, they spared no effort in securing and promoting the finest stage personalities. Ash was not merely an entertainer in B&K employment. The exhibitors worked hard to develop Ash into a marketable brand—a unique offering that would characterize their theaters. Ash did not appear *at* the Oriental; he *was* the Oriental. Many would-be imitators followed in his footsteps, but Ash was inimitable and irreplaceable.

Ash's first weeks with B&K illustrate the method by which the exhibitors cultivated stage talent. In early 1925, the theater chain was in merger negotiations with Paramount, a business deal that would benefit both parties. The merger would give B&K access to first-run motion pictures, and it would give Paramount the opportunity to associate with the nation's premier exhibitors and to implement the B&K model across their family of theaters. As part of the deal, B&K took over operation of the McVickers Theater in Chicago, which was located downtown only two blocks away from the future Oriental. This arrangement came with complications for B&K, since the McVickers was close to their existing flagship theater, the

This publicity photograph of Paul Ash unfortunately fails to capture his vibrant red hair. Theatre Historical Society.

Chicago. To successfully operate the McVickers, B&K needed a new style of stage entertainment that would attract patrons to the area but not interfere with the business of their other theaters. A. J. Balaban was assigned the task of designing this new presentation policy. He had successfully experimented with stage bands in the past, and he suspected that a stage band policy might be perfect for the McVickers.

With this idea in mind, A.J. traveled to San Francisco in January 1925 for the express purpose of tempting Paul Ash away from the Granada Theatre. Ash had already proven himself to be a significant draw in that city, and A.J. predicted that the right marketing would make him a star in Chicago. Ash was not regarded as a great musician in his time. A contemporary columnist remarked, "He plays the piano only fairly well," and added that he did not produce his own orchestrations or design his own stage shows.[63] But A.J. saw great potential in the young man. He noted in his memoirs that Ash had all the qualities of a charismatic host, and this is what A.J. valued. He recalled that Ash invited patrons to enjoy the show with a friendly "listen folks" and introduced acts in a manner that spread good cheer and community spirit.[64] The *Herald* shared A.J.'s view: "It is his sense of audience reaction, his minute-to-minute grasp of the situation beyond the foots, that makes the public demand ever more and more of his stuff."[65] A.J. trusted his evaluation of the band leader and knew that he would be a success at the McVickers. After a three-hour interview, Ash agreed to come to Chicago at a pay cut. A.J. won Ash over with his enthusiastic vision for stage entertainment and the promise of greater fame.[66]

Once B&K had succeeded in securing Ash, they set out upon an extraordinary publicity campaign to make his a household name. The exhibitors were certain that Ash had the potential to be a major draw in Chicago, and they spared no effort to see that he became one. B&K convinced Paramount, their new partner, to make available upwards of fifty of their billboards around town. They then used these billboards exclusively to promote Ash and his shows at the McVickers. Ash was worried that he was being oversold to the Chicago public, but A.J. assured him that he could live up to the advertising.[67] The campaign ran for four weeks and was successful in establishing Ash as a popular entertainer and a fixture of the Chicago theater scene. The new B&K star was duly rewarded for his role in making the McVickers a success. In July 1925, *Variety* reported that Ash was "the highest paid musical director in Chicago and its vicinities," since he had recently been awarded a three-year contract at a salary of $700 a week to replace his initial six-week contract at $500.[68]

When the Oriental opened in 1926, B&K arranged for Ash (along with Keates, who also headlined at the McVickers) to move to their lavish new theater, where Ash assumed the thematically appropriate new title "Rajah of Jazz."[69] The exhibitors wanted their biggest star to perform in a theater designed and built for the theater chain, not one acquired through a merger. B&K, however, found themselves in a delicate position. They had decided to feature Ash as the headliner at their new theater, but they could not risk losing patronage at the McVickers. As a *Variety* reviewer so eloquently put it, "They had to inform the ardent Paul Ash fans that he no longer graces the theatre with his presence and at the same time prevent the Ash fans from interpreting the announcement as a signal to follow their beloved red-head en masse into the new Balaban and Katz Oriental theatre and leave the McVickers flat."[70] It seems that they bungled the affair. First, B&K announced that Ash was to take a "much-needed rest" from his duties at the McVickers, a move that might have facilitated Ash's graceful transition to the Oriental. However, B&K lost control of the situation when they failed to acknowledge Ash's departure from the McVickers, even after a newspaper interview with the star made his move public knowledge. Ash was replaced by another band leader, Henri Gendron, who continued with the stage band policy that Ash had popularized. Ash, however, was much more than a band leader, and the legacy he had built at the McVickers amounted to more than a presentation policy. He was a charismatic performer, and his drawing power lay in who he was, not what he did. Many would imitate his presentation style and some would succeed with the stage band presentation, but Ash himself was unique. The reviewer quoted above concluded with the question: "Will McVickers keep its seats warm after Ash opens at the Oriental theatre?"[71] The McVickers did keep its seats warm—a testament to the appeal of its varied program and superb organist, Helen Crawford—but the Oriental took over as the premier presentation venue in downtown Chicago.

The stage band style of presentation that Paul Ash pioneered became the preferred format for live entertainment in the movie theater. The popularity of this style peaked in 1927, when *Motion Picture News* announced that the B&K Chicago Theatre had just become "the last large de luxe house in Chicago to go into a stage band policy and its success apparently proves the popularity of this type of entertainment beyond any doubt."[72] By this time, the stage band model had also spread beyond the Chicago scene: over two hundred theaters across the nation had implemented what the trade press called "an Ash policy." The Ash policy was a variety stage show for which the band musicians would move from the pit to the stage; the organist was often responsible for providing music during this transition. One famous organist described the Ash policy as suitable for theaters "devoted to the lighter forms of entertainment," in which "the patrons are not adverse to seeing a little clowning from the organist."[73] In other words, it was likely to succeed in a theater that also hosted community singing. Because an Ash show was a stage presentation, it incorporated elements vital to every picture house stage show: lavish sets to create atmosphere and a series of acts to provide the entertainment. The band would remain onstage throughout the show to accompany performers and supply the latest songs. The band leader acted as master of ceremonies, which meant that he provided segues in between acts and chatted with the audience in addition to directing the band. The success of a performer's "turn" on the picture palace stage was determined largely by the context in which it occurred. The theater sought to establish a friendly community of patrons and performers. A show, therefore, was less a performance than a convivial gathering of neighbors with the band leader as host. (The organist occupied a similar role, although only during the organ solo.) To visit the picture palace was to see old friends (on stage) and delight in their company. That atmosphere of congeniality took precedence over the content and quality of the entertainment. As long as the band leader was charismatic and the sets were fantastical, the turns would succeed. This model was very successful at the Oriental, and Paul Ash was responsible for the triumphs of many guest performers.

Ash trained a number of band leaders to emulate his style, such as Al Kvale at the Chicago Norshore and Lou Kosloff ("who does a perfect Paul Ash imitation") at the Chicago Senate and Harding.[74] He also inspired numerous imitators, including Paul Whiteman at the New York Paramount. This is significant, for Whiteman was perhaps the decade's most influential band leader, and the Paramount was arguably the most important picture palace in the world. Ash's influence and reputation in the late 1920s, therefore, can hardly be overstated, and one can only imagine the extraordinary thrill of watching this legend perform live as the star of a show that had been designed expressly for the opulent environment of the Oriental.

Reviewers have left a glut of information about the Oriental stage show the week of October 18, 1927. The sheer level of detail recorded for public consumption reveals the importance of Ash's presentation to the theater's success. As in most picture palace stage shows, all of the acts in Ash's program were unified, more or less, by a theme, even though no plot or narrative connected the turns. Each week an elaborate stage set was constructed to suit the chosen theme, and the guest performers had the option to appear in costume. The band leader would program thematically appropriate music, but the guest performers presented numbers from their own repertoires and made no attempt to integrate their turns into the show. The theme served three purposes. First, it unified a bill of entertainment that would otherwise have no internal cohesion. Second, it provided spectacle, which might not be guaranteed by a given set of acts on their own. A solo singer in a vaudeville show relied on her talent, but in the picture palace presentation she could appear in costume before an extraordinary set and thus become part of an exotic tableau. Finally, the use of a theme provided another opportunity for escapist fantasy.

For the week of October 18, 1927, the theme was "In Spain." The Oriental advertised this theme on the theater marquee, so patrons knew what was in store and were perhaps intrigued by the idea. The *Herald* reviewer reported that the realistic patio scene assembled onstage was so convincing that the patron might in fact believe he had been transported overseas. When the stage show is taken into consideration, one might say that the Oriental offered a fantasy (the Spanish show) within a fantasy (the Indian architecture) within a fantasy (the class-attainment illusion of picture palace culture). The patron had many opportunities to lose herself in the exotic and expensive before the feature film even reached the screen. The *Herald* reviewer added that the show was "Spanish throughout," but this comment must have applied primarily to its appearance. Ash programmed only a few numbers of a Spanish flavor for his band, while the other performers drew their selections from the catalog of recent hits. This meant that the show opened and closed with "Spanish" music but consisted largely of typical American popular songs.[75]

On October 18, 1927, the house band, without Ash, opened the stage show with "Until Tomorrow (Hasta Mañana)," a 1923 song featuring a habanera rhythm. A costumed Jack North provided the vocals while the all-female Abbot dancers, garbed in orange and black, entered from the wings to perform a castanet dance. The Abbot dancers were a house troupe and appeared in all of the shows, sporting costumes and routines that suited the theme. Ash made his grand entrance after the opening number, as was his custom.

While North, who played the banjo and sang in his act, is hardly remembered today as a popular music luminary, he was significant enough in 1927 for B&K to exploit his fame in trade press advertisements for the theater. A spot that appeared in *Variety* the week following the show under discussion featured a caricature of North and proclaimed him to be "The World's Greatest Entertainer"; the advertisement also noted that it was his second week headlining with Paul Ash at the Oriental.[76] The *Variety* reviewer, however, explicitly dismissed North as an act that would not have been strong enough to succeed in the heyday of vaudeville and added that the banjo and singing combination had been worn out already by superior performers. But he countered these remarks with a sharp observation that gets to the heart of Ash's stage band presentation approach: "Jack also gags with Ash and clowns with the band, which is the foremost reason why he stopped this show."[77] North may not have been a stellar musician (neither was Ash), but his ability to project congeniality and to perform intimacy with the host and, by extension, the audience won him the applause.

Ash made his entrance that week costumed as a Spanish don. While this might pale in comparison with his dramatic first appearance on the Oriental's opening night—he was carried in on a litter garbed as a rajah—it still suited his flamboyant stage persona.[78] The patrons came to see Ash, so to make them wait through at least one number was simply good showmanship. After leading the band through "Dream Tango," a 1913 Argentine-flavored instrumental, Ash welcomed local radio tenor Flavio Plasencia to the stage to sing "La Paloma," a mid-nineteenth-century classic that the audience would have recognized. The *Variety* reviewer dismissed Plasencia as a space filler. While his career does not seem to have been extraordinary, it is interesting to note that he in fact recorded "La Paloma," along with three other sides, for Victor only two months after this appearance.

Next the band played "Just Another Day Wasted Away," a 1927 song by Roy Turk of which the Oriental audience was particularly fond. It was at this point that the musical contents of the show began to deviate from the Spanish theme, which would not return until the finale; it was more important that Ash offer audience favorites than that he maintain the exotic illusion. After a round of hearty applause for the instrumental performance, a male trio entered to sing the song and won even greater applause. As one reviewer recalled, "Their harmony in the modern odle-de-do manner sounds well together, but none has a creditable voice in solo."[79] The *Herald* review credits the singers as "The Three Aces," but in *Variety* they are listed as "The Three Rajah Harmonists," known until that very week as perhaps "The Three Collegiates" (the reviewer was not certain). It was not uncommon for ensembles of the period to work under different names, especially when recording. In this case, the trio had been permanently added to the Oriental show by Ash after a very successful first week. For them to perform under a house name such as "The Three Rajah Harmonists" would have been a good advertisement both for the theater and the singers. It is likely that Ash himself insisted upon the change so as to match the name of the group with his own title, "The Rajah of Jazz." The Rajah Harmonists followed up with Walter Donaldson's "My Blue Heaven"—the most popular song of 1927 and prime fodder for movie house musicians. "My Blue Heaven" was heard in every palace across the country and was heavily advertised by the publisher, Leo Feist, in the trade press; organists often programmed it for the purpose of community singing. The Rajah Harmonists closed with "Give Me a Night in June" (1927) and "Are You Happy" (1927), another pair of recent hits.

The Rajah Harmonists were followed by the Dean Brothers, a pair of soft-shoe dancers with an acrobatic specialty who alternated between solo and combined routines. The *Variety* reviewer informs us that the Dean Brothers stopped the show with their eccentric presentation, all in Spanish costume. The music for the Dean Brothers' dancing would have been provided by the stage band, and the audience would have been aware at all times of the dancers, the musicians, and the exotic stage setting. Neither reviewer tells us if the Dean Brothers danced to music of a Spanish flavor, but it is almost certain that they did not. Instead, they would have performed their standard act, identical in content to what they presented in other venues. The theme existed in the costumes, the set, and the band's opening numbers. Each visiting act was woven into the fabric of the show primarily with visual cues, and the performers were not required to learn any new material.

Next to take the stage was Peggy Bernier, a young woman whose history with the Oriental and its patrons colored her reception enormously. Bernier began her career with B&K and was shepherded to stardom by Ash himself. She performed with Ash for a number of weeks at the McVickers and was immediately slated for appearances at the Oriental when that theater opened in 1926 (she sang the recent hit "Tonight's My Night with Baby" in the inaugural program). A. J. Balaban attributed Bernier's success, as well as that of a host of others, to Ash's "encouraging and expert presentation"—that is, his ability to make a performer likable and to elicit a positive response from the audience.[80] By October 1927 she had performed around the country, but the *Variety* reviewer commented that she was rather "tame" when away from the theater that created her. However, it was not Bernier's career that inspired the affection of patrons at the Oriental. It was her love affair with another Ash protégé, Milton Watson, a tenor and stage personality who had worked with Ash throughout the band leader's time in Chicago. Watson opened with Ash at the McVickers and played a supporting role in the presentation of stage shows. During the final weeks before Ash officially departed from the McVickers, Watson served as master of ceremonies in his place, and when Ash moved to the new Oriental, he took Watson with him. Watson sang Irving Berlin's "At Peace with the World" (1926) on the opening-week program at the Oriental, just two numbers before Bernier sang "Tonight's My Night with Baby."

While Bernier and Watson must have encountered one another before the opening of the Oriental, the *Variety* reviewer told the tale of their love in idealized terms: "Where else did Peggy first meet Milton Watson but on the stage of the Oriental? There isn't one masculine Oriental regular who doesn't think he should have been the best man at the Bernier-Watson wedding, nor is there one flapper with the Oriental habit who doesn't think she should have been bridesmaid, at least. And nothing scares up trade faster than a romance that everyone is in on."[81] In this account, the affair was strictly public. The marriage between Bernier and Watson was literally the property of Oriental patrons, and those patrons felt a deep personal connection to the stage performers. As the reviewer phrased it, Bernier and Watson actually met *on the stage* of the Oriental, in full public view, and as participants in a form of public entertainment specifically designed by Ash to make the audience feel as if the performers were their friends. While it is highly unlikely that the two actually met on a stage anywhere, the metaphor is apt. It tells the love story from the perspective of the audience, for whom Bernier and Watson did in fact meet on stage, right in front of their eyes. Because no one in the audience really knew Bernier or Watson, each patron had the power to create the stars in her own image and to imagine their relationship in idealized terms. Bernier and Watson became part of the Oriental fantasy. It is no wonder that the men and women of the audience were disappointed not to be included in the wedding itself. In the public mind, Bernier and Watson were the confidants of everyone who visited the Oriental. They materialized on cue each week in the patron's own home away from home to joke, laugh, and entertain. Although Watson did not even appear at the Oriental in the week of October 18, Bernier's connection to him and to the theater itself assured her place as an audience favorite no matter how she performed. She had long since ceased to be a star and had become a close friend.

The descriptions of Bernier's performance by the two reviewers, representing *Variety* and *Exhibitors Herald*, shed some light on the divergent goals and approaches that characterized the review departments of these publications. Because these two trade journals will play a significant role in the pages to come, it is worth pausing for a moment to examine their motives and techniques. While the *Variety* review focused almost exclusively on Bernier's personal history with the Oriental, pausing only for a moment to describe her (dismissively) from the musical perspective as "a cute little frail-voiced soubret,"[82] the *Exhibitors Herald* reviewer provided a more formal assessment of Bernier's performance, admiring her "capacity for taking any old song, good or bad, and injecting something into it that puts it over with a bang."[83] It is only from the *Herald* that we learn which songs she actually performed: "I Ain't That Kind of a Baby," "He Don't Wanta," and "Miss Annabelle Lee" (the first and third songs were hits of 1927, while the second was probably misidentified). The *Herald* also noted that Bernier had all but abandoned the motion picture stage to take an important role in the Chicago cast of a musical comedy, *Good News.* The *Variety* review painted the picture of an inadequate performer who succeeded on the merit of her personal relationship with the audience, while the *Herald* took Bernier more seriously as a singer and emphasized the legitimacy of her career, not the touching local romance between her and Watson.

After Bernier's highly personal and familiar act—a break in thematic continuity, as she was the only performer not to appear in Spanish costume—the Abbott dancers returned to the stage to present the Kinkajou dance, a popular routine designed and debuted by Edna Passpae at the Dance Masters of America Convention less than two months before. While the Kinkajou failed to take hold in the public imagination as the Charleston had, its presence on the Oriental program demonstrates the fervent desire of movie houses to stay up to date with the latest music and dance trends. The performance won a generous hand due to its incorporation of novel stunts. Next, Jack North returned to the stage to play the banjo and sing

"If You See Sophie Like I See Sophie" (probably misidentified), "I'm Back in Love with You" (most likely the 1927 hit "I'm Back in Love Again"), and "Turkish Towel," a surviving number from 1926. One reviewer described him as "a clever performer" and reported that he was well received.[84]

The last act before the finale demonstrates that picture palace presentation could be highly varied: two children of about five years of age, declared by one reviewer as "the hit of the show," sang, danced, and bantered with Ash. They appeared in Spanish costume to suit the theme and appearance of the show, although the numbers they performed were drawn from their own repertoire. The *Exhibitors Herald* listed the children as Geraldine and Joe while *Variety* called the girl Margery, but either way they seem to have been a typical child act, booked into the Oriental for the standard week-long run. To open, they sang "Hoosier Sweetheart" (a 1927 song coauthored by Paul Ash, misidentified in the *Exhibitors Herald* as "Who's Your Sweetheart"), after which the girl sang "Dew Dew Dewy Day," a 1927 hit that appeared on picture palace bills across the nation for months and had in fact been featured in Keates's community sing the previous week.[85] The *Exhibitors Herald* reviewer noted that the little star engaged in "all the byplay with Ash that the grownup songsters sometimes pull."[86] This suggests that the success of the act was in part due to the performer's ability to joke with the host and connect with the audience on a personal, casual level. It is fascinating to note that even a child performer was conditioned to appeal to the patron's desire for intimate connection with the stage. After another song from the girl, "My Man" (1921), the two youngsters closed with an Apache dance over which the *Variety* reviewer waxed enthusiastic: "Their routine is automatic. But imagine a pair of kids doing a rough-and-tumble apache, good or bad! It is something that can't miss."[87] The Apache dance was linked to a Parisian street gang of the same name (a crude reference to their perceived savagery), and its actions were modeled on the violent discourse between a pimp and a prostitute—although these details must have been lost on the Chicago audience, which would not have accepted such a routine as appropriate for small children.

While Ash and his band were present on stage throughout all of the preceding numbers, they regained the audience's focus for the finale. The band performed "An Old Guitar and an Old Refrain," a 1927 number that was both up-to-date and appropriate to the presentation theme (it bears the subtitle "A Song of Spain"). The responsibility for musically supporting the theme of the show fell to Ash and his regular performers, who both opened and closed each presentation. The Rajah Harmonists entered to sing a chorus of the song, while the Abbott dancers returned, garbed in "beautiful paper dresses and high black headdresses," to perform a "waltz"—a peculiar critical detail, as the song is not in triple time.[88] The *Herald* reviewer described the closing scene of the show: "As the finale begins, they mount small pedestals illuminated with colored lights. The lights shine up in the paper dresses, giving a beautiful illuminated effect, and colored lights appear in the crowns of their hats. The entire effect is extremely beautiful."[89] This climactic visual effect closed out the Ash stage show that had drawn so many to the Oriental that week and ended the exotic journey promised by the stage presentation.

All that was left in the program was the feature itself. It is now easy to frame the film as an afterthought to the Oriental stage show, which boasted dazzling costumes, flamboyant stars, and even a real-life romance. The picture, *Spring Fever*, represented yet another opportunity for escape. The patron, as she viewed the film, could indulge in the fantasy lives of the well-to-do set featured on-screen, just as she might have imagined a journey to India or Spain during other moments in the picture palace experience. She could also escape into the glamorous lives of the movie stars themselves. The film stars could become her friends in the same way that Paul Ash and Peggy Bernier had become her friends. The program came to a close with trailers for the coming feature, which, along with the rest of the show, changed once a week—a promise that the fantasy world would be renewed and made available once again to the weary visitor.

2 THE SING-ALONG TRADITION

As my description of the Chicago Oriental demonstrates, at least some picture palace audiences in the 1920s loved to sing. But why? The answer lies both in the memories that patrons had of past film exhibition practices and in their experiences with community singing outside of the picture theater. Although the community singing conducted in the picture palaces of the 1920s and early 1930s was unique to its time and place, it was neither the earliest example of community singing in the movie theater nor the only instance of community singing activity in contemporary American society. In fact, picture palace singing thrived *because* community singing enjoyed great popularity in American communities during the late 1910s and 1920s.

Picture palace community singing was a product of two other singing practices of the early twentieth century: the illustrated song, which had introduced participatory singing into the earliest movie theaters (ca. 1905–13); and the community singing movement, which had developed in the early 1910s and become mainstream during the Great War as an expression of national unity and patriotism. The illustrated song was in turn descended from older sing-along traditions associated with American vaudeville and the British music hall, in which a performer might call on the audience to "join in the chorus."[1] Indeed, as we shall see, community singing played integral roles both in mass entertainment and music marketing throughout the late nineteenth and early twentieth centuries. Although both the illustrated song and war-era community sing required audience participation, they were essentially unrelated and dissimilar. The illustrated song relied on a solo singer, presented contemporary repertoire, and urged participants to purchase the related sheet music. The community sing eschewed solo performance, presented classic repertoire, and urged participants to support American ideals. All the same, theatergoers in the 1920s remembered the illustrated song and enjoyed reveling in nostalgic reenactments.

Publishing industry practice also linked the two traditions, for which music publishers supplied song slides and performers. Although the materials and techniques had changed when theater sing-alongs were reintroduced in the 1920s, advertising goals remained the same. It was the success of the war-era community singing movement, however, that made sing-alongs viable as picture palace entertainment. In the end, both practices shaped the institution and reception of organist-led community singing.

THE ILLUSTRATED SONG

The illustrated song was a typical component of the program presented in nickelodeon theaters, which—as the first entertainment venues dedicated primarily to motion picture exhibition—were the direct ancestors of the picture palaces. Whether it was offered alongside pictures in the nickelodeon or live acts in the vaudeville theater, the illustrated song was a musical presentation in which a song was brought to life with projected images. A performance required at least two participants: one (or two) to sing and play the piano, and one to operate the magic lantern. While the musician(s) performed the song, the projectionist exhibited a series of pictorial slides designed to illustrate the text. The last slide in the series contained the words to the chorus and, most often, an exhortation for all to join in. At the height of the illustrated song's popularity, the slides were produced by a handful of studios, located primarily in New York City, and featured hand-colored photographs of live models. The best slides—particularly those created by the team of John D. Scott and Edward Van Altena—were artistically conceived and executed using the latest photographic techniques.[2]

The earliest American experiments with song illustration took place during the Civil War, and the initial development of the practice is associated with two men in particular. The first of these was a traveling evangelist named Philip Phillips, who exhibited religious song slides in churches.[3] The second was the famed showman Tony Pastor, who acquired a set of slides to accompany his 1863 song "Heroes of the War." These slides seem to have been a haphazard collection of appropriate images—mostly generals and battle scenes—purchased from a lantern slide company, rather than a set of images commissioned to illustrate the text. For Pastor, the notion of song illustration was indelibly linked with the inflammation of patriotic spirit. After the Civil War was over, Pastor abandoned the illustrated song until an opportunity for revival of his idea came during the Spanish-American war in 1898.[4] Unfortunately, the history of illustrated song development is, at present, hopelessly confused. For example, Pastor's manager, H. S. Sanderson, claimed in 1909 that he gave Pastor the idea of exploiting "tableaux or paintings of song subjects" so as to enhance the performance of a song, but he gives the date of 1873—ten years later than the date provided by other commentators.[5]

This argument over precedence can be put aside, however, for it was not until the early 1890s that the illustrated song became a standard vaudeville turn. During the last years of the century, illustrated songs became popular on vaudeville stages everywhere, as well as in beach resort "concert halls" and dime museums.[6] Certain teams of song illustrators, always made up of a singer and a projectionist, were famous for a particular song, which they would perform hundreds of times as they toured the country. The most famous late nineteenth-century team was that of Joe Maxwell and Al Simpson, who specialized in a "fire" song written and performed by the former. The striking images were always complemented with slides featuring the local fire chiefs, which landed the pair many a sponsored engagement. Simpson went on to become a leader in the production of illustrated song slides for the next two decades.[7]

The mid-1890s saw significant development in the use of illustrated songs, which were becoming more than mere entertainment. In 1894, the song-writing and -publishing team of Edward Marks and Joseph Stern commissioned a set of lantern slides for their song "The Little Lost Child" with the idea that illustrations would help promote the song and increase its popularity. This use of the illustrated song was different from all that had preceded it because Marks and Stern were not interested in the success of any particular performance or performer of the song but were instead interested in the success of the song itself.[8] Over the next few years, illustrated songs became a favorite tool of music promoters, who employed them specifically to create hits and sell sheet music. When illustrated songs were exhibited in movie theaters, the sheet music was often available for purchase at the ticket counter, or even sold in the audience while the show was still underway.[9] For some time, publishers had provided vaudeville singers with free sheet music and cash payments in order to assure the performance of their songs. Beginning in the mid-1890s, publishers provided singers with complementary illustrated song slides as well.[10]

The illustrated song became ubiquitous when it was incorporated into the earliest motion picture shows. These two forms of entertainment were inseparable for most of a decade, and it was through the motion picture show that illustrated songs gained national popularity and lasting fame. The first venue dedicated to motion picture exhibition opened in Pittsburgh in 1905. These theaters quickly acquired the nickname "nickelodeon," a pseudo-Greek neologism combining *nickel* (the cost for admittance) with the Greek word for theater.[11] Nickelodeons were small storefront theaters that offered a mixture of vaudeville, illustrated songs, and motion pictures. The nickelodeon was not often one's final destination but rather a place to stop off for a few minutes of cheap entertainment. For the five-cent fee, a patron could enter at any point in the show and stay for as long as he or she pleased. As one writer noted in 1907, "They are great places for the foot-sore shopper, who is not used to cement sidewalks, to rest. It is much more comfortable than to take street-car rides to rest, and they don't have to pay the return nickel."[12]

Nickelodeons were inexpensive to set up and operate, and they remained small—under two hundred seats—to avoid the steep licensing fees that plagued legitimate theaters.[13] These early twentieth-century entertainment venues were popular in urban neighborhoods and small rural communities. Urban nickelodeons typically offered continuous shows of about fifteen minutes in length, and the program was changed one to three times a week.[14] Nickelodeons were often reputed to attract only the lowest-class patrons—"a section of the population that formerly knew or cared little about the drama"—but in fact they operated across a wide spectrum of respectability.[15] One observer noted that children constituted a third of the total audience. These theaters were also very attractive to urban immigrants, who, for only five cents, could remain all day to study the fashions and customs of the actors and learn English from the songs.[16] Illustrated songs were valued for their assimilative effect, and film scholar Richard Abel notes the upbeat and "blatantly 'American'" element that they contributed to the nickelodeon program, which was often dominated by notoriously bleak French films.[17]

Scholars today usually discuss the nickelodeon's role as the first movie theater, but this is only because movies continued to thrive and develop while the other elements of the nickelodeon program were fated to disappear. In their time, though, nickelodeons were not actually thought of as movie theaters. There was a great deal of doubt concerning the viability of moving pictures, which were often of low quality, usually of foreign origin, and in constant short supply.[18] Vaudeville acts—including the illustrated song, which would soon occupy its own category—were initially incorporated into the nickelodeon program because film production, especially in the United States, had not yet reached the capacity required to supply the necessary length of entertainment. It was only the illustrated song, however, that became established in the nickelodeons. Films and illustrated songs had always appeared together at the end of vaudeville programs (probably because they shared the same projecting equipment), and it seemed only natural that they should continue to be paired.[19] Throughout the first decade of nickelodeon exhibition, featured films alternated with the presentation of one or two illustrated songs.[20] Because of this, contemporary commentators regularly referred to nickelodeons as "pic-vaude" houses and even "moving picture illustrated song theaters."[21] Some nickelodeons advertised their live entertainment more prominently than their films because managers considered the illustrated-song performances to be the biggest draw.[22]

During its brief existence, the illustrated song was plagued by troubles. Song publishers, nickelodeon exhibitors, and singers alike all found the illustrated-song model to be unsustainable. Publishers were overwhelmed by demand for free slides, and their expenses ballooned while profits stagnated.[23] At the same time, exhibitors—in an effort to keep their programs fresh—refused to repeat songs for more than a few days, which meant that the songs were not being adequately plugged.[24] Some slide makers released shoddy sets of illustrations, while reputable slide producers became the victims of both pirates, who copied their slides and sold cheap knockoffs, and unscrupulous singers, who resold complimentary sets of slides below the going rate.[25] Competition drove wages for singers so low that most competent performers left the industry.[26] As a result, inept illustrated song performances damaged the interests of both exhibitors and publishers: they neither attracted patrons to the nickelodeon nor boosted sheet music sales.[27]

Given this litany of troubles, it is not surprising that the illustrated song was on the road to extinction. However, while the illustrated song had all but vanished from the nickelodeon by 1913, no scholar has yet fully explained its disappearance. For example, Rick Altman, a film scholar who has published extensively on the illustrated song, argues that the practice disappeared due to the increase in phonograph use by the early 1910s. The proliferation of recorded music meant that the market for sheet music was shrinking.

Altman argues that, because the object of illustrated songs was to sell sheet music, the disappearance of the product meant that the illustrated song was no longer needed to advertise it. This explanation, which doubtless contains some truth, is not entirely satisfactory. To begin with, historian Matthew Mooney has demonstrated that, after 1908, music publishers had little to do with the illustrated song. It remained a part of the nickelodeon program because it was entertaining, not because it sold sheet music. Second, music publishers continued to plug their songs during live-entertainment programs for decades to come. It is certain that publishers did not lose interest in the movie theater as a plugging venue, for they produced many of the slide sets that were used for community singing in the 1920s and 1930s.

For the present, the conclusion reached by Mooney seems the most plausible: the film program itself was transforming in the early 1910s, and the new approach to exhibition emphasized the feature film, while eliminating variety acts. This new format left no room for the illustrated song.[28] Altman supports this view with his report that theaters were installing second projectors during this period, which allowed continuous exhibition of films. The illustrated song, therefore, was no longer needed to fill the gap created when the projectionist changed reels.[29] Altman also makes the observation that participatory culture was dissipating, due to the replacement of home pianos with phonographs. He suggests that "illustrated songs no longer had a role to play" once theater audiences became passive.[30] It is true that music literacy and home music making were on the decline; the community singing movement, which reached its peak influence during the 1910s, sought explicitly to reverse this trend. However, participation would remain central to film exhibition throughout the 1920s.

In the silent era, every element of the picture show was participatory to a degree. Depending on the character of the theater, patrons clapped, hollered, and booed in response to onscreen events. They also discussed the films with one another during projection, for there was no fear of drowning out the actors' spoken dialogue, which did not exist. "In the old days," recalled organist John Muri, "some people would read the sub-titles out loud, particularly for the illiterates in their families; sometimes they did it just for fun or because they became emotionally involved in the film."[31] In addition, both live and projected entertainment sought explicitly to elicit audience response. For example, the 1927 film Love My Dog invited the audience "to applaud if they want to save the life of a dog, about to be killed at the pound. The customers responded briskly."[32] Only the community sing, however, relied 100 percent on audience participation, and it failed completely if this need was not met.

The transformation of the film program described by Mooney began with the elimination of illustrated songs and variety acts, but this trend was reversed completely with the development of picture palace entertainment during the late 1910s. When palace exhibitors introduced live acts back into the picture show, however, they were not padding a weak film program. On the contrary, they offered live entertainment as a luxury, and picture palace patrons expected it to be of the highest quality. As a result, the stage shows of the 1920s bore little or no relation to the cheap vaudeville of the nickelodeon. This, however, did not prevent exhibitors from exploiting their patrons' nostalgia for the dingy, old-style theaters. Projectionists often employed newly minted announcement slides modeled on those of the nickelodeon era; a favorite theme was the request for ladies to remove their hats, usually accompanied by an outrageous illustration. These slides were meant to evoke laughter, but they also traded on memories of the old-fashioned picture theater (in addition to the fashions of a bygone era).

In capitalizing on fond memories of the illustrated song, organists and vaudeville performers alike would use old sets of slides to accompany the rendition of Gilded Age favorites.[33] In the picture palace, illustrated songs were often presented as part of a complete "old-time" stage show that included nickelodeon-era films and period costumes. Trade press commentators suggested that exhibitors inject as much humor into the novelty as possible; this might be provided by inept underscoring at the piano, primitive projection technology, occasional upside-down slides, or an illustrated singer "in the most approved style"—that is, too loud, out of tune, and maximally melodramatic.[34] The joke was wearing thin in 1933, when a *Variety* reviewer observed that short films burlesquing nickelodeon-style entertainment were "getting to be quite formula."[35] In this way, the illustrated song lived on for another generation, if only as a figure of fun. At the same time, however, participatory singing transcended its historical connotations and found a new home in the organ solo. This came to pass not because of the continuing influence of the illustrated song but because of the entirely independent—and entirely serious—community singing movement, which had taught the practice to Americans across the country during the Great War and thereby established community singing as a part of daily life.

THE COMMUNITY SINGING MOVEMENT

The community singing movement grew out of the efforts of a loosely organized group of community music activists, who labored at the turn of the
century to spread a love of "good music" and develop the habit of participatory music making. These men and women were concerned not with
amusement but with morals, patriotism, and taste; indeed, most of them
would have reacted with horror at the thought that their efforts would cul-
minate in the picture palace sing-along, which was usually comical and
relied on the most ephemeral of popular songs. All the same, Americans
of the 1920s were in the habit of singing publicly with their neighbors only
because Americans of the 1910s were trained in the practice. To understand
the influence of the community singing movement, we must begin with the
spread of Progressive Era politics to a generation of teachers, critics, and
social workers several decades before the first picture palace was erected.

The end of the nineteenth century saw a revolt, headed by social-minded
progressives, against the status quo of European art and music. At the heart
of this effort was a conviction that the time had come to cast off the yoke
of European culture. The United States was emerging as a world leader,
and it therefore required a uniquely American cultural life. American art
needed to be profoundly democratic, to include all and speak for all (or, if
not all, then at least those Americans who held the power). When progressives examined the institutions in place, however, they became concerned
that "good music"—the definition of which they never agreed upon—had
become the property of the elite. Monumental concert halls, formal dress,
perplexing etiquette, and expensive tickets all served to keep the vast majority of Americans from getting to know and love the music that, in the eyes
of reformers, was justly theirs.[36] Reformers were aided in their quest for
cultural uplift by the record companies, who, led by Victor in 1903, marketed highbrow music to the masses in order to boost their overall profits.[37] The campaign to elevate musical taste touched all corners of the nation
and culminated in the community music movement of the 1910s and 1920s.
Community singing—which became a movement of its own—was a favorite tool of reformers, for it brought enormous crowds together in informal
spaces and required no prior training.[38]

The music reformers did not pursue their work just to bring joy into the
lives of Americans, or even to promote their own fields of music education,

composition, and performance. For them, this was a moral issue. As leading reformer Peter W. Dykema put it, "the people as a whole must be educated to believe that music is not an occasional luxury, to be indulged in now and then, but that it is an essential of right living."[39] One could boast neither full humanity nor full citizenship without musical engagement, which Dykema claimed was necessary to "keep our hearts pure, our minds clear, our wills right."[40] Another reformer, Edgar B. Gordon, was concerned that Americans lowered their moral standards in pursuit of entertainment. "Education has stressed vocational training," he wrote in 1916. "Is it not of quite as much importance to train for the proper use of leisure time?"[41] Reformers worried that Americans—especially those involved in urban industry—were debasing themselves in their leisure hours with "rag-time" (that is, African American music) and "the transient song" (that is, commercial music); the urban nickelodeon and its illustrated songs, therefore, represented the lowest and most dangerous form of popular culture.[42] Instead, Americans ought to be engaged in the wholesome process of "spiritual upbuilding," a process that promised contentment, true joy, and complete personhood.[43]

Music reformers genuinely believed that "good music" had the power to cure most of society's ills, and they spread the gospel of "good music" and its "ennobling influence" with missionary zeal.[44] The reformers themselves were largely white, middle class, and educated, hailing from New England or the Midwest. They included music educators, musicians, composers, critics, and members of women's clubs, and each combined shared progressive values with personal agendas. Since the elite already had access to culture, reformers targeted certain underprivileged classes: the urban poor, rural white Americans, and European immigrants. Gavin James Campbell notes the "complicated mixture of humanitarianism and fear" with which music reformers approached their work.[45] They felt compelled to reach out to their brothers and sisters in need, but they also saw these populations as the source of social problems. By offering cultural uplift to the underserved, reformers expected to improve relations between social groups and create a more perfect democracy.

The potential benefits of good music were many. In the cities, an improved cultural life was expected to combat the dehumanizing effects of industrial work, deter immoral behavior, offer an alternative to crime, and take the place of liquor. It would also pacify the working class and prevent social upheaval, while simultaneously improving worker productivity.[46] In the countryside, music would make rural life more appealing and prevent young people from moving to the cities, where they would likely fall victim to vice; reformers also feared that mass migration might result in the collapse of the rural economy.[47] Music, offered in tasteful social settings and with English lyrics, would help to Americanize the immigrant; it provided a common emotional experience that transcended language, and newcomers could understand and participate immediately. Indeed, music had much to offer every citizen, no matter what his social position: it could improve morality, bolster patriotism, solidify citizenship, and promote good values.

There were several avenues through which the dose of good music might be administered. This was the era in which the notion of "music appreciation" was born, and the early twentieth century saw the introduction of classes, preconcert lectures, books, and phonograph records designed to educate the masses about Western concert repertoire. Reformers were certain that the average man could enjoy and understand good music. Arthur Farwell, a music reformer of particular note, proposed the concept of "mass-appreciation," or the idea that citizens assembled in a large group become mentally joined and therefore have a deeper spiritual understanding of the music than if they were to listen alone.[48] John C. Freund, editor of *Musical America*, exhibited a similar belief with his notion of the "mass soul," derived from Emerson's "Over-Soul," in which community singing would literally "weld the people of America into a common ideal and a common purpose."[49] Community singing was favored by many reformers, but it was not the only way to get music into the life of every American. Pageants experienced a surge in popularity, as did community orchestras, bands, and choral unions. Music schools sought to attract adult students and developed community outreach programs.

In all of its forms, the community music movement had a nationalistic aim. Reformers often spoke of the great "melting pot" that was to blend disparate cultures and languages into a homogenous and uniquely "American" society—although this metaphor was usually code for the assimilation of white, progressive, middle-class values. Dykema drew a direct parallel between community music, in which every citizen participated to the best of his ability, and the American political system. He also argued that music—especially community singing—reinforced the ideals of democracy, for it demonstrated "the necessity for unified harmonious cooperation" in a way that any citizen could immediately grasp.[50] "Any group of people singing together," he wrote, "offers a most remarkable example of mutual helpfulness and compensation."[51] Community singing was an exercise in civil discourse and cooperative living. It represented the best of America while encouraging Americans to be their best.

While the ultimate goal of every reformer was to make music a ubiquitous part of American life, many—especially those who worked in music educa- tion—believed that it was most productive to focus their efforts on school children. These children, after all, would grow up to be the musical adults of tomorrow. They were also highly impressionable, and reformers believed that, once they had been taught to love good music, they would demand it at home, thereby spreading the gospel to their families and neighbors. Freund advocated strenuously for this approach. His advice to music reformers was not to start with a symphony orchestra or opera company but to "begin at the beginning, namely, with the introduction of music into the public schools, then build on that with community choruses, music for the people in the parks and piers in the summer and in the school auditoriums in the winter, build on that, then, with other choral bodies and good music in the churches."[52] Once a foundation of interest in music had been laid and latent talent cultivated, the emblems of elite culture might be introduced "as the crown and apex of it all."[53] At this point, Freund was certain that the entire populace would freely offer financial support.

At the same time, few reformers were willing to abandon the adult pop- ulation. "What are we going to do with these thousands and thousands of adults?" asked Dykema. "Are they to remain what our American people as a whole undoubtable are, quite dumb and hopeless as far as artistic expression is concerned? The great democratic surge in music known as community music thunders forth a mighty 'No!'"[54] Dykema and others were convinced that they bore responsibility not only for the youngest Americans but for "the larger children, sometimes the more needy children," and they were certain that community music programs could provide cultural nourish- ment even to the most deprived.[55]

The biggest obstacle to nationwide cultural uplift was aptly summed up in 1915 by the *Baltimore Evening Sun*: "It is maintained that Americans are lacking in the musical instinct largely because we are a nation without folk songs and that our people do not sing naturally as do those of other coun- tries."[56] Although Freund had defiantly announced "the declaration of the Musical Independence of the United States," native artistry was predicated on a store of native culture, and this was where reformers found the United States to be deficient.[57] It was widely agreed that, while American citizens were ignorant of high culture, even the peasants of Italy and Germany sang opera while they scrubbed the pots and pans.[58] Europeans also shared a vast treasury of folk songs, which reformers understood them to sing together at every opportunity.[59] Americans were inferior in this regard, but reformers were committed to uncovering (or creating) a body of American folk song and teaching it to the people. This would remedy an embarrassing shortcoming, promote patriotic feeling, and demonstrate the cultural vitality of the nation.

Music reformers all supported community singing along the lines of European models, but the paucity of shared American folk songs was a real problem. In the early twentieth century, folklorists were just beginning to collect and publish the folk music of white Americans. John Lomax's *Cowboy Songs and Other Frontier Ballads* attracted a great deal of attention in 1910; at the same time, Olive Dame Campbell was collecting ballads in the Appalachians, an area that would soon become a hotbed of folklorist activity.[60] This kind of folk material certainly advanced the cause of white American nationalism, but it was of no use for community singing. These tunes were not part of the collective American consciousness—or at least not that of the northern city dwellers. The reformers needed "folk songs" that everyone could sing.

The creation of a canon and the formal inauguration of the community singing movement might be traced to 1913, when members of the Music Supervisors National Conference (MSNC) met for their annual convention in Rochester, New York. The MSNC had only been in existence for a handful of years; it was founded in 1907 by a group of midwestern music educators who belonged to the music section of the National Education Association (NEA). In part because the NEA meeting that summer was held in far-off Los Angeles, 104 music educators from sixteen states instead gathered in Keokuk, Iowa, under the leadership of music section vice president Francis E. Clark. Most of those present agreed that the aims of their profession would be better served by an independent organization, and Clark became the first president of the MSNC.[61]

In 1913, another woman—Henrietta Baker Low—was concluding her term as president. Low served as music supervisor for the Baltimore school system and was a prominent national leader in music education reform.

Although her career was officially terminated by her 1914 marriage, Low would continue to organize and promote community singing throughout the 1910s. She also played an important part in launching the community singing movement. At the 1913 meeting of the MSNC, a paper was read on behalf of a Kansas music educator and community music activist, Frank A. Beach, who was himself unable to attend. In the paper, Beach observed that less than a third of all American children were provided with music education. To rectify this, he urged the MSNC to adopt a list of twelve songs that every American should know and publish them in a standardized version for use in classrooms across the country. Beach also suggested that members "do missionary work" in rural areas to spread the love of music to otherwise deprived children—a task that Low would later take up with great enthusiasm. The response of those who heard Beach's plea, however, was not supportive: "The members of the convention laughed" in the face of such an ambitious proposal and derided Beach for his unrealistic idealism. Low, however, was so moved that she put aside her prepared address and retorted that "the suggestions were neither preposterous nor too idealistic for realization." She then demanded that a committee be formed on the spot and meet forthwith to create the list of twelve songs, a task for which she reportedly permitted only ninety minutes.[62]

Low appointed Dykema chair of the committee, which immediately began its deliberations. Despite their best efforts, however, the members could not agree on a list of fewer than eighteen songs. Their selections were published later that year as *18 Songs for Community Singing*; Low later hypothesized that this was the first time the term "community singing" had ever appeared in print.[63] While Beach had limited his proposal to a songbook for use in the classroom, the preface to *18 Songs*—signed by the seven committee members, including Low and Dykema—indicated a larger scope for the work. From its opening sentences, the reader learns that the MSNC had "inaugurated a movement to stimulate general singing in the home, the school, fraternal and social societies, and miscellaneous gatherings" with the object of making "an immediate and effective start toward national community singing."[64] While Beach's plan for singing in the schools might have provoked skepticism at the outset, the committee quickly exceeded his idealism with their own vision for a national movement. Although the committee was disappointed with the small number of educators who adopted the songbook in its first four months, the project would soon develop into the enormously successful *55 Songs for Community Singing* (1917), which sold over a million copies in a "Liberty Edition" during the war.[65]

The initial list of eighteen songs set the standard for community singing fare. To create it, the committee brought together patriotic numbers, Stephen Foster classics, and European folk songs that had found favor in the United States. The songs were printed in the following order: "America," "The Star-Spangled Banner," "Old Folks at Home," "Lovely Evening," "Auld Lang Syne," "Annie Laurie," "Home, Sweet Home," "How Can I Leave Thee?," "Dixie," "My Old Kentucky Home," "Drink to Me Only with Thine Eyes," "Flow Gently, Sweet Afton," "Nancy Lee," "The Minstrel Boy," "Sweet and Low," "Row, Row, Row Your Boat," "Blow, Ye Winds, Heigh-Ho," and "Love's Old Sweet Song." Most of the arrangements provided four-part harmony either throughout or for the chorus, while two of the songs selected were rounds. The preface describes the challenge of choosing "correct" versions of the songs, most of which had accumulated a variety of texts and music. The committee settled on the versions that, in their judgment, represented "an approximation of what may be expected from the undirected and hence, rather natural and spontaneous singing of an untrained but musical group."[66] It is worth noting that the committee included the simplified version of the "Star-Spangled Banner," as recommended by the music section of the NEA; that particular song had recently engendered a great deal of controversy regarding the capacity and inclination of amateurs to sing dotted rhythms.

While the repertoire included in *18 Songs for Community Singing* molded the early development of the community singing movement and inspired countless songbooks to come, it did not reflect a universal consensus about what Americans should sing. Some reformers advocated for African American spirituals, although the objection that such music was not "essentially American" largely won out; as countless music historians have observed, the music of black America was seldom accepted as representative of the nation as a whole during this period.[67] Stephen Foster tunes, on the other hand, were widely accepted for community singing and were often referred to as folk songs in the press. Song leaders also employed popular opera choruses, such as the "Soldiers' Chorus" from *Faust*, or the "Pilgrim's Chorus" from *Tannhäuser*. Although Dykema spearheaded the assembly of the community singing canon, he was in fact not content with the available selections. He would have preferred to commission a team of well-trained musicians to compose songs that were simple and catchy but still bore musical merit.[68]

Reformers understood that, if they hoped to achieve their lofty aims, they had to work in stages. To begin with, many Americans had been denied music education, and they lacked both skill and taste. Community singing, which did not require the ability to read music, solved the first problem. The second had to be approached with care. Most reformers agreed that it was acceptable to start with the crass popular tunes that the masses loved and then to introduce "good music" gradually. They firmly believed that any citizen, once exposed to a better class of music, would abandon trite novelties and dangerous ragtime.

Ambitions varied widely, however, and not just in terms of repertoire. Low, for example, conducted community singing all along the East Coast and evangelized for her cause across the nation, but she always had her sights set on the formation of community choruses.[69] She rehearsed her crowds, educating them in proper vocal technique and artistic phrasing. Her contemporary Harry Barnhart, in contrast, conducted community singing in New York without ever teaching technique or part singing; he also saw no value in introducing his singers to the choral classics.[70] Dykema condemned those who abandoned large-scale sings to establish "small sterile glee clubs," while *Musical America* announced that traditional choruses were inevitably to be replaced by community singing, which was "a true movement of our democracy."[71]

In 1915 and 1916 there were some significant experiments with community singing, most notably at the Preparatory Division of the Peabody Institute in Baltimore, Maryland, where Low served on the faculty. With the assistance of the founder and director of the Preparatory Division, May Garrettson Evans, Low began in 1914 to lay the groundwork necessary to ensure that community singing would succeed when it was introduced. Their tactics included regular classroom singing from *18 Songs* for preparatory students and training for public school teachers.[72] Then, on March 5, 1915, Low staged a public community singing concert that attracted four hundred visitors, whom she led in selections from *18 Songs* with the assistance of the Peabody Junior Orchestra and a trained soprano.[73] The success of this event demonstrated the viability of community singing in Baltimore and prompted several repetitions at the Peabody, in public parks, and in the suburban areas of Baltimore, and the two women received inquiries from people around the country who were interested in replicating their community concerts.[74] In all likelihood, however, the practice of community singing would have lost its novel appeal and faded away were it not for a cataclysmic event: the entry of the United States into the Great War on April 6, 1917.

The onset of war presented a series of challenges to the American government. Money had to be raised, troops had to be trained and looked after, and patriotic spirit had to be encouraged in every citizen. Community singing had a role to play in meeting all of these challenges. The fact that community singing became central to the war effort, however, was due to the War Department's authorization of two new administrative bodies to oversee recreation for soldiers in the camps and in neighboring communities. These were, respectively, the Commission for Training Camp Activities (CTCA) and its subsidiary, the War Camp Community Service (WCCS). The architects of the wartime recreation program were Secretary of War Newton D. Baker and the well-known urban reformer Raymond B. Fosdick, who had previously served in John D. Rockefeller's Bureau of Social Hygiene.

In 1916, Secretary Baker tasked Fosdick with assessing the living conditions in military camps along the Mexican border, where troops had been deployed in response to Pancho Villa's raid of Columbus, New Mexico. It was understood that the men spent their leisure time drinking excessively and engaging in illicit sexual behavior. While both of these activities were detrimental to the effectiveness of a fighting force, the military leadership considered the greatest threat to be venereal disease, which had decimated armies in Europe.[75] At the border, Fosdick found that not only were prostitution and alcohol widely available in the vicinity of the camps but that the soldiers had no alternative means of recreation with which to pass the time. He concluded that only a two-pronged attack could obliterate this dangerous threat: the sources of vice must on the one hand be eliminated, while on the other the men must be provided with wholesome and uplifting activities with which to fill their leisure hours.[76]

While Fosdick was uniquely concerned with conditions in army camps along the border, neither his observations nor his solutions were novel: the prominent social reformer Jane Addams had been advocating wholesome recreation for young people since the late nineteenth century and had already experimented with the uplifting influence of music—including community singing—at her Chicago settlement, Hull-House.[77] In one oft-quoted passage from her 1909 publication *The Spirit of Youth and the City Streets*, Addams anticipated Fosdick's conclusions and placed responsibility for preserving the morality of America's children squarely on the shoulders of society: "To fail to provide for the recreation of youth, is not only to deprive all of them of their natural form of expression, but is certain to subject some of them to the overwhelming temptation of illicit and soul-destroying pleasures."[78] When Fosdick recommended morally sound recreation for American soldiers, he was following a trend that had been set in motion by Addams and other early progressive reformers. When he recommended community singing in particular, he aligned himself with Low, Dykema, and other leaders in the new field of community music.

Fosdick and Secretary Baker made limited attempts to improve the situation along the border, but it was not until that onset of the Great War that they had the opportunity to implement a large-scale recreation program. While the conflict in Europe was of course larger and more significant than the border tussle, it also bore an important characteristic that would aid the reformers in their work: the men were to be drafted. For President Wilson, this meant that the government had a sacred responsibility to meet their social and moral needs, and to return boys to their families in perfect spiritual condition. "The career," he wrote in 1918, "to which we are calling our young men in the defense of democracy must be made an asset to them, not only in strengthened and more virile bodies as a result of physical training, not only in minds deepened and enriched by participation in a great, heroic enterprise, but in the enhanced spiritual values which come from a full life lived well and wholesomely."[79] He was supported by a concerned citizenry who associated the soldier's life with drinking and debauchery. Typical fears, expressed here by a community organizer with the Playground and Recreation Association of America, included "broken homes, vice, disease, illegitimate children, brutalized men, disgraced women, lowered standards and moral deterioration."[80] Both parents of soldiers and the residents of towns near the proposed training camps feared the worst and were eager to see reforms in camp life.[81]

The CTCA was officially authorized on April 17, 1917, with Fosdick as chairman. It worked with a handful of preexisting community organizations—most importantly the Young Men's Christian Association (YMCA), the Knights of Columbus, and the Jewish Welfare Board—to provide a wide range of recreational opportunities for men in the army and navy training camps. These included organized sports, theatrical performances, films, clubhouses in which the men could gather and relax, letter-writing materials, libraries, language classes, music-making opportunities, and hostess houses to accommodate female visitors. All of these activities belonged to the "positive program" that sought to combat vice by offering wholesome alternatives. The reformers who helmed the CTCA fervently believed that most soldiers would prefer uplifting and clean entertainment, and they hoped that prostitution and drink would largely disappear once the men had alternatives. All the same, the CTCA saw fit to enact a simultaneous program of suppression that closed vice districts, enacted antiprostitution laws, and relocated undesirable women into detention houses and reformatories.[82]

Community singing was always a part of the CTCA's positive program. Fosdick himself lobbied for its inclusion, and in his 1958 autobiography, he described the event that inspired him: "Four years earlier when I was in Europe—and this, of course, was before the war—I was fascinated by the singing of the German regiments as they swung along the country roads on their practice marches. There was a spontaneity and lift to it, and one got the impression that it brought a relief from tension and eased the long miles under heavy packs."[83] Like Dykema and others, Fosdick perceived Germany as the model for integrating music into everyday life. Americans in these years envied the enriching folk traditions and easy musicality of their wartime foes, even as they feared their political ambitions.

Together, Fosdick and Secretary Baker developed the idea of installing a song leader in every training camp. This person—a citizen operating under the authority of the CTCA—would not only lead group singing as a form of diversion for the troops but would also train enlisted men as song leaders so that the activity could continue overseas. Song leaders were also recruited by camp commanders to lead singing while the men were training or drilling, to organize singing competitions between companies, and even to train officers in the proper use of their voices so that they could give commands more effectively.[84]

The most apparent purpose for singing in the camps was summed up in the CTCA propaganda volume *Keeping Our Fighters Fit*: "A singing army is a cheerful one, and, other things being equal, a cheerful army is invincible."[85] Advocates of the practice, however, ascribed a wide variety of benefits to community singing. One song leader produced the following categorized list of benefits, also included in the above-mentioned volume:

I. The Unit
   1. Team-work
   2. Concerted action
II. Mental Discipline
   1. Memory
   2. Observation
   3. Initiative
   4. Definiteness
   5. Concentration
   6. Accuracy
   7. Punctual attack and action
III. Physical Benefits
   1. A strong back, chest, and lungs
   2. A throat less liable to infection
   3. Increased circulation helps to clear nasal cavities
   4. Strengthens and preserves voice

Others reported great success in using song to teach English to immigrant troops, who at the same time were "Americanized" by the experience of singing patriotic and war-themed repertoire.[86]

The CTCA sought to provide such a quantity and quality of entertainment that men would no longer desire to visit nearby towns, thus eliminating the threat of illicit behavior. There is evidence that leave taking did indeed diminish, but most soldiers still desired to get away from camp, enjoy local entertainment, and meet young ladies. With the aid of the existing Playground and Recreation Association of America, the CTCA established the WCCS to monitor and provide recreation opportunities outside of the camps. This organization worked with local civic and church leaders to ensure that there was plenty of wholesome entertainment available for visiting soldiers. In its efforts to keep the men out of trouble, the WCCS opened hotels and cafeterias, established information centers, sponsored dances, regulated public transportation, and arranged for soldiers to enjoy automobile rides and Sunday dinners with local families. It also organized community singing events outside of the camps. These occasions were intended for the entertainment of soldiers and townspeople alike, and they were headed by the camp song leaders.[87] Finally, song leaders took every opportunity to serve the communities in which they were stationed by providing their services to clubs and school groups. In this way, song leaders became a part of

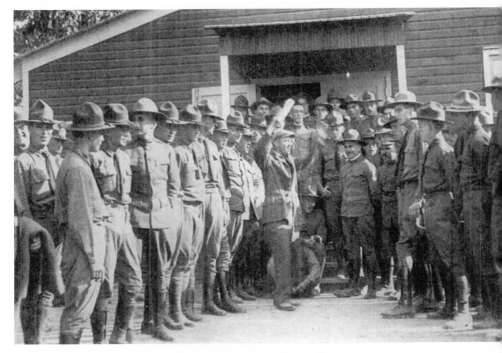

This photograph of CTCA song leader Warren Kimsey teaching officers at Camp Gordon, located near Atlanta, Georgia, appeared in the March 1918 edition of the *Rotarian*.

community life, cultivated goodwill toward the military, and furthered the overarching cause of patriotism.[88]

The community singing repertoire of the war era is represented by the pocket-sized *Army Song Book*, published by the CTCA in 1917 for use in the camps. The booklet was made available to enlisted men at cost and to citizens for a slightly higher fee, and the songs selected for the collection were meant to appeal to soldiers, to promote good spirits, and to instill patriotic feeling. Best represented were the popular songs of the era, including many that dealt with military life and the war. Next came national and patriotic songs, including those of the French, British, Belgian, and Italian people. The remainder of the volume contained folk songs and hymns.[89] This repertoire was disseminated to civilians during and after the war by military song leaders working under the auspices of the WCCS. At the same time, local choir directors and music educators were encouraged by President Wilson to conduct community singing of patriotic songs as a means of building national unity. Wilson's campaign was successful: "The need for singing in the army, to keep up the morale and to maintain spirits during the long grind," observed the *Atlanta Constitution*, "is being transferred to civilian life, where the necessity for patriotic expression is growing keener."[90] By the end of the war, community singing was a fixture in cities and towns across the country.

Community singing was first paired with film exhibition by CTCA and WCCS directors who sought to provide quality entertainment for enlisted soldiers. Such entertainment was staged in the camp's Liberty Theater, in public parks, in municipal auditoriums, and in urban vaudeville and movie houses.[91] Song leaders collaborated with local theater managers to offer community singing alongside the regular program of films, usually for the purpose of raising money for the war effort.[92] At the same time, various State Councils of Defense began producing and circulating song slides to encourage community singing. These slides, which contained the lyrics to various American anthems, national anthems of the Allied forces, and favorites like "My Old Kentucky Home," were distributed without charge to movie theaters for use in patriotic exercises.[93]

As the war drew to a close, interested parties—music industry leaders, educators, social reformers, and professional entertainers—began to perceive the revitalized community singing movement as a valuable tool that could aid in the pursuit of their own agendas. Although wartime singing was dominated by men, female music reformers were quick to take advantage of the popularization of community singing. In Georgia, for example, Annie May Carroll, state chairman for community music under the Council of National Defense, organized the spread of community singing throughout her state. She was joined by countless other women at the local level who were enthusiastic about using voices to win the war and saw long-term advantages to the community singing habit. Carroll and other organizers appealed to Georgia's musicians, educators, and tradespeople to become involved, with the promise that building public interest in a respectable style of music—that is, patriotic and folk song in place of ragtime—would profit them in the long run.[94]

This promise was kept. Once the war had concluded, members of the music industry quickly commandeered the practice of community singing. The organization behind the largest effort to capitalize on the practice was the National Bureau for the Advancement of Music, which was founded in September 1916 to further the interests of two existing trade organizations, the National Piano Manufacturers Association and the Music Industries Chamber of Commerce.[95] Writing for his peers in the *Music Trade Review*, director Charles M. Tremaine described the mission of his organization: "This has been the principle of the Bureau—to help the trade at its foundation by increasing the interest in music among the general public."[96] Tremaine spent the first decade of his tenure working to establish a National Music Week. This annual celebration would encompass a wide variety of activities, but it would rely first and foremost on public community singing. The idea of committing an entire week, on a national scale, to the pursuit of a single task emerged during the Great War. Weeks dedicated to the Red Cross, to the YMCA, and to various drives mobilized the population in support of the war effort. According to Tremaine, the idea was often employed after the war by "organizations that have some interest to promote or by individuals who have something to sell."[97] The industry journal, *Music Trade Review*, described the goal of Music Week as follows: "It may not result, of course, in people dropping other pursuits and rushing into piano or music stores to purchase, but it will turn their minds towards music, and having accomplished that much, open a way for musical instrument purchases in the future."[98] This transformation of the community singing movement foreshadowed the development of picture palace community singing in the next decade: although organists led sing-alongs in order to entertain their patrons, the practice was encouraged and supported by music publishers who saw an opportunity to plug their songs.

The first local Music Week celebration took place in Saint Louis in November 1919.[99] This was quickly followed by other city-wide celebrations, which were typically organized by members of the music trade. Organizers won broad support for the celebrations by including government officials and representatives of community organizations.[100] During these events, community singing migrated once again, this time from the public parks and auditoriums into places of learning and commercial activity. During an Arkansas-wide Music Week of 1920, "more than 10,000 persons attended twenty-one sings . . . in schools, clubs, industrial plants, department stores and theatres."[101] Organizers in Little Rock brought community singing into churches, public and private schools, theaters, restaurants, cafés, the capitol building, and Liberty Hall. Special sings were conducted for industrial workers, business men, school children, and, as a separate group, "negro" children. "In this way," reported the *Music Trade Review*, "practically everybody in the city will be reached." These efforts, however, were not philanthropic. The columnist concludes, "It is expected that the Music Week program will prove a great factor not only in stimulating musical interest generally, but in bringing about increased sales of musical instruments."[102]

While Tremaine and his colleagues spoke frankly about their motivations and goals in the pages of the music industry trade journal, they presented a different agenda to the public. Following the successful inauguration of National Music Week in May 1924, Tremaine published a book-length account of the event in which he outlined a lofty ideology aligned with that of the music reformers. "Missionary work done to aid the progress of music as an art consists chiefly of bringing under the influence of music those who have hitherto felt it was out of their sphere," wrote Tremaine. "The benefit to the public of a more general appreciation of music is attested by too many poets, philosophers and leaders in business life to need emphasis here, and Music Week is but one factor in extending that appreciation."[103] The volume opens with a letter of support from President Calvin Coolidge, who had accepted the position of Honorary Chairman of the National Music Week Committee. This is followed by a preface made up entirely of quotes from politicians (Coolidge himself gets the first word), philanthropists, writers, philosophers, and musicians, all of whom praise the uplifting power of music and advocate for its inclusion in everyday life. In making National Music Week a reality, Tremaine went to great lengths to involve community members and organizations that were invested in the promotion of musical uplift, including clergy, music teachers, factory managers, women's clubs, music clubs, public libraries, public schools, and music schools.[104] In the end, he was successful in leveraging the work done by music reformers in the 1910s—which was in turn reinforced by war-era community singing practices—to promote the interests of the music trade.

Alongside the success of Music Week, community singing also became a part of American culture through other channels. Service clubs, such as the Rotary, integrated community singing—of "good, honest-to-heaven, he-man songs, with good melodies and worthwhile words"—into their activities.[105] Rotary leaders pointed out that they abhorred song parodies, in which comical lyrics were attached to familiar melodies, even though these were popular at camps and parties; parodies would later become ubiquitous in the picture theater.[106] Community singing was also introduced into workplaces—especially department stores, factories, and mining camps—as a regular exercise, where it was believed to act as "a safety valve for the release of social unrest and economic discontent."[107] Once again, organizers placed the emphasis on the uplifting and therapeutic aims of group singing.

The safety valve issue also stood at the heart of escapist picture palace entertainment, in which the organist combined elements from a number of community singing traditions. Sometimes the organist invoked a Rotarian sense of camaraderie; other times, he created the atmosphere of a college party. He might select traditional repertoire, or rely on sidesplitting parodies. With every performance, however, the theater organist distracted his patrons from their daily concerns. Seminal theater historian Ben Hall evocatively describes the role that picture palaces played in the lives of urban Americans:

> The people loved it. After all, it was for them that this sumptuous and magic world was built, and they thoroughly enjoyed being spoiled by indulgent impresarios. Ladies from cold-water flats could drop in at the movie palace after a tough day in the bargain basements and become queens to command. Budgets and bunions were forgotten as noses were powdered in *boîtes de poudre* worthy of the Pompadour. From a telephone booth disguised as a sedan chair, Mama could call home and say she'll be a little late and don't let the stew boil over.[108]

The picture palace allowed lower- and middle-class patrons to imagine that they were better off than they were. In this way, the palace system preempted any social unrest that might have arisen between the starkly divided haves and have-nots of the 1920s.

To trace the path by which community singing became a part of picture palace entertainment, however, we will have to return to the war era, during which film exhibition and community singing first appeared in tandem. Although the practice began when government-employed song leaders brought their activities into the movie theater, exhibitors were quick to see the commercial potential in community singing and to establish it as a regular part of the program. By doing so, theater managers were also investing in the reputation of their institutions. Because President Wilson himself had called on cities, clubs, and societies across the country to engage in community singing to support the war effort, managers were able to secure local goodwill by inviting song leaders and their wholesome fare into the picture palace. George W. Beynon of *Moving Picture World* assured his readers that patrons would "praise the patriotism" exhibited by entertainers who rehearsed audiences in "America," "Columbia, the Gem of the Ocean" (1843), and other such selections. "In the second place," Beynon continued, "it will add yet another laurel wreath to the head of the fifth industry because of its musical educational facilities."[109] The exhibitor to most explicitly draw attention to the patriotic and enriching attributes of his singing program was George Fischer, manager of the Alhambra Theater in Milwaukee, Wisconsin. When he initiated community singing in June 1918, he invited a crew of journalists to tour his theater and witness the sing, which was directed by veteran song leader Frederick Carberry.[110] Following this stunt, Fischer enjoyed months of regular press coverage. Notices of his sings appeared in most of the trade journals, and he was even (mistakenly) credited with starting "the movement."[111]

In reality, it appears that community singing first caught on in the theaters of Buffalo, New York, where it was reported in March 1917 that "moving picture men are watching with interest the community singing craze which has hit this city."[112] Interest was especially high in Buffalo because of weekly sings conducted in the local high school by Harry H. Barnhart, a founder of the community music movement who at that time served as a CTCA song leader. Community singing soon became a staple in Buffalo theaters, where several times a week patrons joined together to sing wartime favorites such as "There's a Long, Long Trail" (1914), "Pack Up Your Troubles in Your Old Kit Bag" (1915), "Over There" (1917), "Keep the Home Fires Burning" (1914), and "The Star-Spangled Banner." As was typical of picture palace sings in the war years, these sessions were accompanied by the theater orchestra and directed by a professional song leader. The manager of the Elmwood, Edwin O. Weinberg, reported that his audiences greatly enjoyed community singing and called regularly for encores. He suggested that the stunt's success could be attributed to the fact that "a man or woman is most pleased with his or her own entertaining."[113] Weinberg also observed an additional benefit: "The singing awakens the audience between pictures, puts new life into them and consequently the entertaining qualities of the feature are greatly enhanced."[114] This notion—that singing improved appreciation of the films—would be echoed by commentators throughout the 1920s.

Another pioneer in picture palace community singing was theater manager Ralph R. Ruffner, who got audiences singing in Spokane, Portland, and Butte.[115] Ruffner, who claimed to have first exploited community singing at a midnight show in 1916, experimented with many of the techniques that would later become standard in organist-led community singing. First, he formed his audience into an official "Patrons' Chorus," which had the effect of building community spirit and theater loyalty; the term soon caught on with other exhibitors and can be considered a forbearer of the many "organ clubs" that would emerge in the next decade. Ruffner also relied more heavily on humor than his contemporaries. During sings held in his theaters he called for whistling choruses, instigated competition between sections of the audience, and projected comical slides to encourage participation. These included: "The ushers will now pass around the birdseed to those who are not singing," "Go ahead and sing; we'll keep it dark," and "Gee, that was great! Now the other barrel."[116] All of these tricks would persist in the picture palace sing for well over a decade, although they would later be deployed by the theater organist instead of the manager.

Trade professionals who witnessed the early popularity of community singing in the picture theater were not sure what to expect. "Some theatre managers are of the opinion that it is successful only because of the patriotism inspired by the war and will not be practicable or desirable in peace times," reported one commentator, "while others contend it is both practicable and desirable whether the country is at war or not."[117] In general, trade press commentators advocated for the trend but linked it with the war effort, suggesting that community singing would no longer have a place in American life after the conflict drew to a close. But community singing in the theater did maintain its commercial viability—whether due to the efforts of music educators, tradespeople, or exhibitors it is impossible to say. It persisted, however, in a new form: as an organist's specialty.

It is difficult to pinpoint the occasion—or even the year—when a theater organist first incorporated community singing into his portion of the picture palace program. In the first place, organ solos were not regularly discussed in the trade press until the mid-1920s. The earliest reference to community singing in the context of organ music that I have discovered is a brief, deprecating jab in the August 31, 1918, issue of *Exhibitors Herald and Motography*: "If that community singing will drown out some of the wheezy pipe organ playing a number of the theatres furnish, we're for it."[118] While this one-liner is good for a laugh, it is hardly evidence of a burgeoning practice.

In more recent decades, a number of theater-organ enthusiasts have attributed the community singing idea to different performers. In 1972, a columnist for *Theatre Organ* credited Ted Meyn—more famous for his staged productions of song lyrics, which he termed "organlogues"—with starting the community singing trend at the Kansas City Pantages Theatre, remarking that "some old song pluggers insist" that he was the first.[119] A number of accounts from the same era give precedence to Earl Abel, who ostensibly inaugurated the practice in 1924 while working at the Auditorium Theatre near Chicago. "It took some showmanship to put this across," he is said to have recalled, "but it worked and the audience enjoyed it. Officials in the trade couldn't believe an audience would sing. Only when they heard it were they convinced."[120] In 1969, a reporter for *San Antonio* magazine—doubtless working off of Abel's own recollections—explained that song pluggers used to visit his theater with lyric slides to advertise their wares. "Abel got the idea of using the slides only, not the song pluggers," she wrote, "and having the audience sing along with the music."[121] Abel also took credit for passing the community singing idea on to the McVickers Theater's Henri Keates, who soon became known as the "man who has put community singing on the map" and whose success, according to Abel, was responsible for the national craze.[122] Interestingly, both of these accounts invoke the practice of song plugging, suggesting that community singing developed out of publishers' techniques for advertising popular songs. They also indicate that song slides predated participation—which leads us to the second problem in pinning down the earliest examples of organist-led community singing.

When organists directed community singing, they almost always projected lyrics for the audience to follow, either via slide or film. Therefore, it is tempting to read references to the incorporation of lyrics as references to community singing. For example, one early account of projected lyrics describes a 1921 solo presented by Keates while he was at the Liberty Theatre in Portland, Oregon. "The song is not featured by the usual method of a slide," wrote the columnist, "but by a special reel of motion pictures."[123] Since some five years later Keates's name would become synonymous with community singing, it is tempting to assume that this is a description of that activity. Nonetheless, because there is no actual mention of singing in this review, we cannot do so, for slides and films that contained lyrics were not employed only to facilitate community singing. As we shall see, organists who performed popular numbers but did not invite singing usually projected song slides as well. In these cases, the audience was expected to read the lyrics and to follow the interplay between text and music but not to vocalize. Sing-along films also found success with nonsinging audiences, and they were often appreciated for their artistic or comedic value instead of for their song-leading utility. Consequently, early accounts of projected lyrics need not imply that community singing had taken hold in the organ solo. The presence of organist-led community singing cannot be demonstrated until the trade press began to explicitly review the practice in 1925. By that point, though, it was clear that community singing had been developing for some time.

3 PRACTICES AND TOOLS

Much of this study engages with individual organists and their work in specific theaters. Because every picture palace offered a unique program tailored to the interests and values of the audience it sought to attract, it is difficult to generalize about the moviegoing experience. Individual patrons tended to feel at home in a particular theater, where they took pride in the resident performers and came to cherish the house traditions. We have already seen this process at work in the Chicago Oriental, where patrons shared an imagined relationship with performers such as Paul Ash and Peggy Bernier and developed a taste for Henri Keates's "hoked up" community singing. All the same, the basic mechanisms of the organ solo and community singing were common across theaters. In this chapter, I will describe how each element of the organ solo, from repertoire to lighting to the organist's appearance, was typically presented. What follows is a survey of the techniques and materials that were available to every theater organist when he or she planned a community singing session.

COMMUNITY SINGING DURING THE ORGAN SOLO

In those theaters that practiced community singing, it was almost always directed by the organist as part of his organ solo. The organ solo was the portion of the program given over to the organist to use as he or she saw fit. This means that the organ solo was not necessarily a solo at all, for it often incorporated guest performers or audience participation. It was usually about ten minutes long and took place soon after the overture, but picture show programming was quite flexible, and neither the length nor the position of the organ solo were rigidly determined. Programming depended somewhat on the strengths of the organist but was primarily determined by the character of the theater.

Needless to say, organists played a large role in the success of community singing. Most organists chose or developed their solos with care and presented them in unique settings that surprised and entertained. They played with great skill, carefully articulating each word with the organ and maintaining correct tempi, and they often memorized the music to heighten their effectiveness as performers.[1] Organists who were new to community singing had to work especially hard to ensure that their song-leading efforts were successful, and trade press columnists often warned organists against forcing their patrons to sing. As one writer put it, "They must be cajoled and good-naturedly guided into enjoyable ensemble vocalizing."[2] One organist suggested that, despite the popularity of community singing, it was always best to distribute a handful of plants throughout the audience. By the time the sing-along medley was over, he claimed, the organist would be "unable to hear the organ above the voices."[3] All of the trade commentaries indicated that community singing, while enjoyed by audiences across the country, needed to be carefully sold by the organist.

It might be noted, though, that community singing occasionally took place outside of the organ solo. In 1926, for example, the popular banjo player Eddie Peabody led community singing in theaters across the country as part of his stage act.[4] Comedians, song pluggers, and masters of ceremony also encouraged community singing from the stage, while orchestra directors led singing from the pit.[5] In 1929, one trade commentator described an entire program of community singing led by the orchestra at the Tivoli Theatre in Chicago, a practice that he labeled the "orchestral vogue"; ten years earlier, of course, orchestra-led community singing was the norm.[6] Slides were regularly used in conjunction with the orchestra but do not seem to have been employed by visiting performers. Community singing led by the stage band would become popular in the 1930s, when organists had largely disappeared from theaters, but it does not appear to have been a significant factor in the 1920s, when the theater organ was still ubiquitous.[7]

The theater organ developed with the picture palace. The organ first found a place in the theater because it offered the wide range of tone colors also associated with the orchestra. The organist, however, had an important advantage over the orchestra for he could easily improvise film accompaniments.[8] He was also less costly. The first organs were built in the style of church instruments, but a unique theater organ was quickly developed to suit the needs of picture palace exhibitors.[9] A British organ builder, Robert

This slide, which contains lyrics to "Song of Love" from the 1921 operetta *Blossom Time*, is from a Quality Slide Co. medley. Each slide in the set features a different pastoral background. American Theatre Organ Society.

This example comes from the Standard Slide Corp. set for the 1928 song "After My Laughter Came Tears." Each of the slides features a unique color illustration set against a repeated grayscale background. From the author's collection.

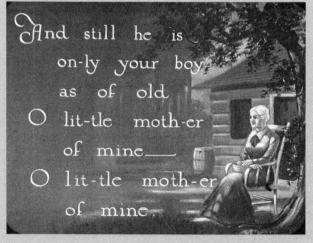

This is the concluding slide from a Fowler Studios set for the 1917 song "Little Mother of Mine." Fowler Studios was located in Los Angeles and seems to have specialized in sentimental songs, but only a few of their slides can be found in archives today. From the author's collection.

Hope-Jones, was responsible for most of the innovations behind the theater organ. He died soon after the first picture palaces were built, but his name was linked with the famous Wurlitzer "unit orchestra" organs for many years. A theater organ was defined by a number of characteristics. Some of these were technical, such as electric action, double touch key operation, unification of ranks, high wind pressure, and the iconic (if not universal) horseshoe console. Some concerned the sound of the instrument, such as the presence of a tremulant on every rank, the prominence of the tibia voice instead of the diapason, and the incorporation of a complete range of percussion instruments and sound effects.[10] By the late 1920s, some theater organs could be operated from several consoles at the same time, and the primary console was usually situated on a lift so that it could rise up from the pit for the organ solo.[11]

As the theater organ became an integral part of the picture palace experience, exhibitors sought new ways in which to turn their investment into a box office draw. The organ solo soon emerged as a regular picture palace feature. There is not much information about organ programming before the trade press began to review organ solos in the mid-1920s, but the evidence indicates that the earliest organ solos were of a strictly classical nature. Even after community singing became the norm, many organists continued to present serious art music. Organists were free to draw from both art and popular repertories, which they often combined in a single solo.[12] Organists also introduced creative additions to the organ solo, such as vocal soloists (often hidden from view), films, costumes, decorations, fanciful lighting schemes, and even miniature stage presentations.[13]

Almost every organ solo employed projected slides, and these served several important functions. Most often, slides contained the lyrics to the popular songs performed by the organist. This did not necessarily mean, however, that the audience was expected to join in. Lyric slides were a staple in many houses where community singing was never practiced, and it was uncommon for an organist to perform popular repertoire without them. The audience knew whether to sing based either on the house's custom or on an invitation from the organist. Other slides allowed the organist to communicate with his audience. In the late 1920s, public address systems were introduced into most picture palaces and organists began to speak directly to the patrons. Before the public address system, however, an organist required slides in order to tell a story, deliver a joke, or give singing directions. The text on these slides was usually set to a well-known tune, which the organist would play. The audience could thus read the text in time to the music. There is some indication that patrons might hum the melody, but it appears that they never sang the words.[14] Finally, slides were used to project frames and backgrounds. These large-format slides were associated with the Brenograph projector, and they could be used to create extraordinary effects.[15]

It is difficult to determine just when organ solos began to feature community singing. There is no reliable information about this matter until the trade journal *Exhibitors Herald* launched its weekly Organ Solos column in March 1927. This was a significant moment in the history of theater organ entertainment, for it indicated that the organ solo had achieved a high level of national importance. The advent of this new column, however, only indicated the peak of the organ's popularity. Readers had been requesting a column dedicated to organ entertainment for nearly two years, and organ solos had been reviewed under the heading Current Presentations since November 1925.[16] The other main trade publication for motion picture exhibitors, *Variety*, discussed organ solos under House Reviews, Presentations, and New Acts beginning in March 1925. *Film Daily* reviewed New York City organ solos, in the context of complete presentations, starting in 1926. All of these trade journals, with the addition of *Motion Picture News*, published supplementary articles on organ entertainment and community singing from around the same time.

The Organ Solos column in *Exhibitors Herald* provides a glimpse of community singing's popularity through the years. The data set that can be derived from the column, though, is of limited value because it represents only the handful of theaters that the journal chose to review, and the breadth and style of this coverage changed dramatically over the period in question. All the same, the numbers are revealing. In April 1927, for example, 18 percent of the organ solos included in the column featured community singing. In April 1928, 27 percent of the solos featured community singing. In 1929, this number rose to 38 percent, and in 1930 it was 70 percent. By April 1931, 77 percent of the organ solos featured community singing. The number eventually fell to 55 percent in 1932, the last year in which *Exhibitors Herald* published reviews.

Nonetheless, based on these figures and on additional commentary in the reviews, one may draw two conclusions. First, community singing

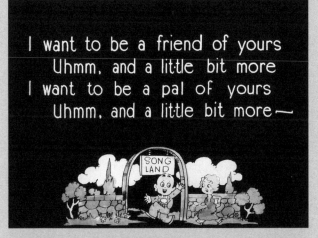

This style is typical of Ransley Studios, whose slides almost all feature colorful cartoon figures positioned below a text block against a black background. In this case, the text—which appears in the 1927 volume *Parodology*—is a parody of the fraternity song "I Want to Be a College Man." American Theatre Organ Society.

This is a narrative slide from the Quality Slide Co. set "Moon Dreams." The accompanying image appears throughout the set. American Theatre Organ Society.

This is the last slide in a cowboy-themed Quality Slide Co. set. None of the slides contain song texts or titles. Instead, they offer humorous exhortations to join in the singing of whatever songs the organist chose for his solo. These might have been suited to the theme but probably were not. American Theatre Organ Society.

established a significant presence in the organ solo during the mid-1920s. Most mid-decade reviews refer to the practice, if only to denigrate it or remark upon its absence. Clearly, community singing had already made its mark on the exhibition community. One must remember, though, that organists had a wide variety of entertainment options available. Some historians have developed a nostalgic association between community singing, the "mighty Wurlitzer," and the glamorous picture palaces of the 1920s, but in reality this iconic image represents only one practice among many.[17] All the same, Chicago organist Harry L. Wagner, who contributed a regular column to the *Herald*, was able to announce in 1926 that "of all the different kinds of solo stunts and novelty ideas, the one that stands out alone as the most popular of all is community singing. It never fails to make a big hit and leaves the audience clamoring for more."[18]

Second, community singing experienced a dramatic rise in popularity upon the widespread introduction of talking pictures in the late 1920s. This occurred for two reasons. On the one hand, the installation of sound equipment reduced the need for live entertainment and eliminated opportunities for audience participation. Theater patrons were not accustomed to sitting in silence throughout the film, and the trade presses report that they often became restless. Patrons also missed the "flesh element" that live musicians and stage performers provided. Community singing introduced an opportunity to release excess energy and to engage with the organist, who, by 1930, was the only live entertainer to remain in some theaters. On the other hand, the Great Depression changed the landscape of film exhibition. Before the 1930s, picture palace exhibitors were highly class conscious. As we shall see in the next chapter, those who directed important flagship theaters often prohibited community singing on the grounds that it was not dignified. After the onset of the Depression, however, exhibitors became less concerned with such matters. The top priority of every picture house was to draw patrons into the theater and entertain them at a reasonable price.

During the years in which community singing was a popular organ solo activity, the organist always grappled with the same set of elements. First, he or she had to decide what kind of repertoire would appeal to the audience and encourage participation. Each singing session normally consisted of about five popular songs, but organists made their selections from a broad range of stylistic categories, including traditional favorites, recent hits, comical ditties, sentimental ballads, parodies on well-known melodies, specially written tongue twisters, or any combination of the above. The choice of songs was influenced by a variety of factors, including organist preference, singability, and the interests of publishers. The practice of song plugging had a decades-long influence on popular musicians in all types of entertainment venues. In the picture palace, music publishers pressured organists to program recent commodities, and they encouraged compliance by supplying song-leading materials free of charge. Such programming choices could be detrimental to the organist's popularity, however, since audiences could not sing numbers that were brand new and therefore unfamiliar. Organists and publishers were most successful when they introduced a new song at the end of a medley of familiar numbers. That way, the audience was in a participatory mood by the time they encountered the fresh selection and were usually willing to give it a try.[19] Wagner encouraged his colleagues to take advantage of publishers' materials but advised them to avoid numbers that were "right off the press."[20] Instead, he suggested that they listen to popular dance orchestras, radio programs, and recent phonograph releases in order to have a sense of what music the patrons might know. While publishers tried to inject new material into the organ solo, the use of sing-along films, which usually featured old songs, had the opposite influence on repertoire. Most films were designed to profit a studio, not a publisher, so new material was excluded because it was less conducive to community singing, as well as for copyright reasons. When left to his own devices, an organist usually programmed the music that was most likely to inspire singing: recent hits, but none so recent as to be unfamiliar.

The age variation among picture palace patrons also presented a challenge for organists. Trade press commentators noted that young people did not know the old songs and therefore could not sing them.[21] At the same time, they worried that older people were not excited about the jazzy new tunes that constituted the standard community singing fare and that community singing, therefore, appealed only to the "flaming young folks."[22] While some commentators proposed that only the young were interested in community singing, it is clear that a large spectrum of patrons enjoyed it.[23] For example, the popular Chicago organist Henri Keates was credited with appealing to both "old timers" and "young moderns" when he offered a blend of traditional favorites and "hot tunes" for a 1928 solo.[24]

Next, the organist had to decide how (and if) to provide the lyrics—by slide or by film. Although slides were by far the most popular method, I have

I'll walk down the lane
With a hap-py re-frain
And sing-in' -
just sing-in' in the rain.

This slide is from the Maurice Workstel set "Hits from Metro-Goldwyn-Mayer's 'Hollywood Revue of 1929.'" The film was one of MGM's first sound releases and popularized the song "Singin' in the Rain." American Theatre Organ Society.

dedicated the final pages of this chapter to an in-depth discussion of the sing-along films that were produced during the silent era. An organist could either use professionally manufactured slides—supplied by a dealer, rental exchange, or publisher—or create slides specifically for his solo. Some of the larger theaters commissioned sets of slides for their organists on demand, but for most houses this was prohibitively expensive.[25] Any organist could create rudimentary slides by hand. In 1992, the son of organist Stanleigh Malotte recalled the process by which his father produced slides for community singing: "I remember watching Dad prepare the song slides in his dressing room, typing the gels with two fingers (he never learned to touch-type), and then putting them between glass (about three or four inches square) and then inside the slide frames."[26] Many of these handmade slides can be found in collections, but most extant slides were created by a handful of companies that specialized in the production of attractive slides for use in picture theaters. The most prolific included Bond Slide, Quality Slide, and Ransley Studios in Chicago; Kae Studios, National Studios, Cosmopolitan Studios, and Maurice Workstel in New York City; and Kansas City Slide in Kansas City.[27] Despite their ubiquity, some organists spoke out against the use of slides. Lew White, who sat at the impressive console of the New York Roxy, warned the organist against "building his reputation and his success

This example comes from the Maurice Workstel set for the 1925 song "I Never Knew." The slides still reside in their original cardboard box, on which is printed the line "Kindly return to the publisher." From the author's collection.

around the slides he is employing rather than around his own ability and personality."[28]

The appearance of slides varied enormously. Each studio developed a distinct style in terms of coloration, lettering, and art work, and there was a predictable trade-off in terms of quality versus speed of production. "Ransley could be depended upon to get slides of consistent quality out in a hurry," recalled organist John Muri. "Ransley's lettering and cartooning usually followed a single pattern, however. They didn't have much variety."[29] The finest commercial sets included illustrations on every slide. These were suited to the character of the composition: comic songs were adorned with cartoon-style drawings, while sentimental numbers featured realistic figures and romantic landscapes. Semiclassical songs, which were likely to receive the most attention from the audience, sometimes appeared with detailed illustrations and composer attributions—an unusual touch.[30] Muri reported that Quality Slide offered the greatest variety in art work but that Workstel "produced the most imaginative, interesting and humorous cartoons."[31] Some of the most unusual slides came from the British firm of Morgan's Slides, whose founder, Henry Moorish Morgan, copyrighted a process in 1924 that involved coating glass slides with a colored substance that could be cut away to form words and images. Most slides, however, contained only clear text on a black background. The song lyrics were usually hyphenated as necessary to indicate a note change. This simple tool helped participants adhere to the melody, which was seldom represented with musical notes; when a musical staff did appear, it seems to have been included largely for visual effect.

Slide sets also ranged in terms of complexity. A single song might be represented on one or more slides, in which case the organist was expected to make individual selections for his solo. The fact that most slide sets are of this type indicates that it was typical for an organist to put together a customized program. By 1925, however, slide makers competed to produce elaborate presentations that averaged thirty-two slides but could exceed fifty. When intended for community singing, these sets combined a number of songs and tied them together with a theme or story. The narrative texts were composed to suit a preexisting melody, which the organist would render as the slides were displayed. Muri reminisced about these packaged productions with great skepticism: "There would be the tale of the deserted lover who had asked the organist to tell his love to return, or there would be a song to be sung whenever some important event or crisis occurred in the narrator's life. Because of the pressures of time and quantity production, some of the writing was poor; often the poetry that is essential when words are set to rhythmic music was downright bad. . . . Sometimes the material was in bad taste."[32] Muri's criticisms are born out in extant slide sets such as Quality's "Some Girls I Have Met" (a medley of songs that bear women's names) and "Moon Dreams" (a medley of moon-themed numbers). The former contains the sort of off-rhymes that Muri disliked, such as "melody" with "memory," while the latter repetitively deploys a small number of sentimental illustrations and floral designs across the range of slides.[33] Other sets, such as "No More Jazz" (maker not identified), provide a narrative into which the organist is invited to insert his own selections. This set describes a dream in which the organist goes to heaven and is interrogated by St. Peter. It contains opportunities to include a variety of repertoire but does not mention any selections by name.[34] Other popular themes for medleys included travelogues, in which the audience would sing selections representing different stops in a trip; holiday celebrations, in which the organist provided selections suitable for a specific occasion, such as Mother's Day or New Year's Eve; and imagined activities, in which patrons might assemble a cake or stage a horse race through song.[35]

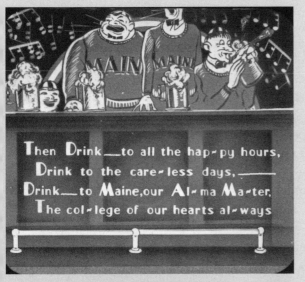

This slide for the "Stein Song" comes from Consolidated Advertising Corp. in Detroit, which produced slides of various types in the late 1920s and early 1930s. The University of Maine "Stein Song" became a hit when Rudy Vallée recorded it in 1930. From the author's collection.

This example comes from a Quality Slide Co. set entitled "Chestnuts." In addition to the 1891 classic "After the Ball," the set contains choruses to "In the Shade of the Old Apple Tree," "Sweet Adeline," and several other old favorites. In between the choruses are slides containing texts such as "I'll bet Pop remembers that one," and "Ah, me, Thems was the days!" American Theatre Organ Society.

This National Studios slide contains lyrics from the alternative "Charleston Chorus" to the 1925 song "I Wonder Where My Baby Is To-Night." The chorus, which features comedy lyrics and added syncopations, was included in various period recordings. From the author's collection.

Song lyrics were not the only subject for these presentations; slide-production firms also created sets to introduce a new organist, to demonstrate the capacities of the instrument, or to guide listeners in appreciating classical fare. The archives of the American Theatre Organ Society contain several extraordinary examples of this type from Morgan's Slides, including the fifty-five-slide set "Members of My Orchestra" and the forty-six-slide set "The Story of the Opera." Both of these sets were designed to accompany the performance of concert excerpts and do not contain song lyrics—with the exception of Enrico Toselli's popular "Serenade," included near the end of the operatic saga, which may or may not have been sung by the audience.

Many of these slide sets were produced on behalf of music publishers for the purpose of plugging songs. As one *Variety* columnist put it, the picture palace, "with its vast audience over and over each day," was the perfect venue in which to reach a large number of potential customers.[36] During the 1920s, all of the major publishing firms maintained "special service" departments that developed and circulated organ solo materials. These departments commissioned sets of song slides that contained lyrics to their latest numbers. Slide sets were then booked by theater chains and rotated among the houses along with films and stage shows.[37] Publishers usually offered these slides to organists at no charge in return for the publicity.[38] The organists were expected to return the expensive slides so that they could be reused, although the presence of these slides in theater collections confirms the publishers' complaints that they were often kept.[39] Evidence from the trade journals suggests that publishers' slides were most prevalent in the late 1920s. In early 1926, Wagner took it upon himself to proselytize on behalf of the publishing companies; he was concerned that many organists and exhibitors were not aware of the complimentary materials that had been made available for their use.[40] A year later, however, Ransley was able to announce that "the number of theatres using slides as a regular part of their exploitation and advertising campaign is growing by leaps and bounds."[41]

While the relationship between organists and publishers was mutually beneficial, their divergent goals generated some tension: organists needed to entertain, while publishers needed to sell. Sometimes a publisher might directly undermine an organist who was using his slides by placing the same song with the stage band. This practice increased exposure for the song but decreased its entertainment value for the picture theater and often annoyed patrons.[42] All the same, organists were grateful for the high-quality materials that publishers provided, and they took advantage of the commercial angle by convincing local sheet music merchants to underwrite their plugging efforts in the theater, which could become quite expensive when professional singers or stage sets were involved.[43] As we shall see later, organists were also quick to alter publishers' slide sets to suit their own purposes.

Publishers such as M. Witmark & Sons, Remick, and De Sylva, Brown and Henderson described their slide offerings with full-column advertisements in the *Exhibitors Herald-World*.[44] Most of the slide sets mentioned in these advertisements contained only single songs, the verses and choruses of which were distributed across a handful of slides, but some included a narrative as well. In 1926, for example, Henry Murtagh used a set of fifty song slides released by Leo Feist that exploited five different Feist songs and was the work of L. Wolfe Gilbert, a "special material expert" at the company.[45] Publishers also released medleys in which choruses from old favorites that had no commercial value introduced a new song that the company wanted to sell—a tactic that appeased organists, who were more concerned with entertaining their patrons than with advertising hits.[46] For example, the aforementioned "Some Girls I Have Met" contains only old favorites, but the final slide bears the text, "I hope you've liked my old-time pals, / And now be-fore I go / May I pre-sent my new-est love, / You'll like her, folks, I know"—a clear invitation to conclude with whatever fresh song needed to be plugged. Finally, a publisher would sometimes alter the lyrics to one of his own songs in order to suit an organ presentation. In 1926, Feist released a set of slides for the song "Too Many Parties, Too Many Pals" that incorporated an address supposedly given by a judge from his bench; the subject of the song, a fallen woman, was to be sentenced for her crimes. To heighten the impact of the address, which was to be delivered by an actor from the stage, Feist put the final chorus in the past tense. In another example, Irving Berlin issued a slide version of his 1926 hit "Gimme a Little Kiss, Will Ya, Huh?" in which the last chorus shifted from the male perspective to the female—at which point "kiss" was replaced with "coat."[47] Both of these solos contain elements—melodramatic excess on the one hand, stereotypical gender relations on the other—that were typical of picture palace entertainment.

Many organists preferred to obtain professionally designed slide presentations that were created and distributed independently of the music publishers. The advantage to these solos was that they served only the interests of the organist. "In a service of this kind," the *Herald* was pleased to report,

These two Quality Slide Co. examples are part of a presentation that pairs gilded-age favorites—in this case, "Silver Threads among the Gold" (1873)—with modern parody versions. Only the parody slide belongs to the set; the organist was expected to supply straight slides from his library. American Theatre Organ Society.

"there is obviously no song-plugging." The disadvantage was that such solos were not free but rather had to be purchased or, more likely, rented from a slide exchange. The Paramount Slide Rental Service in Chicago, for example, offered an arrangement by which any organist could receive two presentations a month, guaranteed to be up-to-date and suited to "seasonable subjects," including holidays, upcoming boxing matches, and recent political news. Depending on the type of theater, the organist could request either "straight solos" or community singing medleys, while the biweekly schedule left the organist free to tailor his or her own presentations on the off weeks. Most of these solos, whether straight or of the community singing type, were designed such that "any song suitable at the time" could by interpolated into a clever narrative.[48] The archives of the American Theatre Organ Society contain a presentation of this type that has been augmented with sing-along numbers selected by the organist. The basic set, manufactured by Quality and titled "Some Sweetheart Songs," contains ten colorful slides that outline the theme and introduce each song, but no titles are mentioned; instead, the songs are described as "the 'sweetheart' song of yesterday," "one for the 'lonely Hearts,'" "the favorite 'sweetheart' of all the College Boys," and so on. An unknown organist has interpolated slides from six other Quality releases, including both individual songs and excerpts from medleys. The slides come from different eras in the company's history and feature a variety of illustrations, lettering styles, and color palettes.[49] A set like this gives us an invaluable glimpse of the theater experience and brings the sing-along to life in a way that reviews and descriptions cannot. At the same time, it leads one to wonder whether audiences were ever put off by the incongruous mixture of slides. Although interpolation was a common practice, there was at least some pushback: organist Henry Murtagh was once criticized by a reviewer for employing "two or more sets of slides that didn't mingle so happily as could have been desired."[50]

In the final years of the decade, the role played by slide exchanges grew in importance as publishers gradually lost interest in plugging their wares via song slides. *Variety* reported that the expense was "estimated to run into the thousands" and that the effect of slides had been dampened by sound films, since many theaters did not retain an organist.[51] Music publishers turned to Hollywood for their advertising needs, leaving organists to rent slides from exchanges or rely on stock slides—including generic exhortations to sing— that they had accumulated over the years.[52] By 1929, a *Variety* article was able to proclaim that organists were only the sixth most valuable plugging outlet after talking films, radio, bands, discs, and acts.[53] At the same time, however, a new source of slide presentations emerged as the national exhibitor-producers took control of organ solo development. By the early 1930s, all of the major chains had established centralized organ departments. Dan Parker, who was in charge of organ solos for RKO, published a complete description of his duties in the *Herald* in which he emphasized the collaborative nature of organ solo production, the central role of music publishers, the tight schedule on which organists worked, and the freedom with which organists tailored the solos to their audiences:

> My writer and myself discuss an idea for an organ presentation. (An "organ solo" does not mean enough.) The idea must appeal to audiences everywhere. The topic must be appreciated by all of our varied audiences. Then again, it must be flexible for different types of work. Religion, prohibition or other controversial subjects cannot enter into any organ presentation, for we endeavor to serve all. Music, a very important item is next. Songs, which the publishers are exploiting and which are appropriate, are selected. The writer now has his foundation.
>
> When he returns with the finished product, a few minor changes are probably made, then it is ready for the okay. The presentation is then discussed with the general music director. By him it is either rejected or accepted. If accepted, the work goes on.
>
> While music for the parodies is being obtained, the lantern slide manufacturer and his artist are called in. The writer, the manufacturer, his artist and myself take infinite care in the next step. Each slide is gone over, cartoons are thought of and drawn. When the slide man has the proper information, he is off. In a day or so, I received hand-painted cards. This gives me an idea of just what the slide will look like. These are okayed and the slides are delivered.
>
> Sufficient sets of slide, music and cue-sheets are made ready for the theatres. Now for the routing. Popular music is soon forgotten, therefore the presentations must be played very soon. Few presentations can be used after six or seven weeks. This being the case, the theatres are grouped for such a purpose, bearing in mind that the geographical location of each is of vital importance.[54]

Parker and others in his position were eager to collaborate with music publishers. Boris Morros, who was in charge of the creation and distribution of organ solos for all Paramount organists, explained that "cooperating with the publishers in plugging their songs" kept the chain's organists "well acquainted with the latest tunes."[55] The partnership was probably most valuable, however, because the exhibitor-producers themselves possessed vast catalogs of popular music and needed the cooperation of others in the industry to profit from their own products. Film production companies also created slide specialties that plugged songs from their recent musical releases. These usually featured stills from the picture and might have been used to advertise films as well as songs.[56] At the same time, this account of painstaking preparation distracts from the fact that most organists did not put much effort into crafting a novel presentation. Even in the 1930s, it was typical for an organist to provide a generic title for his solo—something like "Let's Sing," "Let's Sing and Be Happy," or "It's Time to Sing"—and then to lead patrons in a string of unrelated tunes.[57]

When an organist did choose to employ a professionally crafted slide presentation, whether issued by a publisher, a rental service, or an exhibitor's organ department, she was always provided with a "lead-sheet" to guide her through the slides.[58] These were necessary because organ solos, whether designed by a publisher or assembled by a player, could become very complicated, combining not only narrative and song but contests, parodies, gags, tongue twisters, and special effects. While most of these instruction sheets have been lost, the American Theatre Organ Society retains a single folder of eighteen typewritten guides for the presentation of commercially produced slide solos. Each set of instructions replicates all of the text found on the slides for a given presentation. The corresponding slide numbers are printed next to each text block, along with—in most cases—an indication of the slide type: "explanation," "warm up," "chatter," "fun maker," "community finish," and so on. The song selections—both for singing and underscoring—and additional instructions for putting over the presentation are printed either to the right of or below the slide text. It is clear that these instruction sheets have been used by organists, and they bear a number of annotations indicating that slides were added or removed, songs were swapped out, or new participation techniques were employed. Most organists carefully renumbered the slides after making a change—evidence of which remains both on the instruction sheets and on the slides themselves.

The instruction sheets and slides also support a further conclusion: community singing in the picture palace was usually a lighthearted affair. Indeed, it was often sidesplittingly comical, and community singing was known to provoke hilarity among the patrons, even to the point of disrupting the

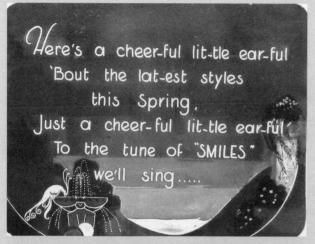

This slide, from a spring-themed Quality Slide Co. set, introduces an alliterative tongue twister to be sung to the tune of "Smiles." This text slide can be sung (or read) to the same tune. The next slide opens with the text, "Sim-ple styles, sweet smiling Spring shows / Sil-ly styles some shops shall sell." American Theatre Organ Society.

This Ransley Studios slide introduces a parody in which male and female audience members act out a risqué scene: Jack tries to convince his fiancée to join him for a drink and then spend the night, while the fiancée responds with lines such as "You must be-have, you see" and "Then you can sleep out-side." American Theatre Organ Society.

This example of a "lisping chorus" comes from National Studios. The song in question is the 1925 hit "Cecilia," which was common fare for community singing. From the author's collection.

picture palace program. The comedy was sometimes introduced by the song lyrics themselves. This could happen when the organist programmed a comic song such as "Down by the Winegar Woiks," a 1925 community singing number that was wildly popular in theaters across the country.[59] More often, however, special comedy versions of popular songs were devised by organists or slide producers.

One of the extant instruction sheets, "A Musical Meal," offers examples of almost every technique used to provoke hilarity during the organ solo. No slide maker is indicated, but most of the songs—including the last and newest, "You're Simply Delish" (1930)—were published by Robbins Music, indicating that the purpose of this presentation was to plug that company's catalog. At the head of the sheet are instructions to play "You're Simply Delish" behind all additional trailers and announcement slides exhibited during the program—a stunt that would obviously benefit the publisher but that might also benefit the organist by integrating the rest of the theater experience with his solo. The entire presentation is cast as an imagined meal, starting with oysters and ending with the after-dinner coffee. The instructions indicate that the first two explanatory slides were set to the tune of "Tea for Two" (1924), while the third slide was set to Robbins's "Cooking Breakfast for the One I Love" (1930). Presumably the patrons would have noticed that the songs used for underscoring were food themed, even though the words were neither sung nor displayed. After the first community singing number, the instructions called for a whistling chorus—a popular tactic for introducing variety. Next, the organist was to display a slide reading "THOUP / my girl friend lisps" while playing "My Baby Just Cares for Me" (1930). This indicated to the audience that they were about to sing a lisping chorus (on the topic of food, of course) to the familiar tune. The text of this chorus began with "My baby don't care for clams / Or smoked 'Virginia' hams / My baby just cares for THOUP." The next community singing number was followed by a tongue twister to the tune of "Anchors Away," a 1907 Robbins publication: "Say slow Sam saw some spooks / Sam shrieked so scared" and so on. This was followed by parody versions of "Yes! We Have No Bananas" (1923) and "You're the Cream in My Coffee" (1928), both of which were to be sung by the audience before the final plug of "You're Simply Delish."

It is unusual to find such a variety of comedic approaches in a single solo, but all of these techniques were widely employed in picture palace community singing. Lisping choruses and tongue twisters abound in slide collections, as do stand-alone slides with announcements, such as "Here's Your Whistle Chorus," which could have been inserted into any presentation.[60] Parodies were restricted to older tunes that the audience would recognize. In 1930, for example, the Brooklyn Paramount duo of Earl Abel and Elsie Thompson performed a parody of "When You and I Were Young, Maggie" (1864) that "had some extremely funny and catchy lines that not only had the audience singing lustily but nearly rolling out of their seats with laughter."[61] Gilded Age classics were usually subjected to age-based derision, such as in this parody of "After the Ball" (1891), which was issued by Quality on two slides complete with cartoon illustrations: "After the ball was ov-er / She took out her old glass eye / Put her false teeth in the ba-sin / Washed off the paint and dye. / Threw her peg leg in the corn-er / Hung her false hair on the wall / The rest of her went to 'bye-bye' / Af-ter the ball."[62]

Additional techniques for adding humor to the organ solo were also widely employed by slide manufacturers. When even whistling became a bore, patrons might be instructed to hum or clap for all or part of a selection.[63] Singing was also directed by way of graphic notation, in which words were enlarged or misshapen to suggest performative techniques. Interjections and echoes were often indicated with text situated in parentheses or shaded in a different color. Sometimes, slide producers seemed to delight in making the text as hard to read as possible; the lyrics might run in all different directions, or certain words or syllables might be replaced with images. Other solos were designed to make the resulting community sing as cacophonous as possible. In such cases, the slides might instruct patrons to sing two different songs at the same time or to choose their favorite parody version of song lyrics from several on offer.[64] For example, one set of slides offered alternative lyrics to Irving Berlin's 1919 hit "A Pretty Girl Is Like a Melody." These included "A goofy gal is like a bad nightmare" and "A dizzy dame is like a mickey finn"; the final simile, "euphonical pastorale," might be replaced with "discordant passacaglio [*sic*]" or "cacophonous capriccioso" respectively.[65] A later example suggested an "argument" based on straight and parody versions of the 1942 song "Who Wouldn't Love You." Each slide contained the original lyrics on the left-hand side (e.g., "You're the breath of spring that lovers gad about, are mad about") and alternative lyrics on the right-hand side (e.g., "When I hear you sing I want to run on out, and hold my snout"). The slides originally instructed the audience to choose sides based on seating ("upstairs" vs. "downstairs"), but at some point an organist taped over the text in question.[66] In these cases, it is likely that the organist gave verbal directions regarding which line to sing.

Apart from the material included on the slides, organists employed various techniques for introducing humor. They often sought to make participation more difficult—and therefore more amusing. Sometimes an organist would quit playing until the audience could no longer keep together. At the Chicago Oriental, Keates once "stopped playing and let the customers shout through six lines of a number"—a practice that particularly appalled critics of community singing, who saw silence as the ultimate offense to the organ.[67] The organist might also plant an accomplice in the audience to cause trouble, or choose to interrupt the singing to comical effect.[68] At the Brooklyn Paramount the organ duo of Merle Clark and Elsie Thompson once directed a rendition of "Making Faces at the Moon" (1931) in which "the number was started by the audience six different times but after singing a few lines some different thing would interrupt them. At each interruption Merle would explain to the audience just what had caused it and would then suggest that they start anew."[69] The organist might also challenge and amuse his patrons by providing a deliberately disruptive accompaniment. One such approach was to change keys every few measures.[70] On rare occasions, an organist would abandon slides altogether. When this occurred, it was usually done as a memory test for the participants, in which case the temporary absence of slides provided both a challenge and a change from standard practice.[71]

Organists also employed gimmicks that, while humorous, were primarily intended to encourage participation. One of the most popular stunts involved placing a barometer-like device on the stage that was meant to register the volume of the patrons' singing.[72] Another strategy was to inform the audience that a representative from the radio or film industry was in the house and was seeking out the next big talent. In 1929, Adolph Goebel of Loew's Theatre in Yonkers, New York, used the latest technology to put over a particularly effective version of this stunt: "With the assistance of an usher, Goebel endeavored to have persons in the audience sing into a 'Mic' which the usher carried around the house. A few people, especially one man, sang very well. . . . The embarrassment that Goebel caused some of the audience, when he asked them to sing individually, was lost when all were to sing, as every one responded and gave Goebel a very fine reception."[73] A third strategy was to inform the audience that the evening's community sing was being broadcast live over the local radio station—a fiction made all the more believable by the fact that some theaters did in fact broadcast their live programs.[74]

Perhaps the most popular method for lightening spirits and boosting volume was to stage a singing competition between different factions of the audience. Common divisions were men against women, single patrons against those who were married, and balcony seating against orchestra.[75] Some organists and slide makers became quite creative with their competitive sings. New York organist Leo Weber, for example, pitted "fatties" against "slenders," while one particularly adventurous set of slides divided the audience into "hen-pecks," "blondes," "college-boys," "old maids," and "jitter-bugs."[76] The practice of competitive singing—which was directed by annotations on the slides—helped to build enthusiasm in every theater and usually added to the humor as well. Sometimes the divisions produced conversation in place of competition. For example, a popular version of "Let Me Call You Sweetheart" (1910) invited boys and girls to alternately holler out lines from the song while the other gender whispered responses such as "does he mean just me?" and "do my ears hear right?"[77] Other conversational sings were less amiable, such as when girls were instructed to respond to a male rendition of the title lyric from "I Don't Want to Set the World on Fire" (1941) with the line "Well, you can just bet / You won't do it, PET!" (although this is a late example, the sentiment is typical).[78]

Organists always played an important role in the presentation of slides, but the most prominent also developed their own specialties, often in collaboration with a publisher or slide producer. In 1927, organist Ted Meyn of the Pantages Theatre in Kansas City, Missouri, devised a clever setting for the recent hit "What's the Use of Crying" (1926). Meyn would begin his solo by playing a verse and chorus of the tune with lyrics projected on the screen. Then, during the second verse, a plant in the audience would sing "out of key, loud, mournful and very sour."[79] After a second interruption, Meyn would ask the man to please remain quiet. The plant would beg Meyn to teach him how to sing, and the organist would oblige with a series of slides containing solfege. After leading the plant through his vocal exercises, Meyn would invite him to sing a chorus of "What's the Use of Crying" for the crowd. In his column for *Exhibitors Herald*, Meyn informed his readers that his presentation was now available from the publisher of the song at no cost.[80] Stanleigh Malotte's son also reminisced about his father's work developing original solos for the Alabama Theatre in Birmingham: "Dad's

SAY it is-n't SO ___Hold it___

SAY it is-n't SO ___hold it___

Ev.'ry-ONE is SAY-ing
you don't LOVE me

SAY it is-n't SO ___hold it___

This Quality Slide Co. example contains lyrics for Irving Berlin's 1932 hit song "Say It Isn't So." The deformed text (larger means louder) and performance instructions ("hold it") suggest a particularly humorous interpretation. American Theatre Organ Society.

+ EL👁N

MY ✝ E

AT

4 U 👁

This example from Quality Slide Co. replaces words and syllables with images. Participants would have puzzled over the slide for a few moments before deciphering the lyrics to the 1903 favorite and perennial community singing number "Sweet Adeline." Quality produced several sets in this style. Fox Theatre Archives, Atlanta.

But lest we forget the real significance of Independence Day, I think we'd better close with a patriotic chorus.

EVERYBODY SING !!!!

This slide concludes an Independence Day–themed Ransley Studios set titled "Safe and Sane." The only song specifically mentioned in the slides was the newly adopted national anthem, which was accompanied by a "telegram" from President Hoover requesting that it be sung. American Theatre Organ Society.

shows included a lot of satire on current events. He was a comedy writer at heart, and he'd take a current news item and have fun with it by putting his rhymed comments to his own or familiar tunes and play and sing them during his act."[81] Malotte had both the skills and the resources to create custom presentations, as well as the capacity to perform as a vocalist to his own accompaniment.

When organists used commercially produced slides, they typically felt free to alter them for their own use. "With few exceptions," wrote organist Albert F. Brown, "the material offered by the publisher is flexible, and if used at all should be revised and adapted to the especial requirements of the theatre, if only to reflect the personality of the performer."[82] When working with a publisher's specialty, the organist might incorporate his audience's favorite songs or replace worn-out numbers with up-to-date hits. Although the interpolated set described above, "Some Sweetheart Songs," was designed with the intent that the organist should contribute his own selections, performers did not hesitate to apply the same practice to slide sets supplied by publishers. If an organist broke up a commercial medley to use the songs individually, he might add introductory or instructional slides. Chicago organist Edward Meikel suggested that "publisher's versions can easily be used, . . . the only additional material needed being four or five slides to create the club atmosphere."[83] An organist could easily change the annotations on commercial slides by placing masking tape over unwanted words. The organist who created the "Sweetheart" medley, for example, taped over the subtitle on the first slide, which read "Past—Present and Future." Perhaps he felt that these time periods did not reflect his selections, or perhaps he just thought the text was silly. Organists reused old slides in a variety of ways and displayed great creativity when it came to making use of the materials at hand. An organist at the Atlanta Fox, for example, taped over the title of a song ("In the Shade of the Old Apple Tree") in order to make use of the singing instructions: "Give this old-timer a 'glee-club' rendition by singing the BIG words LOUD." The same organist might also have taped over the introductory phrase "First on the Hit Parade some months ago—now you never hear it much—" on the title slide for "I'm Always Chasing Rainbows." Perhaps he had been playing the song frequently and the comment was inappropriate for his audience. The reasons for which organists removed texts are difficult now to decipher.[84]

Organists could also introduce attractive nonmusical elements into a community singing solo, including console decorations, costumes, or even

---

Week to Week Stunts— **ATTENTION!** —Vocal Variety

ORGANISTS!
"JIMMY SAVAGE" offers for **RENTAL**
ORGAN SOLOS
The Last Word in Community Singing
805 Woods Theatre Building, Chicago, Ill.
Community Comics — Exclusive Rights — Original Organlogues

Jimmy Savage created organ novelties for Chicago theaters. His solos were used by Henri Keates and Preston Sellers at the Oriental and by Edward Meikel at the Chicago Harding. Savage advertised heavily in the trade press and his work was highly considered among organists and exhibitors. This advertisement appeared in an August 1927 issue of *Exhibitors Herald*.

actors. Organist Art Thompson of Clarksburg, West Virginia, for example, once placed prison bars around his console and engaged an assistant to play the role of an armed prison guard. After sounding a shot the guard chased Thompson, dressed in prison stripes, to his console. Thompson played a few measures of "The Prisoner's Song" and then begged the audience to secure his release by singing the recent hit "My Fate Is in Your Hands."[85] Thompson was not the only organist to stage this routine, but he added his own touches to make it unique.[86] Some organists also employed illustrative film segments. These were not sing-along films but rather contained short narratives or visual effects intended to enhance the organ solo.[87] In an extreme example, organist Ted Meyn created a film especially for his presentation of the song "I'm Walking around in Circles." The segment, exhibited in the middle of Meyn's organ solo after he had left the stage, featured the organist himself in conversation with a friend who had come upon hard times. The "friend" then joined Meyn onstage to present a dramatic recitation over organ underscoring. According to Meyn, "the applause thundered."[88]

However an organist chose to present his solo, he also had to take his personal appearance and demeanor into account. The organ solo contributed to the overall fantasy that picture palace entertainment promised, and the organist had to be careful not to dispel the illusion. In most theaters, the fantasy included a sense of informal intimacy and friendship between the performers and the patrons. The elements of appearance and demeanor, however, always had to reflect the character of the theater, and some venues called for a more formal persona. In a 1932 trade press article, organist Ted

Organ novelties were available from a variety of producers. This advertisement appeared in a July 1931 issue of *Motion Picture Herald*.

Crawford noted that a tuxedo might be appropriate for an elite house, while a dark suit or sport clothes were preferable for most venues. Crawford provided a simple rule to govern the selection of apparel for any theater: "The organist should dress primarily to make people want to like him the minute the spot hits him."[89]

Organists also had to consider their bodily motions when not seated at the console. Writing in 1927, organist Clark Fiers considered the problem of awkward bowing to be so severe that he offered precise instructions for the correct execution of a bow. "The way in my estimation is to stand and face the audience and bow the head and shoulders about twice," he wrote. "Woe to the fellow who can't summon a smile when he bows. Let them think that you are having as much fun as they are and they will eat it up."[90] Fiers warned the organist, however, against any affectation and recommended the same casual attitude that Ted Crawford extolled. According to his assessment, the audience "can quickly sense a ritzy organist."[91]

In 1927, the use of public address systems became widespread and organists suddenly had to take even more care with their speech than their dress.[92] Crawford's rule for speech, published in 1932, echoes that for appearance: "In speaking to the audience, one should indicate an attitude that says as simply and sincerely as possible, 'I like you and I want you to like me.'"[93] The speaking organist was well equipped to present himself to the audience as a friend, and many were successful in developing close—if illusory—relationships with their patrons. The installation of public address systems also allowed the singing organist to emerge, and a handful of performers developed a reputation for vocalizing to their own accompaniment during the organ solo.[94]

Exhibitors programmed community singing in order to entertain, but they were aware that it had other effects on the audience as well. In particular, community singing promoted a sense of community. According to Josef Zimanich, head of the Paramount Publix music novelties department in 1931, "It is an established fact that community singing creates an intimate, 'get-together' atmosphere in a theatre, the institutional value of which cannot be underrated."[95] To capitalize on this effect, exhibitors exploited singing to put the audience in a good mood for the film or the other acts.[96] As early as 1926, a *Herald* reviewer was able to editorialize in his account of Henri Keates's solo at the Oriental that "undoubtedly these cheer-leader organists serve a purpose in warming up the crowd for what is to follow, but why not give them ukuleles or mouth organs to do it with and employ an organist to get some good out of those $50,000 pipe organs?"[97] This commentator sought to voice his objection to the practice of community singing, but he freely admitted that it served a valuable purpose from the exhibitor's point of view. Patrons, it seems, became more receptive to the entertainment that was to follow after a round of community singing. The reasons are clear enough. First, and quite simply, the sing-along was fun and exciting, and it promoted good humor. Theatergoers who participated in the entertainment themselves also seemed to develop a special sympathy for fellow performers, which in turn allowed them to forgive shortcomings in the professional turns. Finally, community singing helped the audience to feel as if they belonged to the picture palace community. After the warmth of a community singing session, patrons began to perceive the stage entertainers as personal friends instead of anonymous professionals.

Exhibitors were also aware that community singing helped patrons to forget their cares. Organist Edward Meikel recalled that Americans had used community singing to lift downtrodden spirits during the Great War; as he wrote in a letter to the *Herald*, "The psychological effect was the same then, as it is now—it cheers them up."[98] Meikel encouraged organists to bring joy to their patrons via community singing whatever their personal or artistic reservations might be. Spreading good cheer became increasingly lucrative in the 1930s, when most patrons desired a momentary escape from their often-difficult lives. "In these days especially," observed Louis K. Sidney,

ORGAN
PRESENTATIONS OF
GREAT SONGS

SMALL SLIDE SETS

-MY SIN-
MEAN TO ME
OLD FASHIONED
LADY
BUTTON UP YOUR
OVERCOAT
I'LL NEVER ASK
FOR MORE
THE SONG I LOVE
WHEN THE WORLD
IS AT REST
SALLY OF MY
DREAMS
(Theme of "Mother Knows Best")
MY TONIA
(Theme of "In Old Arizona")
TRUE HEAVEN
(Theme of "True Heaven")

We Also Have Chorus Sets for All
of These Songs, As Well As a Few
Not Listed

SPECIALS

"ROMANCE AND MELODY"
Introducing
THE SONG I
LOVE
(A Presentation That Is a Classic)
"OPEN SECRETS"
Introducing
THAT'S HOW I
FEEL ABOUT
YOU
(Perfect for Community)

Write for All Slides and
Information to
SAM LERNER, Mgr. of Publicity

DE SYLVA, BROWN &
HENDERSON, INC.
745 7th Ave., New York City

head of production for Loews theaters, in 1931, "the orgainst [*sic*] who can do things to make people happy and forget their cares, if only for ten minutes, is valuable to the theatre in which he works, and it has been proved that he is a box-office attraction."[99] By this time, organists were in need of some cheer themselves, for the combination of sound technology and the economic downturn was driving them from their jobs. They leapt at the chance, therefore, to ingratiate themselves with patrons by lifting their spirits with song.

Exhibitors also noted that community singing encouraged their patrons to be more polite to one another. One columnist from 1930 suggested that once audience members began to sing together they realized that they "are among other people like themselves, there to have a good time."[100] Patrons then experienced the feeling of belonging to a sympathetic community, and they behaved with courtesy as a result. In the age of talking pictures, the issue of courtesy became very important. Early sound systems were mediocre, and patrons had to maintain perfect silence in order to understand the dialogue. In the early 1930s, therefore, commentators redoubled their effort to urge community singing as a means to promote social harmony within the audience. "It is a rather intimate proceeding," wrote *Herald* columnist W. S. Russel in 1930, "this singing together in the theatre, and it has a value in it that makes for a more congenial and solicitous audience.

This advertisement for song slides from the publishing firm of De Sylva, Brown, and Henderson Inc. appeared in *Exhibitors Herald-World* in May 1929. During the late 1920s, every issue of the *Herald* contained multiple publishers' ads in this style.

And in having a good time together in this manner, it reminds people that others like the same things, and consequently, there is probably more consideration given in this day of taking pictures, when it is so easy to disturb someone."[101] Patrons were sometimes distressed by the requirement that they remain silent throughout a talking film, which was contrary to their established moviegoing habits. Organist Dale Young found in 1930 that community singing was also useful after the feature film, since it allowed the audience to engage with the entertainment and, finally, make some noise. "In the age of 'talkies,'" he told his own audience via slide, "they are useful in introducing theme songs, and also when audience gets a chance to sing, they relax after being quiet all through the feature picture."[102]

By most accounts, patrons enjoyed community singing enormously. The clearest evidence of community singing's popularity is that it persevered in the picture palace for over a decade, despite constant opposition from certain quarters of the exhibition trade. Chicago organist Edward Meikel, writing to his peers, explained as early as 1926 why the practice could not and should not be eliminated: "Regardless of what you and I may think of community singing stunts as entertainment, one thing is certain in my mind, and that is that the audiences at the present time want them, and enjoy them."[103] Other commentators also noted the overwhelming popularity of the practice, and exhibitors regularly reported a high demand for community singing to the trade press.[104]

Firsthand accounts of community singing do exist, although they are scarce. In 1930, the *Chicago Daily Times* interviewed six theatergoers about their experiences with community singing. The responses provide an unusual perspective on the practice: that of the participating audience member. While the six interviews constitute a miniscule sample, they provide a coherent picture of the community singing experience:

The women's answers come first. Here they are.

"The theatre is a place of amusement, and I have a great time singing with the rest of the people. Singing alone I would feel bashful, but when everybody is singing, I am braver. I prefer to sing the latest songs, and enjoy every new one more when I hear a great number of people singing it. It sounds like opera."

"I think singing with the audience in the theatre is loads of fun and at the same time we are receiving singing lessons. Most people just can't resist singing in the theatres, because everybody else is singing. It makes people more friendly and everyone is happy. Sometimes it reminds me of singing in church. Everyone from the smallest to the tallest is singing."

"Singing with the audiences in the theatres is one of my favorite sports. It affords an opportunity for everyone to exercise their vocal cords and have lots of fun at the same time. Whenever I go to a theatre and the audience sings to the music of the organ I feel at home because everyone is singing and I have my exercise too."

And now we hear from the men.

"Although I am not a frequent visitor to the theatre, every time I do go, and the audience is singing, I try to do my best, too. It is all in fun, and usually the organist has some funny songs up his sleeve which makes everybody laugh. Even when I do not feel like singing I do just the same, because I do not like to appear different from other people."

"I enjoy singing with the audience in theatres. It is a maker of fraternity, and gives the more backward ones more confidence to express their pleasure. It also gives occasion to people who have no other opportunity to participate in what we call congregational singing in churches. Let the theatres keep it up, louder and funnier."

"It gives me a great deal of pleasure to sing with the audience in theatres or at any other gathering where singing is permitted. I enjoy singing and not having a particularly good voice, I get a lot of fun out of singing in a crowd where my voice cannot be distinguished from the others. However, some people sing in theatres at the wrong time and thereby spoil the fun for others."[105]

All of the interviewees indicated that community singing was fun, and several mentioned the central role that comedy played in the experience. For these patrons, community singing provided lighthearted entertainment above all else. But another important theme emerges from these answers: the community-building power of group singing. Community singing, as an innate "maker of fraternity" among theater patrons, affected participants in several different ways. Some of the answers indicate that singing improved the general mood, while others reveal that singing in a community allowed the amateur to enjoy music making without embarrassment. This in turn built up excitement in the theater and allowed patrons to engage directly with the entertainment. One woman observed that community singing made her feel at home in the theater, as if the other patrons were friends instead of strangers. Yet another idea represented in the interviews is that singing in a theater was analogous to singing in a church. In the eyes of some theatergoers, these two institutions had much in common. Just as the church provided community and like-minded companionship, the picture palace—and its community sing—brought people together and created a bond between them.

SING-ALONG FILMS IN THE SILENT ERA

Throughout the 1920s, organists had the option of projecting lyrics via silent film. Although these films were less prevalent than song slides, they deserve careful consideration. I have chosen to discuss sing-along films separately because they were not the exclusive tool of organists. Films, unlike song slides, were incorporated into various parts of the program, and they could be accompanied by the organist, the orchestra, or even a synchronized sound track. Also, some of these films still exist, which means that they can be experienced in a way that the typical picture palace sing cannot. Finally, the genre of sing-along film underwent explosive growth in the sound era, and in the 1930s these films often served to replace the theater organist—the topic to which I will turn in the final chapter.

As we have seen, organists often procured song slides directly from music publishers. Although a few publishers also produced sing-along films to advertise their own products, these have not survived. There is a small amount of information about publishers' films in the trade press, however, and records suggest that they most often contained live-action scenes outlining rudimentary plots. After the mood had been set, the song lyrics faded in and the organist became responsible for coordinating his accompaniment with the text.[106] The film used by Henri Keates in 1921 to accompany the song "Why, Dear?" might have been of this sort.[107] By 1926, publishers' song films were described as "passé."[108]

Far more prominent were the films released by production companies. These films were not intended to advertise songs. Instead, they were marketed to theaters as entertainment and rented in the same manner as other short subjects. In the 1920s, two series of silent sing-along films were available for organists to use: Norman Jeffries's Sing Them Again (1923–24), distributed by Educational Pictures, and Max Fleischer's Ko-Ko Song Car-Tunes (1924–27), carried by the Fleischers' own distributional organization, Red Seal Pictures.[109] Educational specialized in short subjects, and the series, directed by Russell Shields and filmed at Betzwood Studios near Philadelphia,

fit comfortably into its catalog of live-action turns familiar from the vaudeville stage.[110] The Song Car-Tunes were directed by Dave Fleischer and produced in the Fleischers' own New York studio. These animated shorts were
intimately linked with Fleischer's Out of the Inkwell series (1919–29), which
had already established the Fleischer studio as a major player in American
short subject production, and they featured the popular Inkwell character
Ko-Ko the Klown.[111] Both studios were responding to the rising popularity
of theater sing-alongs, but their unique products reflected diverse values that
were emerging within the practice of community singing.

Both series featured classic American songs, including Stephen Foster
and early Tin Pan Alley hits. Jefferies, however, accompanied medleys of
choruses with nostalgic live-action scenes, whereas Fleischer set complete songs against backdrops of animated gags. All of these films could be
screened with orchestral or organ accompaniment, and—depending on the
source of the music—they could be suitably programmed either among the
short subjects or as part of the organ solo. While each Song Car-Tune reel
arrived at the theater complete with an eighteen-piece orchestration, organists often disregarded the studio's preference and instead used the films in
place of song slides.[112] Likewise, Educational designed "a complete music
score" for every issue of Sing Them Again, "so that while the action preceding the singing of the chorus is taking place, the verse of the song is being
played."[113] These arrangements were available for orchestra, organ, and—in
the final year of the series—player piano.[114]

The first issue of the Sing Them Again series, Close Harmony, was released
on August 1, 1923.[115] To develop a rough estimate of the series, one need
only read the titles of the issues, which were released at the rate of one per
month: Companions, Golden Gems, Memories, Home Again, Lest We Forget,
Old Friends, Long Ago, Heart Throbs, Lost Chords, Echoes of Youth, and
Melodious Moments. Producer Jefferies, who was known to audiences as a
veteran stage performer, sought to appeal to the nostalgic streak in 1920s
movie patrons. The title of the series itself explicitly states the purpose of the
entertainment: to revisit old favorites and remember bygone days. Opening
titles explained to the audience that these shorts were "modernized revivals
of the songs you used to sing," although it seems that the songs were considered to have been "modernized" simply because they were presented on
film.[116] The Sing Them Again films have been almost completely lost; only
a severely damaged reel of Echoes of Youth survives today. However, the

releases were extensively reviewed in the trade journal *Film Daily*, and as such it is possible to examine the contents of the films, the responses that the films provoked, and the ways in which the films were used.

An *Exhibitors Herald* article from 1925—at which point the Sing Them Again series was still being actively promoted—lists each of the songs used in the twelve films. All of the titles mentioned belong to old songs, including American favorites, traditional songs from the United Kingdom, and patriotic or wartime numbers. For example, the first Sing Them Again release, *Close Harmony*, featured "Sweet Rosie O'Grady" (1896), "In the Shade of the Old Apple Tree" (1905), and "Sweet Adeline," the 1903 barbershop classic.[117] The release title refers to barbershop singing, which by the mid-1920s was already an idealized and explicitly nostalgic form of male music making.[118] For the first film in his series, therefore, Jefferies not only chose songs that dripped with nostalgia but presented them in the revered and nostalgia-laden guise of barbershop.

In each of the films, the singing of a well-loved chorus was preceded by a short live-action scene suited to the lyrics of the song. For example, before the audience sang the Civil War song "Tenting Tonight" (1863) in the film *Lest We Forget*, they watched as a group of young soldiers sat around the campfire and wrote letters to their distant loves ones. After a short sequence accompanied by a wordless verse from the organ or orchestra, the soldiers broke off their activity and began to sing the featured song, although without voices: the audience provided the soundtrack. The next song in the same film, "Wait till the Sun Shines, Nellie" (1905), was preceded by a scene in which Nellie and her young man were caught in the rain while on a picnic outing—a slight variation on the events described in the song.[119]

In an environment where the tone of community singing could range from the saccharine to the ludicrous, Jeffries's films seem to have fallen in the middle of the spectrum. On the serious end, a film like *Lest We Forget* carried "several titles pleading for universal peace and brotherhood of man," and opened with the somber "Tenting Tonight."[120] At the same time, reviews of the series suggest that not all of the films struck such a solemn note. *Heart Throbs*, for example, was described in the trade press as an issue that "may not occasion [as] many laughs as some of the previous ones, owing to the songs chosen"—a clear indication that some of the eight films preceding it *did* provoke laughter.[121] In another report, one exhibitor saw fit to substitute a Sing Them Again issue for a comedy in his Brooklyn theater "on the theory that it contained sufficient humor."[122] Still, it seems that the films never incorporated the more ridiculous elements of organ-based community singing, such as lisping choruses, tongue twisters, gags, and parody lyrics. The songs in this series were presented with reverence, but for the sake of entertainment.

Sing Them Again films received excellent reviews, and trade professionals expected them to succeed in a wide range of theatrical environments. *Memories* was described as "a peach of a number for any house," while *Old Friends* "might well be used on any program."[123] These comments suggest that the films were appropriate even for high-class, nonsinging houses like the New York Paramount in Times Square, discussed in the following chapter; and indeed, the most prestigious of all theater organists, Jesse Crawford, was reported to have used a film with song lyrics while presiding at the console of the Balaban and Katz Chicago Theatre—a house that seldom permitted the crass activity of community singing. In 1925, a reviewer praised Jesse and Helen Crawford for their perfect synchronization with an unidentified film, *Waiting for You*, in which "the words are very faint and as the note is struck it becomes bold. Intermingled between the first and second choruses are violin and piano solos showing a closeup of each instrument."[124] Just as the Sing Them Again issues maintained a reserved and elegant demeanor that did not offend high-class audiences, this film struck a tasteful balance between entertainment and pedagogy. This account also reminds us that sing-along films, like song slides, could be used without encouraging participation.

All the same, Sing Them Again films usually were expected to inspire community singing. Many reviewers noted the importance of pairing the films with a skilled song leader, who would personally urge participation and keep the audience in time with the picture. While the organist could assume this role, it appears that some theaters took the opportunity to procure the services of a popular song leader from the community. In Malcolm Cook's account of the films, he describes a long association between the Sing Them Again series and song leader John Henry Lyons, who was first recruited in 1923 by the Strand Theatre in Seattle. After experiencing initial success, Lyons went on tour and appeared with Sing Them Again releases in several western states during the following year.[125] The presence of a song leader would have allied the films more closely with the community singing movement than with commercial picture palace entertainment, and Educational took advantage of this possible new market. Cook has documented the use of Sing Them Again films in conjunction with the 1924 Kentucky Home Coming celebrations and a community singing week in Philadelphia and has also uncovered plans laid by Educational to exhibit them in 106 army training camps.[126]

For theater managers, Sing Them Again films appear to have had promotional value. The aforementioned Brooklyn exhibitor not only screened an unnamed Sing Them Again reel in place of the comedy but also billed it alongside the feature on the marquee and promoted it in the weekly advertising materials—tactics he would only have pursued if he expected the film to be a significant draw. However, not every critic was satisfied with the quality of the films. After the series had already concluded production and was apparently waning in popularity, one reviewer dismissed the entire oeuvre with the following assessment: "Would be more valuable if developed with greater musical and pictorial taste."[127] This was among the final trade press mentions of Sing Them Again.

Max Fleischer's Ko-Ko Song Car-Tunes series was significantly more successful and longer lived. Indeed, Daniel Goldmark notes that the sing-along series was among the Fleischers' best-known products of the silent era and helped bring their animation studio to national attention.[128] The Song Car-Tunes were also significantly more influential than Educational's product, both in the United States and abroad. Pathé brought the series to England in 1926 where, as Malcolm Cook demonstrates, their popularity inspired at least six additional British-produced sing-along series.[129] The first Song Car-Tunes were released in March 1924, just as production of the Sing Them Again series was drawing to a close. Only 150 theaters booked the films in 1924, but 1925 saw three thousand houses exhibiting Fleischer's sing-alongs, and the films were heavily advertised and reviewed in the trade press.[130] Thirty-eight films were released between 1924 and 1927, most of which are extant, and the popularity of the series spawned a sound-era sequel, Screen Songs, that ran from 1929 to 1938.

While Fleischer was no doubt aware of the Educational films, no one associated with the Song Car-Tunes ever mentioned the other series as an influence. Instead, the various genesis stories for the Song Car-Tunes link the series with the illustrated song and organist-led community singing. Out of the Inkwell Films, established by the Fleischers in 1921, was composed of

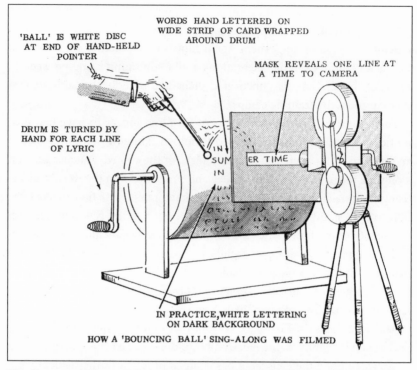

This diagram, which reveals how the bouncing ball portion of a Fleischer Song Car-Tune was filmed, appeared in the October 1969 issue of *Theatre Organ Bombarde*.

three brothers: Max, Dave, and Lou. Bernard Fleischer, son of Lou, claimed that it was his father who came up with the idea of a sing-along series. Lou had worked as a pianist in nickelodeon theaters and provided accompaniment for illustrated songs, but he always wished—according to his son—that there could be a marker on the screen to indicate which word was being sung. Bernard credits his uncle Max with the idea of marking the text with a white ball, filmed in live action as it "bounced" over lyrics pasted onto a rotating drum.[131] Animator Richard Huemer, however, recalled that the idea for the series came from Max and Dave, who wanted to provide an animated alternative to the static song slides used by organists.[132] As a third option, Max's son Richard credited Charles K. Harris with inspiring the animated sing-alongs. Harris—a composer and publisher whose 1891 "After the Ball" is remembered as the hit that launched the American song publishing industry—toured the Fleischer establishment in the early 1920s, and reportedly complained to Max about the song slides that were used to advertise his music in theaters. According to Richard, "It bothered him that the musicians who accompanied the slides set the tempo, sometimes too fast, sometimes too slow, depending on their mood. Audiences would frequently get out of synch with the lyrics when the projectionist was too early or too late with the next slide."[133] Whoever was responsible for the idea, the Song Car-Tunes were intended to repair a significant shortcoming—unreliable synchronization—in the practice of slide-driven community singing.

Harris's involvement in the Song Car-Tune series is undeniable, but its extent is unclear. The first two mentions of the series, both of which appeared in *Film Daily* in early 1924, emphasized the role played by Harris.[134] His name was listed before that of Max Fleischer in both cases, and the first review of a Song Car-Tune stated that the films were "presented by Charles K. Harris, the music publisher who is responsible for the songs."[135] At first blush, it would appear that the Song Car-Tunes were to be a plugging vehicle for Harris's wares. However, Harris's name was not mentioned again in the trade press after March 1924, and only two of the films, both from the first round of releases, featured songs published by his firm. This mystery has yet to be unraveled.

Each Song Car-Tune presented a single musical number. The sing-along portion, which featured the bouncing ball, was preceded by the animated shenanigans of Ko-Ko the Klown and his "Kwartet," all of whom were habitually conjured from the inkwell at the start of each film. The on-screen lyrics, which followed a descriptive title and invitation to sing, were often paired with illustrative line drawings reminiscent of those seen on song slides. The body of songs is similar to that used in the Sing Them Again series, with several overlapping numbers. After the first release, which presented the contemporary song "Oh Mabel" (1924), all of the cartoons featured either a nineteenth-century favorite like "Old Folks at Home" (1851) or "Dixie" (1859), or an early Tin Pan Alley hit like "By the Light of the Silvery Moon" (1909) or "When the Midnight Choo Choo Leaves for Alabam'" (1912). If the series was ever meant to be a vehicle for Harris's songs, it quickly came to resemble the nostalgic Educational films in terms of content. It seems evident, however, that the choice of repertoire for these films was motivated not by the desire to wallow in memories of the past but by recent copyright laws. The shorts trade only lightly in nostalgia: traditional

What Others Think

8.

MISSOURI THEATRE:
"Have used your Ko-Ko Song Car-Tunes as Featured Organ Solos and want to say they pleased the audience immensely."
—*Milton Slosser, Organist.*

729 7th Ave.   N. Y. C.

Edwin Miles Fadman, Pres.

This spot belongs to an extended series of advertisements that appeared in *Exhibitors Herald* in 1925 and 1926. Milton Slosser was a renowned theater organist who led community singing with slides and films.

brass bands and barbershop singers (the aforementioned Kwartet) regularly introduce the sing-along, but the settings are facetious, not sentimental. All the same, many of the songs were popularized on the minstrel stage and, as Nicholas Sammond and others demonstrate, the conventions of minstrelsy were commonly resurrected in cartoons of the 1920s and 1930s. For this reason, Sammond describes the Song Car-Tunes as facilitating "an affectively positive experience of collective and distributed racism."[136] Although the following discussion will focus on the trade press discourse surrounding these films, we cannot forget the social conditions they embodied and perpetuated.

Some trade professionals expressed concern that these old songs would not appeal to youthful theatergoers. In January 1926, Red Seal Pictures, the series distributor, heavily promoted the Song Car-Tune *Has Anybody Here Seen Kelly?*, which featured an Irish-themed number from 1908 suitable for St. Patrick's Day.[137] The film was well received, but one reviewer observed that while "this old-time song will no doubt bring back memories to the adults in the audience, [. . .] it will mean little to the younger generation."[138] Later that year, perhaps the same reviewer noted that the film *Sweet Adeline* "should appeal to the new and old generation, for here is one of those songs that is perennially popular."[139] The use of Song Car-Tunes in children's matinee programs—a topic of chapter 5—is also well documented. One New York City reviewer reported that "the youngsters join lustily in the singing" whenever the films were screened—clear evidence that Song Car-Tunes had cross-generational appeal.[140] The songs may not have been youthful, but the clever and irreverent settings created by the Fleischers were entirely up to date. While the repertoire of the Song Car-Tunes resembled that of the community singing movement, the approach was that of the theater organist, who sought to promote good humor in his audience. The films are genuinely funny, even from a modern perspective. Reviewers often emphasized Ko-Ko's "comedy antics," and in 1925 the president of the National Motion Picture League applauded the clown for "vitaliz[ing] the song with bits of humor."[141] In addition, the Song Car-Tunes were heavily promoted each year as part of National Laugh Month, an exploitation scheme devised by film exhibitors to boost traditionally low January ticket sales.[142]

As mentioned at the outset, each Song Car-Tune reel arrived at the theater bundled with an eighteen-piece orchestration and an organ reduction, which allowed any house to present the cartoon with live, synchronized music. Unfortunately, only a few of these scores survive.[143] Daniel Goldmark has examined the keyboard score for the 1926 film *Has Anybody Here Seen Kelly?* and published a detailed analysis in the volume *Beyond the Soundtrack: Representing Music in Cinema*.[144] Although the extant sheet music represents accompanying practices incompletely, it tells us much about the creation, distribution, and execution of Song Car-Tune scores. The staves are interlaced with text to indicate various points at which the musicians must synchronize with the film and paired with instructions for how best to do so.[145] For example, the score examined by Goldmark suggests that the orchestra should be "led by a single instrument such as the violin or cornet, the player of which carries the melody, and *follows it by watching the screen*" (emphasis in original).[146] Editorial notes included, it seems, in all scores indicate that each arrangement had been premiered successfully at the Capitol Theatre in New York City—and that all of the parts should be immediately returned to Red Seal Pictures upon conclusion of the rental agreement.[147]

Although the score makes no mention of the fact, *Has Anybody Here Seen Kelly?* was one of a number of the cartoons to be released with recorded soundtracks, provided courtesy of Lee de Forest's Phonofilm sound-on-film process. Max Fleischer, who had collaborated with de Forest for some years, intended from the start to incorporate recorded sound into the Song Car-Tunes. The first screening of a Song Car-Tune with "canned" sound took place in June 1924 at the Circle Theatre in New York City, and according to animator Huemer, it was a resounding success: "It brought down the house, it stopped the show. They applauded and stamped and whistled into the following picture, which they finally stopped and took off, and put back the 'Oh, Mabel' cartoon again. They ran it again to the delight of the audience. I always say that was an indication of what sound would do for animated cartoons."[148] Most theaters, however, were not equipped to exhibit sound films, and the musical accompaniment was almost always provided by live musicians.[149]

Because of their flexibility when it came to exhibition practices, the Song Car-Tunes could find a home in various parts of the program. Although they were usually exhibited along with the other short films, they could also be used by the organist during his solo. In these cases, the Song Car-Tune replaced the usual lantern slides used to facilitate community singing. The cartoons were employed in this fashion by organists Milton Slosser of the Missouri Theater, Billy Muth of the Texas Theater, and Milton Charles of the Chicago Theatre, among many others. Theater organists sought constantly to provide novelty in their solos, and it seems that the incorporation of a sing-along film delighted audiences. When Muth screened the Song Car-Tune *Has Anybody Here Seen Kelly?*, for example, the *Herald* reviewer was able to report—with only a hint of disdain—that his patrons "liked it better than they like the singing lessons customarily thrust over here."[150]

While most trade press reviewers indicated that the Song Car-Tunes were best suited to the singing house, they also appealed to an audience beyond the habitual warblers. One writer remarked that the value of the films "consists in the reaction on [sic] your audience. If they can be induced to join in the singing, it is a success. If not, it becomes just

LOOK!

"Has Anybody Here Seen Kelly?"

BOOK!

For Week of March 14th
St. Patrick's Day Special

One of Max Fleischer's Great Ko-Ko Song Car-Tunes Hand Colored By Brock'

RED SEAL PICTURES CORP

729—7th Ave., N. Y. C.
DISTRIBUTORS

Has Anybody Here Seen Kelly? (1926), featuring the popular 1908 British music-hall song, was the most heavily advertised release in the Fleisher Song Car-Tune series. This spot was one of many that appeared in *Exhibitors Herald* in 1926.

PRACTICES AND TOOLS 121

filler."[151] Another noted that the cartoon *My Bonny Lies over the Ocean* failed at the Los Angeles Metropolitan Theatre because "the audience didn't have its singing voice with it and refused to join in the chorus."[152] However, there is no question that these films met with success in nonsinging houses. The audience at the above-mentioned Chicago Theatre, for example, almost never sang. In addition, the Song Car-Tunes were regularly premiered at New York's majestic Capitol Theatre, where the films were brought to life with an eighty-piece orchestra. There is no evidence, however, that the Capitol audience ever engaged in community singing of any sort.[153]

Other large theaters also got more than singing out of the Song Car-Tunes. In 1925, the newly opened Mosque Theatre of Newark, New Jersey, staged an enormous presentation act based on the Song Car-Tune *My Bonnie Lies over the Ocean*.[154] Live stage presentations were standard in all picture palaces of the 1920s, and they often set the scene for a feature film, in which case the presentation was termed a "prologue." A prologue for a short film, however, was unusual, and the trade press noted that this was perhaps the most elaborate stage presentation ever to accompany a one-reeler. *Moving Picture World* explained that the managing director of the Mosque was "so impressed" by the Fleischer shorts that "he proceeded to stage this Red Seal release precisely as though it were a feature picture."[155] The idea for this prologue might have come directly from the score for *My Bonnie*, which contains text suggesting that the Fleischer sing-along films were particularly well suited to stage promotion. "By opening the act with singers in costumes appropriate to the song," reads a notice on the first page of the score, "the stage number can be blended into the film and the audience will unconsciously be drawn into the spirit of participating in the songs."[156] (This notice was not unique to *My Bonnie* but rather appears to have been included in all of the Song Car-Tune scores.) The prologue staged at the Mosque Theatre contained elements prescribed by the studio, but producers H. M. S. Kendrick and Colby Harriman conceived of it as an "epilogue" to the film instead of as an introduction. An overture by the fifty-piece Mosque orchestra segued into the film score at the sound of a whistle emanating from the percussion section. During the first chorus of "My Bonnie," a male quartet joined the singing from off stage; the disembodied voices would have helped lead the audience in song without distracting from the film. At the conclusion of the film, the stage lights were raised to reveal a traveler gazing admiringly upon a "Scotch mountain scene" as bagpipes sounded "My Bonnie" in the distance. Soon the pipers appeared onstage in the company of "twenty Scotch lassies" (in reality the house ballet troop) and proceeded to offer a program of characteristic music, dance, and song. Finally, the orchestra joined in with the pipers as "the curtain came down amidst a veritable tumult of applause."[157] Several trade journals noted with admiration that the presentation required the service of forty onstage performers.[158]

Moving Picture World revisited the topic of Song Car-Tune prologues the following year with an article entitled "'Ko-Ko' a Presentation Knockout." In it, the trade journal offered advice for exhibitors hoping to exploit the films, including the suggestion that life-sized cutouts of Ko-Ko and his Kwartet be prepared. Song leaders were to stand behind the cutouts and sing through openings in the faces while operating the arms in a "mechanical gesture" peculiarly at odds with Ko-Ko's own realistic movements, which were animated using Max Fleischer's innovative Rotoscope technique. The journal also recommended that exhibitors introduce "a character made up as 'Ko-Ko' . . . to lead the audience in the singing."[159] These accounts confirm the commercial success of Flesicher's Song Car-Tunes. They also suggest that the presentation of the films was often facilitated by a song leader—a practice common in community singing outside of the theater but nearly unheard of in the organ solo.

4 COMMUNITY SINGING AND THE "CLASS HOUSE"

Although the organ solo could feature a wide variety of entertainment styles, in certain theaters it was always dedicated to community singing. But which theaters were these? The popularity of community singing was not limited by geography nor was it limited by the size of a theater. Community singing was practiced with great enthusiasm in every major city and was equally successful in tiny neighborhood houses and cavernous, five-thousand-seat showpieces. Nor did its popularity depend on a theater's age, expense, or scale of luxury. No one exhibition chain was more likely to program community singing than another. Indeed, two houses located only blocks from one another might appear to be identical in all respects but one: the presence or absence of community singing.

The difference had to do with class-based cultural aspirations. Community singing was not an appropriate activity for picture palaces that presented "high-class" entertainment. The exhibitors who programmed entertainment for "class houses" (a trade term) were not concerned about the performance of popular music per se; organists and stage performers presented popular song in even the most elite theaters. What these exhibitors objected to was audience participation. This prejudice was not new to the picture palace: in the early 1910s, impresario B. F. Keith took the lead in eliminating low-class elements from the vaudeville stage when he prohibited performers from addressing the audience directly.[1] Vaudeville theater managers were soon in agreement that audience participation discouraged attendance by sophisticated theatergoers who were accustomed to the conventions of the playhouse.[2] When patrons of the next decade joined the picture palace organist in song, they were often viewed as disrupting the atmosphere of cultured consumption that was the hallmark of a class house. First, by collaborating with the organist they upset the audience/performer dichotomy that characterized artistic performance. Second, singing patrons behaved physically in a manner unbecoming for the consumer of art. Third, they produced a sound that was itself inartistic. And finally, participation eliminated the possibility for musical edification.

The identity of a class house was determined partly by geographic location and partly by exhibitor decree. Motion picture exhibitors in the 1920s built massive empires consisting of production companies, distribution exchanges, and theater chains. Every large chain boasted a variety of theaters; in this way, the exhibitor could appeal to all of the potential customers in a city. The picture palace industry as a whole catered to middle-class patrons, but this does not mean that all patrons had the same taste in films and stage acts. In order to maximize profit, each of the theaters in an exhibition chain offered a specific style of entertainment designed—in conjunction with architecture, location, and other elements—to attract a unique patronage. The class house, which offered artistic entertainment in a dignified atmosphere, was usually located in the heart of the city. These class houses were often flagship theaters: the chain's preeminent picture palace, where films were premiered and stage shows were inaugurated. A flagship represented the best of what an exhibition chain had to offer and, therefore, pretended to a higher level of cultural sophistication than the average house. However, almost any theater had the potential to develop and cater to a "class" patronage.

This paradigm will be explored with case studies of two important picture palaces, one of which featured community singing and one of which did not: the Brooklyn Paramount and the New York Paramount (located in Times Square). Both of these theaters thrived in New York City, a major metropolitan center rich in community singing activity. Both belonged to the Paramount Publix chain, which means that they shared access to films, stage presentations, and contract performers. Both were first-run houses. Both were large and first-rate in terms of adornments and service. Both engaged famous organists with national reputations. However, each theater built a different public image by providing live entertainment suitable to its own specific class of patron. Before we can approach these case studies, however, we must understand the significance of community singing to a theater's reputation in the picture palace era.

The class connotations of community singing were frequently addressed by trade professionals. In fact, the late 1920s witnessed a heated discussion on the topic of community singing in the organ solo. This exchange took place primarily in the trade periodical *Exhibitors Herald*. The *Herald*—a weekly publication dedicated to all aspects of motion picture exhibition—was uniquely positioned to offer a forum for ideas on the topic of live picture palace entertainment. When exhibitors and other trade commentators wished to voice their opinions about the motion picture industry, they turned to the *Herald*. At the same time, the *Herald* editors and reviewers demonstrated strong opposition to community singing, sharing their opinions in signed articles, reviews, and op-eds. The strongest editorial statement came from the Presentation Acts department in May 1927; terse excerpts from this manifesto, prematurely titled "Last Word on Community Singing," will be included throughout the following account.

The *Herald*'s main assault on community singing played out in 1926 and 1927. Although the trade journal's own writers produced the bulk of the criticism, several notable theater organists contributed as well. The attack had three focal points: the organ, the organist, and the patrons. In each case, contributors attempted to demonstrate that community singing was harmful to, or did not fulfill the potential of, one of these three elements of picture palace entertainment. It is important to note that, although the *Herald* seldom invoked the issue of class by name, class was always at the center of the controversy.

The first writer to aggressively oppose community singing was William R. Weaver, a *Herald* critic who penned a regular column on stage presentation in the picture palace. In two short articles published in the summer of 1926, Weaver introduced all three of the focal points that would characterize the journal's criticism of community singing in the coming year. His initial article, titled "Why Not Play the Organs?," highlighted the first objection made by critics of community singing: the organ, a "great instrument" installed at enormous expense, was wasted on community singing.[3] In his follow-up a month later, Weaver emphasized the "prestige effect" of the organ, an attribute that was permanently undermined by audience participation.[4] Weaver viewed the organ as a high-class instrument that should be reserved for dignified entertainment. He was not alone in this opinion; organist Albert F. Brown, who boasted a reputation for artistic organ presentations but also led community singing, argued that every organist must fulfill the potential for prestige inherent in his instrument.[5] While this position relies on the notion that certain instruments and repertoires are objectively more valuable, it was the editors of Presentation Acts who most explicitly evoked class.

"Persistence in sing thing cheapens organ in opinion of patrons qualified to appreciate instrument's real worth," they wrote, with the result that community singing "destroys prestige of instrument."[6] An anonymous *Herald* commentator also rested his evaluation on the quality of the patrons, blaming "the weaker-willed part of an audience" with dragging the organ down to their level and thereby "robbing it of its value."[7]

After establishing that community singing was inimical to the inherent greatness of the theater organ, Weaver turned to the figure of the organist to illustrate the negative effects of the practice. In both of his 1926 articles, Weaver warned that community singing was dangerous on two fronts: on the one hand, it allowed inept players to disguise their lack of skill, while on the other, it prevented capable organists from fulfilling their potential. He predicted that the end of the community singing craze would bring with it the separation of wheat from chaff in the theater organ community. The value of the true "artists," he claimed, would finally be acknowledged, while the "near-comics getting away with the current murder" would disappear into ignominy once they could no longer use community singing to mask their incompetence.[8] A variety of trade commentators supported Weaver's hypothesis that community singing enabled unskilled organists. Brown observed that community singing was employed only "by those suffering from lack of ideas or musical ability, or both," while the editors of the *Herald's* Presentation Acts department described the practice as "grapenuts for beginners willing to work cheap to break in."[9]

Despite widespread evidence to the contrary, there appears to have been broad critical agreement with Weaver's postulation that community singing could damage the career of a skilled organist. In 1927, the editors of the *Herald's* Presentation Acts department suggested that the practice could destroy the reputation of a "name" organist and reduce his value as a box office draw; in an open letter to concerned theater owners, the journal even suggested that community singing could spell the end of the organ solo. After dismissing the rumor that the practice was encouraged by devious exhibitors who sought to cut organists' salaries after "letting them hang themselves," the editors encouraged all organists to avoid community singing and to return to the "classical solo number" that had represented the high point in organ entertainment.[10] The next month, the same editors offered a terse analysis of the situation: "Community singing—save occasionally as novelty—slow suicide (and not so slow, either, at present rate) for organists with talent."[11] In 1970, organist John Muri subscribed to this way of thinking when he blamed the downfall of the theater organist on community singing: "The seeds of his destruction were planted the day he ceased to be an artist-performer and became a song-leader."[12]

After establishing the threat to both organ and organist, Weaver addressed the issue of audience response to community singing. On this point, however, he suffered from inconsistency. In the first article, Weaver had suggested to managers a simple test expected to reveal that audiences almost always preferred a straight, classical solo over community singing.[13] In his follow-up, however, Weaver blamed audiences for the fact that the community singing scourge could not be easily eliminated. "It is unlikely," he concluded, "that the public will consent to accept [organists] as anything save the clowns they now insist on being. The public's that way."[14] Other commentators insisted that community singing was not desired by audiences. "Plenty of objections to community sings," wrote the Presentation Acts editors. "No known instance of majority singing when requested."[15] The editors offered no evidence to support their first claim, however, while the second can be refuted by countless reviews published across the trade press.

This inconsistency exposed the central problem with the attack on community singing: most audiences actually enjoyed it. Organist Edward Meikel was the most prominent advocate of community singing on these grounds. Late in 1926 Meikel admitted that he himself had reservations about the practice, but he concluded that the audience must always have the final say in entertainment. So far as Meikel himself had observed, the audience wanted community singing.[16] Other advocates fought the rhetoric of Weaver and the *Herald* editors when they described community singing as a valuable tool for organists and exhibitors. Organist J. Newton Yates of Berwyn, Illinois, summed up the practice as "a great boost to the organ game in general," while Walter Hirsch, a well-known songwriter and creator of organ solos, reported in 1927 that "community singing conducted by the organist is directly accountable for much of the profits."[17] While Hirsch might be accused of trying to further his own interests, the fact that community singing would become increasingly common in the coming years supports his claim, for exhibitors were no more likely to permit an unprofitable practice than were audiences to support entertainment they did not enjoy.

Other critics joined Weaver in the attack on community singing but provided a more nuanced analysis of the audience. One popular argument was that theater patrons paid to be entertained, not to entertain. When patrons participated in community singing they were entertaining themselves, each other, and even the hired performers who worked in the theater. A reviewer who heard Keates at the Oriental suggested that patrons would soon be expected to bring instruments and accompany themselves: "If this singing thing continues in some of the picture theaters," he wrote, "it will not be long before the payees will be asked to provide the music that goes with the vocalisms with which they entertain organists and band leaders."[18] This was counter to the natural order of entertainment, in which professional artists presented their art and paying visitors sat in receptive silence. Critics also claimed that the patrons themselves did not want to provide their own entertainment. The Presentation Acts' editors, never shy to make a statement, declared: "People who pay way in to be entertained consciously or subconsciously resent being made to do the entertaining."[19] Despite the editors' hard-to-disprove argument concerning the subconscious, however, there is little evidence that this was the case.[20]

A final faction in the debate echoed the rhetoric of the music reformers, who had launched the community singing movement over a decade before. Just as the reformers had hoped that singing simple folk songs would elevate participants' taste and inspire more ambitious musical engagement, some trade professionals hoped that patrons would develop their skills and eventually be able to tackle more serious repertoire. Henri Keates was well-known for his comical sing-alongs, but he once confided to a journalist, "I'm working to get them so that they will finally sing opera."[21] He was supported in his endeavor by the head of the Music Research Bureau of Chicago, who reiterated the goals of the original community singing movement in a letter to the organist: "I take much pleasure in heartily congratulating you on the great success of your Community Sings at the Oriental Theatre. If I may be permitted to make a suggestion, you are afforded a splendid opportunity to raise the level of the class of music which is now placed on the screen."[22] Other organists hoped that their patrons' tastes would improve to the point where community singing was no longer of interest. Edward Meikel, another Chicago organist with a reputation for song leading, shared this opinion in a 1927 edition of the *Herald*: "I don't really believe there is an organist today playing community sings, who would not prefer to do something along more legitimate lines. Personally, I have an idea for solos that I am ready to spring as soon as I am convinced my audience is tired of the sings.... I am constantly on the alert looking for the handwriting on the wall."[23] Unfortunately, the era of live picture palace entertainment would not last long enough for either Keates or Meikel to realize their goals.

Writing after the controversy over community singing had largely petered out, the Presentation Acts editors made the following observation: "By the type of organ music and solo stunts offered in your theatre you can judge the class of people attending your house."[24] Despite the acrimonious conflict surrounding the issue of audience participation, no one seemed to disagree with this fundamental position. Whether a contributor warned that community singing would lower the class of a house or argued that patrons must be entertained at whatever level they demanded, he always conceded that community singing was inherently a low-class affair. To demonstrate the practical effect of this consensus, we will turn to our case studies.

THE BROOKLYN PARAMOUNT

At the height of the picture palace era, Brooklyn was a hotbed of community singing activity. A number of large palaces in downtown Brooklyn—most notably the Fox and the Paramount—competed for the singing patrons. The Paramount never had an organist who stayed for more than a few months. This was a typical arrangement; major exhibitors, such as Paramount Publix, often shuttled organists between theaters in order to provide variety for the patrons. Despite the changes in leadership, community singing was practiced at the Paramount for many years and remained a cornerstone of that theater's entertainment style well into the sound era.

The character, appeal, and status of the Brooklyn Paramount were grounded in the reputation of the surrounding neighborhood. Brooklyn itself carried important connotations for a 1920s exhibitor, such that the character of the borough determined the class of the theaters contained therein. In the late nineteenth century, Brooklyn had expanded rapidly following the development of trolley lines and the construction of the Brooklyn Bridge. The growing city had been formally annexed in 1898, when it became a borough of New York City. Completion of the Williamsburg Bridge and the expansion of the New York subway system in the early twentieth century had made Brooklyn even more accessible, all of which contributed both to casual tourism and to immigration.[25] Most of the newcomers were eastern, central, and southern Europeans, and many were Jewish.[26] Public transportation had also allowed Brooklyn to develop an amusement destination of

mythological proportions: Coney Island. It might be said that the amusement parks of Coney Island anticipated the picture palaces that would arise
a decade later, since they sought to attract a diverse, middle-class patronage
with a mixture of fantasy and education, all for a low entrance fee. The early
twentieth-century parks also cleaned up Coney Island's seedy reputation in
the same way that picture palaces transformed moviegoing after the era of
the nickelodeon.[27] Although Brooklyn's major picture palaces were located
downtown, not at Coney Island, they nonetheless reflected the same spirit
of carefree escape and attracted the same crowd of patrons: middle-class
adventure seekers from Brooklyn and Manhattan who were looking for a
few hours of fun.

It was the Paramount that introduced community singing to Brooklyn.
Exhibitors at the Paramount realized that community singing—which
had been popular in other regions for years—was a perfect match for the
class of patron that Brooklyn attracted, and they expected that patrons
would embrace the practice with enthusiasm. The exhibitors were not disappointed. Following the opening of the Paramount, community singing
became a local craze, and reviews of organ solos indicated that the popularity of the practice in Brooklyn matched that in Chicago, the city where
organist-led community singing had first been established. The 4,305-seat
Fox Theatre, which opened on August 21, 1928, would be the Paramount's
main competition in the years to come. The Fox soon became notorious,
like the Paramount, for raucous community singing led by a string of
famous organists.[28]

The 4,084-seat Paramount was designed by the architectural firm of Rapp
and Rapp, and it was located, like many urban theaters, in an ordinary-looking
office block. The Paramount presented the entering visitor with a series
of increasingly splendid impressions. She would enter the dour facade
and pass through the comparatively modest lobby and restrained lounge,
only to then find herself in the theater's dazzling auditorium, which the
Theatre Historical Society of America today considers to be "easily the most
flamboyant of all Rapp & Rapp designs."[29] The chief designer behind the
Paramount, Arthur Frederick Adams, regarded the theater as "a compos-
ite palace," a theater, that is, that combined the elements of "atmospheric"
and traditional architecture.[30] Atmospheric theaters were popularized in
the mid-1920s by the architect John Eberson, who designed auditoriums
so as to resemble exotic outdoor courtyards. To create the illusion, Eberson

The main lounge of the Brooklyn Paramount, in which visitors waited for the next show to begin. Terry Helgesen Collection, Theatre Historical Society.

The alcoves of the Brooklyn Paramount auditorium were painted sky blue, to create the illusion of an outdoor theater, and vines hung from the ceiling. At the same time, the statues, busts, and plaster ornaments echoed the European splendor that informed traditional picture palace design. Terry Helgesen Collection, Theatre Historical Society.

studded his dark blue ceilings with electric-light stars and projected moving clouds from a hidden Brenograph machine. Plaster masonry, real trees, fountains, and stuffed birds completed the effect.[31] The atmospheric touches in the Paramount were applied to the auditorium, which featured potted plants, a latticework trellis suspended above the balcony, and side bays of sky blue.[32] The impression that Rapp and Rapp sought to create was one of refined natural beauty. As the Theatre Historical Society puts it, "The audience felt like they were in a great garden pavilion, surrounded by fountains, flowers, vines, and songbirds."[33] In many aspects, however, the auditorium resembled those in other Rapp and Rapp palaces. The space was conventionally divided into orchestra seating and balcony, with a mezzanine tucked between the two. The magnificently decorated main console of the Wurlizter organ was positioned on a lift in the orchestra pit; a second console that could be moved onto the stage was later added. Wurlitzer modeled the organ on the instrument that the company had built for the New York Paramount some years previously. As in most theaters, the sound emanated from ostentatious grilles positioned on either side of the main stage.[34]

An extraordinary parade of organists passed through the Brooklyn Paramount, each of whom was at the top of his or her field. Each organist who graced the Paramount's console displayed unique and distinguishing characteristics, and each boasted a diverse résumé of picture palace experience. However, each of the organists suited his or her style to the Brooklyn Paramount and sought to entertain the patrons in the manner to which they had become accustomed.

Consider, for instance, the career of Stuart Barrie, who took over the Paramount console in October 1930. Barrie was an experienced organist who had worked in a variety of theaters, each of which required a different mode of organ solo. For each of his posts, Barrie reinvented his presentation style to suit the theater and its patrons. By 1930, Barrie had many years of experience conducting community sings. His first appointment of national significance had been at the Grand Central Theatre in Saint Louis. There, at least as early as the first half of 1925, Barrie had led community singing on a regular basis, and he was credited with starting the Saint Louis vogue for community singing.[35] In 1926, he moved downtown to open Saint Louis's Ambassador Theatre. The 3,005-seat Ambassador was a new palace, built that year by the Rapp and Rapp firm of architects. Barrie, however, did not offer community singing during his year at the Ambassador, and his solos tended more toward the serious or high minded than the comedic. A

Organists at the Brooklyn Paramount

Organist	Years as Soloist
Henry Murtagh	1928–29
Bob West	1929–30
Earl Abel	1930
Stuart Barrie	1930–31
Elsie Thompson	1931*
Merle Clark	1931–32
Dick Leibert	1932†

* Elsie Thompson appeared in conjunction with other organists both before and after her tenure as a soloist. As early as 1929, she joined Bob West at the console. Her last recorded appearance was in 1932, alongside Dick Leibert.

† The trade journals ceased to review live entertainment at the Brooklyn Paramount while Dick Leibert was at the console.

typical concept for a solo—one used by organists all over the country and by Barrie at the Ambassador—was that all modern jazz hits were based on pieces of classical music. To prove this to the audience, Barrie performed pairs of numbers so as to illustrate the elements that they had in common.[36] Such a presentation favored art music as the only form of original musical expression and dismissed popular music as derivative, ephemeral, and second-rate. Solos of this sort were designed for patrons who took pleasure in learning and valued art above popular culture (or, perhaps, for patrons who desired to be perceived in this way).[37] In short, at the Ambassador Barrie targeted an audience with cultured tastes.

Barrie expanded his highbrow programming for Ambassador patrons by initiating a series of Sunday afternoon organ recitals, the first of their kind in Saint Louis. The Sunday afternoon organ recital—a popular feature in urban American theaters—always featured classical and semiclassical works. It attracted a cultured patronage who enjoyed art music and did not want to be distracted by community singing or other live acts. The organ recital was the most highbrow variation of picture palace entertainment and always exceeded the culture standard set by the regular program. At the Ambassador, Barrie added an educational element by giving a short talk before each number. In these talks he described each piece and gave "an anecdote about its composition" to facilitate appreciation.[38] At his first recital, which featured works by Chopin, Kreisler, and Rubinstein, Barrie was joined by violinist Joseph Winters, concertmaster of the Ambassador orchestra. The recital was reviewed with great enthusiasm. "With an organist like Barrie and a four-manual instrument like the Ambassador's," reported the reviewer, "these concerts are destined to have capacity audiences. The first one was great!"[39]

For his first appearance at the Brooklyn Paramount in 1930, Barrie transformed his performance style once again. Most organists were skilled at this type of self-reinvention; it was the duty of the organist to adapt to the preferences of each new audience and to provide entertainment in the appropriate register. Barrie's inaugural solo consisted of three popular numbers for community singing, which he offered in the form of a contest. He received high praise for his skills as a song leader from the *Herald* reviewer, who observed that "the audience [joined] in the singing as if Barrie had always been at the organ."[40] Barrie, however, did not excise high-toned artistry from his solo completely. After the second of the three sing-along numbers, "When It's Springtime in the Rockies" (1929), Barrie offered a series of instrumental variations on the tune that showed off his virtuosity at the console and established his authority as a highly skilled organist. This nonparticipatory interlude, however, was unique to Barrie's introductory presentation. Like most of the Paramount's organists, Barrie marked his arrival at the theater with a combination of low- and high-class elements. In subsequent appearances he would employ solo performance only as an introduction or for comedic effect.[41]

Not every organist needed to transform his performance style to this degree. Some, either through chance or conscious decision, worked in a series of theaters that all catered to similar audiences. Others forced their preferred style of entertainment onto unwilling audiences. Sometimes these headstrong console artists succeeded in cultivating a preference for their presentations—and sometimes they did not.

Henry Murtagh, the first organist to perform at the Brooklyn Paramount, numbers among the successful. Murtagh built his career around community singing, and he repeatedly introduced the practice to reluctant audiences with excellent results. He was a natural choice for the Paramount and was no doubt hired because of his fame as a song leader. Murtagh made his name with community singing at the New York Rivoli, where he began to perform in August 1926.[42] Located in downtown Manhattan, the 2,270-seat

Rivoli had been standing for nearly ten years and was no longer a fashionable picture palace. The New York Paramount was to open just a few months later, one in a string of increasingly large and lavish exhibition houses erected in downtown Manhattan. The Rivoli was operated by exhibition magnate Samuel L. "Roxy" Rothapfel, who would open his magnificent 5,920-seat Roxy Theatre early in the following year. The Rivoli, a flagship presentation venue for Rothapfel in 1917, was by 1926 a small and outdated palace that could not hope to attract the class crowds.[43] The Rivoli's programming reflected its status: about two-thirds of Murtagh's organ solos were community sings. When the patrons were not invited to join in, he played popular songs without slides, offered comic variations on a song, provided verbal humor, or illustrated a serious song with images projected from slides onto the scrim curtain.

While at the Rivoli, Murtagh demonstrated that an organist is not always wise to maintain the status quo. Murtagh's predecessor at the Rivoli, Harold Ramsay, had sought to introduce community singing but had met with little success; a *Variety* reviewer present at his final attempt observed that Ramsay inspired only "a small choir of voices which represented about 1 per cent of the audience" to join him in singing some old numbers, after which he abandoned the practice.[44] Murtagh, however, saw that community singing could be successful if properly administered, and for his first solo at the Rivoli, Murtagh pulled out all the stops to make his audience enjoy themselves. To open the solo, Murtagh informed the audience via slide that his doctor had claimed he was going deaf and that he wanted to use their singing to test his hearing. After they failed to respond well to his first number, Murtagh mourned the horrible truth of the diagnosis before switching to a better-known song. To this the audience responded energetically, at which point Murtagh switched back to the first song. The amused patrons gave a much better try the second time around. At the conclusion, all were in good humor and Murtagh had demolished any resistance to singing.[45] It would seem that community singing initially failed at the Rivoli for two reasons: the practice was new to the theater, and Ramsay was incompetent at leading the sings. Murtagh demonstrated that the Rivoli patrons were happy to participate in well-led community singing, and he would continue to introduce community singing to audiences and encourage their appreciation of the activity for the rest of his career. Before initiating the community singing craze in Brooklyn, however, Murtagh took a detour through Chicago, where he performed in quite a different style of theater.

When organist Jesse Crawford came to New York to assume the prestigious position at the New York Paramount, Henry Murtagh took over Crawford's previous post—also very prestigious—at the Chicago Theatre in Chicago. Murtagh conducted community singing at the Chicago, but the atmosphere in which it took place was wholly different from that at the Rivoli. The Chicago was the flagship theater for Balaban and Katz and was therefore committed to high-class entertainment. As a result, the trade press condemned Murtagh's impudence and lambasted the practice of community singing. The *Herald* reviewer, for example, described Murtagh's sings as "happily infrequent," wisely avoided, not to be overdone, and undesired by the audience, who preferred sober and highly musical efforts.[46] When Murtagh omitted community singing, on the other hand, the reviewer reported that he "gave the folks an idea of what a real organist can do with a real organ," an underhanded compliment that simultaneously denigrated the alternative practice.[47] In short, there was disagreement over whether the Chicago Theatre was an appropriate venue for community singing. The trade commentators found that it was certainly not. Murtagh waffled.[48] And in the end, the patrons developed a taste for occasional community singing, as long as it was well presented.[49]

For his first appearance at the Brooklyn Paramount, Murtagh offered an atypical presentation. Opening night was a grand occasion for any picture palace, accompanied by lights, crowds, special guests, and all the pomp that could be mustered. The inaugural program, which was to be repeated throughout the first week, would be sure to feature outstanding performances, a dazzling stage show, and an exceptional feature film (the star of which might even be in attendance). The Brooklyn Paramount did not disappoint: opening night featured Paul Ash in one of his trademark stage shows and the dancer Maria "Gamby" Gambarelli—famous from the "Roxy and His Gang" radio broadcasts—in an original number. "Never before," gushed the *Herald* reviewer, "have we witnessed such a gala event in either Brooklyn or New York."[50] To match the glamor of the occasion, any opening-night organist would take special care to present a solo that was both highly entertaining and appropriately dignified.

The entirety of an inaugural program was special, but in some ways its organ solo portion required even more careful attention than the other elements. The organ ranked among an exhibitor's largest investments, and in the era of sound films (the Brooklyn Paramount was wired for sound from the start and never relied upon live musical accompaniment for films), the organ was expected to draw patrons as a major attraction in its own right. For these reasons, the organist had to impress the audience with the entertainment value of the organ from the very first performance. The theater owners did not want their investment to go to waste, and the organist did not want to lose his job—an inevitable result if he failed to entertain the patrons.

For the opening of the Brooklyn Paramount on November 24, 1928, therefore, Henry B. Murtagh presented "A Trip through the Organ," a solo popular with organists across the nation. Presumably, he used the fifty-eight-slide set produced by M. S. Bush of Buffalo, New York, which was accompanied by a detailed cue sheet and the guarantee of exclusive showing rights.[51] The solo was typical fare for house openings because it showcased the complete range of the instrument and permitted the organist to display his virtuosity. Indeed, a press release promoting the Bush presentation noted that it would "create an intelligent interest on the part of the audience in the organ" and was "a splendid set for an opening, for it will serve to call your audience's attention to one of the most expensive pieces of equipment in your theatre—the organ."[52] Not every organist favored the idea, however; some felt that "letting the audience understand our mechanical mysteries" detracted from the mysterious power of the organist and his instrument.[53] In his solo, Murtagh introduced the audience to all of the timbres and effects that the new Wurlitzer 4/26 was capable of producing. He demonstrated "the violin, piano, tuba, tambourine and castanets, xylophone, mandolin, saxophone, banjo, a whole German band, vox humana, darkey quartette, then followed by birds, dogs barking, storm, harp, flute, chimes, trains, auto horns, marimba, Scotch bagpipes, calliope, cat fight, hand organ (without monkey), bugle and many others." Finally, Murtagh incorporated all of these sounds into "a classical number" that exploited the entire range of the instrument in pitch and volume and evoked a thunder of applause.[54]

Patrons at the Paramount would not have expected this opening-night solo to set a precedent for organ entertainment at the theater. The "Trip through the Organ" solo provided a high-class tone for the first week but did not commit the Paramount to high-class entertainment in the long run. This was true for two reasons. First, this number was a perfect house opener, but it could only be exploited on that special occasion. Its novelty faded after a single performance. Second, it was natural for the Paramount, or any picture palace, to program high-class entertainment for the opening show regardless of the theater's character. A theater opening was a dignified occasion, and "A Trip through the Organ" was more appropriate than community singing because the solo—notwithstanding its barking dog and banjo impressions—lent an air of gravity to the proceedings. The performance of a grand classical number for which the audience sat in silence outclassed any of the solos that were to follow. Based on the reputation of the neighborhood, patrons would have expected comedy and light entertainment in the weeks to come—and indeed, Murtagh offered a regular program of community singing, with occasional vocal solos, for the remainder of his tenure. Opening night was the audience's one opportunity not to participate in the creation of the entertainment but to appreciate the power of the organ and the artistry of Murtagh.

To get a sense of how community singing worked at the Paramount, we will turn to another organist and another opening night. In May 1929, Murtagh was replaced by Bob West. The introduction of a new organist was always a major event for the Paramount. Each Paramount organist was highly visible to the public, and he was promoted on the basis of his individual character and unique presentations. Often, an organist would accrue a devoted following, and patrons might attend the theater primarily to see and hear their favorite performer. The organist was heavily promoted because the theater relied on him to become a big attraction, but this created a problem for exhibitors: when an organist moved on, they had to convince the audience that a new performer was equally gifted. For this reason, an organist's opening week was crucial both to his success and that of the theater. The new organist had to win over the patrons as quickly as possible. To do this, he needed to demonstrate both that he could fill the shoes of his predecessor and that he brought something new and special to the theater.

West was introduced to the Paramount audience in 1929 as "The Man You'll Love to Sing With," a slogan that left no doubt about his anticipated role.[55] As such, West—unlike Murtagh—did not try to impress the audience with highbrow music at his initial appearance. Instead, West demonstrated his capability to carry on existing traditions with a program of community singing entitled "Smile, Grin and Giggle." In this program he asked the audience to sing "Carolina Moon" (1928), held a laughing contest between the boys and girls, offered special lyrics to the tune of "Smiles" (1917), and concluded with the singing of "Sweetheart of All My Dreams" (1926). The laughing contest in particular indicates the lighthearted tone of the solo. The contest was set to the tune of "That's My Weakness Now" (1928), the slides for which replaced all words other than the title phrase with "ha-ha."

The special lyrics to "Smiles" may have been humorous as well, or they may have concerned West's arrival at the Paramount. From beginning to end, there was nothing serious or classy about West's presentation. His goal was simple: to generate excitement and introduce an element of good humor. West did make a point, though, of exhibiting his skills as an organist. As the console rose out of the pit, he showed off with "a 'hot' tune." Such a flashy entrance not only drew attention to the new organist and stirred excitement among the patrons but also demonstrated that West was a capable player, even if his primary task was to accompany community singing.[56]

West, however, did not just carry on the Paramount's community singing tradition. Immediately upon his arrival in early 1929, West permanently transformed the presentation style of organists at the Paramount. After emerging from the pit for his first appearance, West left the bench, stood beside the organ console, and spoke to the audience with the aid of a public address system. This was something new: Paramount patrons had never heard their organist speak before. West's predecessor, Henry Murtagh, had communicated with the audience solely through slides, which he provided in advance to the projectionist to be displayed at the appropriate points in his solos. In this way, Murtagh had been able to make jokes and otherwise express his personality indirectly, but he never communicated with his auditors face to face.[57] When West spoke aloud, he tore down in an instant the barrier that had existed between audience and organist since the opening of the Paramount. In doing so, he changed the role of the organist permanently. The organist, who formerly provided only music, now also offered personality and the chance for intimate connection.

The trade press was quick to comment on West's innovation. One reviewer noted, for instance, that West's "pleasing personality and intimate manner of talking to [the audience] won out"—a comment suggesting that the patrons may have been initially resistant to a new organist but were enthralled by West's manner of presentation.[58] West had become an instant friend and confidant, and he had gained the patrons' trust and affection by opening up to them on a personal level. The result was exuberant singing and a warm reception. West's decision to speak in May 1929, however, was not made lightly, for it too was linked to the perceived class of the theater. The reviewer did not note the fact that, while West's approach to organist-audience relations may have been uniquely suited to a theater like the Brooklyn Paramount, it would have been utterly inappropriate for a class house. West's relationship with his patrons was that of a regular fellow with his friends, all of whom made music together as near equals. A *Washington Post* reviewer who heard West at the Fox Theatre a year later summed up the dynamic perfectly: "In his introductory organlogue he goes in less for musicianship and the artistic potentialities of the console than for breaking down the barriers and getting acquainted with his audience. This he accomplishes in no uncertain manner by means that are unique. When it is all over, the customers are not sure whether Mr. West is part of the audience or they are part of the show, but out of their perplexity they derive a vast amount of hilarious fun and Mr. West enough laughter and handclapping to compensate him handsomely for ten minutes of teasing and tricky tunefulness."[59] This reviewer was not at all critical of West's personal style; indeed, he was enamored of the organist's easy manner and inclusive approach to entertainment. In a class house, however, the boundary between performer and audience was less permeable. This was in part the case because the performer was perceived to offer not mere entertainment but art. The presentation of art in the picture palace required clearly defined roles: the performer produced art, while the patron consumed it. The use of a public address system, while too familiar for the class theater, was the perfect complement to the practice of community singing. It removed the organist from his pedestal and helped to further a sense of community during the sing.

The *Herald* reviewer who heard West at the Paramount week after week was evidently taken with the organist's personal manner and his habit of speaking directly to the audience: "Bob's personality has dominated his audience to the extent that a few spoken words from him starts them all singing."[60] The image of domination is a powerful one and perhaps well chosen to describe West's influence on his patrons. West quickly won the audience's affection, and they responded instantly to his entreaties. Over the course of West's tenure, the *Herald* reviewer continued to refer in every review to West's practice of speaking, usually with the distinction that West communicated something "orally" instead of by slide. While we might take the element of speech for granted today, in 1929 it was a new idea for organists and a distinctive feature of the Brooklyn Paramount's entertainment. Another review—this one from *Variety*—also remarked on the organist's habit of speaking to the audience: "West turns around and faces his audience to talk and encourage better vocal outbursts. And they love it."[61] The reviewers were in perfect agreement concerning the motive for and effect of West's approach to community singing. His speeches broke down the barrier of formality, fostered an intimate atmosphere, and encouraged exuberant participation.

We have seen that community singing was, in general, much maligned in the trade press. The reviews just cited, however, are entirely positive. In fact, community singing at the Brooklyn Paramount never met with a word of criticism. The Paramount's first organist, Henry Murtagh, conducted community singing every week after his opening solo, and his sings evoked overwhelmingly positive reviews. One reviewer wrote that he had "created a fine following" with his community sings and had "become a showstopper."[62] The reviewer, clearly satisfied with community singing as it was practiced at the Paramount, also noted the big hand received by Murtagh at the end of every solo and remarked that it was well deserved.[63] Not a hint of criticism emerged in a year of published accounts across trade journals—but this had not been the case when Murtagh conducted community singing at the Chicago, a dignified flagship theater. And this was also not the case when patrons dared to open their mouths at the upscale New York Paramount, to which we now turn.

THE NEW YORK PARAMOUNT

The New York Paramount—or as historian Ben Hall puts it, the *paramount* Paramount—dwelt at the pinnacle of the picture palace system.[64] This Paramount opened on November 19, 1926, to much fanfare in the trade and popular press and set a box office record of $80,000 in its first week.[65] The Paramount was not the largest palace in New York City—the Capitol, also in midtown Manhattan, boasted a staggering 5,230 seats—but it was by far the most glamorous and up to date. Like the Brooklyn Paramount, the New York Paramount was a Rapp and Rapp design—the first Rapp and Rapp palace to be erected in New York. It created a sensation with its luxury and decadence. From a modern perspective, the Theatre Historical Society of America succinctly describes the Paramount as "less flamboyant than some other Rapp & Rapp endeavors, but not by very much."[66] The Paramount's design drew freely from the finest of European art and culture. The lobby was modeled after the Paris opera house, complete with white marble columns and a sweeping double staircase. The public spaces were outfitted with thirty-odd bronze statues of all sorts, an even larger collection of marble pieces, and dozens of oil paintings by well-known artists.[67]

The lobby of the New York Paramount. Theatre Historical Society.

The proscenium and stage area in the New York Paramount's auditorium.
Theatre Historical Society.

The Paramount's organ was a major showpiece. While not the largest Wurlitzer ever built, it was widely considered to be the finest.[68] *Variety* printed a description of the instrument and its architectural setting alongside coverage of the opening performance. From this, patrons learned that the organ "is equipped with every conceivable stop," as well as crystal grilles over the openings that could be illuminated with colored lights during performances.[69] Even more talked about than the organ, however, was the organist. Jesse Crawford, for whom the organ was specially designed, arrived from Chicago in 1926 to take the post at the Paramount, and he remained there until 1933. He was and is by far the most famous of all theater organists and much has been written about his life and career. Jesse Crawford's wife, Helen, was a fine organist in her own right. She often appeared at the Paramount's twin console, and the two organists specialized in different styles of music: Jesse played popular ballads exquisitely, while Helen had a gift for rhythmic, fast-paced numbers.

The New York Paramount marked the apex of Jesse Crawford's career, but he had spent many years building his reputation as he advanced through the ranks of theater organists. Born in 1895, Crawford grew up in Our Lady of Lourdes orphanage near Seattle, where his impoverished mother had placed her two-year-old son after his father passed away. He taught himself how to play the cornet while at the orphanage and later took to the piano as well. Crawford obtained his first post as organist in 1911 at a small theater in Spokane. In 1913 he moved to Billings and, shortly thereafter, to Seattle, where he played in a number of theaters before returning to Spokane in 1915 as a featured artist. Crawford stepped onto the national scene when he moved to San Francisco the next year to work for the exhibitor Sid Grauman. He spent some months performing in Los Angeles theaters, where his most prestigious post was as organist at Grauman's Million Dollar Theatre. In 1921, A. J. Balaban convinced Crawford to move to Chicago to open the Balaban and Katz (B&K) Tivoli Theatre, for which he assisted in the design of the Wurlitzer. Crawford also provided advice on organ voicing and installation when he moved to the new Chicago Theatre later that year.[70]

We have already encountered the high-class Chicago Theatre—B&K's flagship house—in the context of Henry Murtagh's career, which brought him to that theater in 1926. In the early 1920s, when his predecessor Crawford sat at the organ console, the director of the fifty-two-piece pit orchestra programmed symphonies and operatic excerpts, and Crawford often joined in the performance of these works. Crawford was highly regarded for his renditions of popular song, but his repertoire at the Chicago consisted mostly of opera arias, symphonic arrangements, and light classics.[71] There is no clear indication in the trade press that Crawford ever conducted community singing at the Chicago. All the same, a close reading of the reviews from his Chicago years reveals that community singing was often out of earshot but never out of mind.

A handful of reviews from 1926 give a glimpse into the organ solo culture at the Chicago. One *Herald* writer remarked on a typical presentation: "Jesse Crawford at the organ playing excerpts from 'Sylvia' ballet, a straight classical number giving the crowd no chance to sing and getting a great hand. The number was worth it on straight merit and here's a guess that relief from the singing thing generated additional appreciation."[72] But why mention that there was no community singing when the only music in the program was from a ballet? There are two possible explanations. The first is that Crawford had sometimes led community singing. The second is that community singing was so popular in Chicago that an organist who offered any other form of entertainment was anomalous. Because of the absence of community singing accounts from Crawford's 1926 reviews, the second explanation seems more likely. Either way, as noted earlier, this reviewer's negative view of community singing represented the typical attitude of trade professionals toward entertainment at the Chicago. (Henri Keates, on the other hand, was encountering no such opposition at the nearby Oriental.) Other reviewers of Crawford's solos at the Chicago echoed the establishment position: they would mention explicitly that "the deadly community sing" was not included and then praise Crawford for eschewing audience participation.[73] In most of his solos Crawford performed popular numbers that could be sung, and he regularly projected the lyrics via slide. He did not ask the audience to join in, however, and this appears to have been all that was needed to prevent singing.[74]

There is no indication that Crawford, at any point in his career, explicitly directed an audience not to sing. Instead, he developed an arsenal of strategies to discourage participation. One of his techniques was to display a great deal of artistry in his rendition of a tune—using special effects, for instance, or providing a number of variations, which made participation difficult. This technique worked well: many reviewers would comment over the years that audiences preferred to sit and listen to Crawford's exceptional playing over singing along. Crawford biographer John Landon reported yet another tactic employed by the organist to keep his audience quiet: whenever patrons burst into song, Crawford would reduce his registration so as to become inaudible. To hear the organ, the patrons would have to abandon their singing and listen carefully. It is also possible that this tactic would have caused some embarrassment to those who had sung.[75]

In addition, we have some information about Crawford's own attitude toward community singing. In 1939, the *New York Times* sought out the increasingly forgotten Crawford and published a nostalgic piece on the decline of the organist's career. In it, we learn that Crawford, "the man who taught the movie theatre organ to sing," was supposedly the first organist to project the lyrics to the tunes he played, "so the audience could mentally follow [the organ's] singing."[76] Crawford would continue to do so throughout his career, but he never intended for the audience to sing out loud. The article contains the following parenthetical disclaimer: "[Crawford] says disgustedly that the idea of the audience joining in, too, was a later corruption." According to the *Times*, therefore, Crawford was indirectly responsible for the community singing phenomenon but was opposed to it from the start and never participated willingly.[77] Perhaps this is why *Variety* claimed in 1928 that Crawford, along with stage show producer Ted Koehler, was "responsible for the organ community singing idea in the film houses of this town [Chicago]."[78] Or perhaps Crawford himself rewrote history in order to better suit his exalted position at the Paramount.

Crawford was the major star of the theater organ world, but for most of his career he did not work alone. In 1923 he met and married Helen Anderson, also an organist in the employment of B&K. While Jesse was performing at the Chicago, his wife was usually at another major B&K house, the McVickers, where she took over the console after Henri Keates left to open the Oriental. Helen also sometimes performed with her husband, and on such occasions she used a side console installed for her at the Chicago.[79] The McVickers was only a few blocks away from the Chicago, in that city's downtown entertainment district, but the theaters were remarkably different in character. The McVickers was not a B&K design, but rather one of the many theaters that the exhibitors had taken over during their expansion in the 1920s. The McVickers was all but replaced by the B&K–commissioned Oriental in 1926 and was relegated to the bottom of the heap upon the departure of Keates and Paul Ash. With the new Oriental featuring B&K's top talent around the corner and the flagship Chicago offering high-class entertainment just down the road, the McVickers struggled to attract an audience. In a bid for widespread appeal, Helen Crawford abandoned any artistic aspirations and offered entertainment in the style of her predecessor Keates—that is to say, community singing.

Despite a lack of virtuosic display in her presentations, reviewers noted that Helen Crawford had a great deal of skill at the console. After her first performance, one writer noted that she played "infinitely better than her predecessor, Henri Keates," although the singing response was weak due to greatly diminished attendance—most of Keates's fans had followed him to the Oriental.[80] After a time, it seems that Helen moved away from community singing, perhaps inspired by her husband's success at the Chicago. On one occasion she offered a song accompanied by lyric slides "without making the audience sing," while the next week she invited the audience to sing without insisting (in contrast to the tactics employed by many organists).[81] Throughout her tenure, critics admired her raw talent—Helen had never taken a piano or organ lesson in her life—and her ability to make challenging performances look quite effortless.[82] Of course, Helen gave up community singing entirely once she arrived with her husband at the New York Paramount. Once again, we see that every fine organist was able and willing to adapt his or her style to the clientele of the theater that offered employment.

Jesse Crawford's first solo at the celebrated Paramount in Times Square was highly anticipated and exhaustively reviewed. He did not disappoint. The *Variety* review, published as an independent article in the Presentations section, was overwhelming in its adulation: "At the new Paramount, New York, opening, he knocked an elite audience for a score of 1,000 to 0 with a demonstration on an organ no one on Broadway believed was in a player or the instrument."[83] For this momentous first appearance at the most important theater organ console in the world, Crawford crafted a unique solo that was ideally suited to his new position. Entitled "Organs I Have Played," the solo narrated Crawford's personal history as a theater organist—a career, moreover, that doubled as a classic American success story. In his solo, Crawford described and imitated each of the organs he had performed upon, doubtless to humorous effect. He noted both the progress from each instrument to the next and his own development as a performer and concluded that the Paramount organ was at last the instrument he had always dreamed of. The Paramount, in other words, was his destiny.

Crawford could not have designed a more effective inaugural presentation. His appearance at the Paramount organ was the culmination of an entire career, the moment to which all of his experiences had led. This account would have allowed the patrons to encounter Crawford as a real person, and it would have given them a sense of privilege to be there, in the Paramount, at the pinnacle of Crawford's career. At the same time, the solo boosted the Paramount's magnificent organ. While every new theater needed to promote its organ, Crawford took this concern to a new level when he explicitly compared the Paramount organ to every other instrument he had played—and proclaimed it to be the greatest.

While the promotional elements of this solo would have been equally at home in the Brooklyn Paramount, in another respect this solo was uniquely suited to a flagship house. In the words of the enthusiastic *Variety* reviewer, Crawford made the presentation "educational for the masses."[84] The idea that picture palace entertainment should be both uplifting and educational was nearly universal among the class houses. Community singing, such as that practiced in Brooklyn, could hardly be expected to improve one's mind. A theater like the New York Paramount, however, sought to better its patrons by offering the finest music coupled with informative presentations. In the trade press, there was a generalized debate over whether or not it was the responsibility of exhibitors to improve the tastes of their patrons. At the Paramount, however, this matter had been settled. The Paramount existed to entertain *and* to enlighten.

After the Paramount's opening week, reviewers mentioned community singing—or its absence—on a regular basis. Even though it was not incorporated into the entertainment at the Paramount, community singing was indeed popular in New York, and every visitor to the theater was aware of its role in motion picture entertainment. It took some time for Crawford to convince critics that the Paramount was a nonsinging house—and even more time for him to convince his patrons.

In place of community singing, the Crawfords offered an eclectic mix of musical genres and performance styles. On occasion, Jesse Crawford staged a miniature recital of classical works, such as his all-Tchaikovsky program in December 1926.[85] Other times he featured "stirring march tunes" or solo excerpts from popular operas, such as *Cavalleria Rusticana*.[86] He often performed popular songs, sometimes alone and sometimes with the assistance of a concealed singer.[87] Helen Crawford was renowned for her skill at syncopated playing and therefore did not often present classical works. When Helen joined him at the twin console, she would usually offer uptempo, jazzy numbers, and the pair would close with a duet rendition of a hit song.[88] Helen, however, was also a flexible performer: in April 1927, to celebrate Easter, she joined her husband in a dignified recital of religious songs.[89] In addition to the standard "great" console, which rose out of the pit on a lift, the Paramount added three additional consoles over the years: a "slave console," installed on the other side of the pit, and two "skeleton" consoles that could be positioned anywhere on the stage. All consoles controlled the same organ.[90] This feature gave the Crawfords an enormous degree of mobility, which they used to enhance the drama of their performances. While they did project simple effects onto the scrim curtain, the Crawfords did not typically employ production elements or additional performers, as did some of the other upscale organists. Jesse Crawford was his own biggest draw and wisely chose to remain in the spotlight.

Even though Crawford never intentionally led his patrons in singing, popular songs constituted the bulk of his repertoire, and when he performed a popular song, he almost always projected the lyrics onto the screen via lantern slides. To read the slides was part of the entertainment, and they added a textual dimension to the performance. Early on there was considerable criticism of Crawford's use of lyric slides. The general complaints were that they "cheapened" the organ solo and were inappropriate for a class house.[91] These objections seem to have hinged on the association between song slides and the practice of song plugging. For the most part, critics were willing to accept Crawford's plugs tongue-in-cheek; one reviewer noted, for example, that Crawford played a new Walter Donaldson number "just to be nice" to the publisher.[92] Another, however, concluded his comments with the sarcastic observation that "the 20-song medley . . . is great stuff for the sheet music lobby sales' gross."[93] Song plugging was not Crawford's own idea. As a Paramount employee, he was obliged to promote Paramount Publix products, including songs from Paramount films and music that was available for purchase at the theater.[94] Most reviewers made peace with the practice, which was universal among the major studio-owned picture palace chains.

Crawford did not only use slides to project song lyrics. They also constituted his sole means of personal contact with the patrons. That Crawford communicated with his audience via slides on opening night can be explained in terms of the available technology: public address systems were not installed in theaters until 1927, and they did not become widespread for another year.[95] However, even though Crawford remained at the Paramount until long after public address technology had been perfected, he never spoke to his public; as a *Variety* reviewer put it in late 1930, "Mr. Crawford does not speak to his audiences."[96] Other organists quickly adopted the new development and used the public address system to promote a sense of intimacy with their patrons—but it was precisely this informal intimacy that was considered to be inappropriate in an upscale house. Instead, the class organist cultivated an image of artistic authority. Crawford's projected messages revealed him to be personable, and even funny, but his silence assured that he remain distant and unattainable.

The delicacy of this boundary between organist and audience is illustrated in the review of a June 1929 solo by Helen Crawford. In a message to the audience, projected onto the screen via lantern slides, Helen informed the patrons that her husband was away on vacation, having left herself and the baby behind. While we might interpret this message as a simple explanation of Crawford's unusual absence, the *Variety* reviewer objected to the gesture on the basis that the "Paramount is a pretty high class picture house to have considerable personal stuff thrown upon the sheet."[97] Although Helen's announcement was well received, the reviewer's discomfort with the revelation of personal information tells a great deal about what was expected at a class house like the Paramount.

In early reviews, critics did not know how to react to the potential for community singing at the New York Paramount. It is possible that Crawford himself was unsure whether or not the Paramount audience wanted to engage in community singing, although it is clear that he never encouraged it. The first two *Variety* reviews of his playing, probably penned by the same critic in late 1926, engaged with the issue of community singing head-on. Crawford's second-week solo at the Paramount was a "miniature organ recital" featuring four items: a new organ composition, the novelty piano number "Nola," the finale from *William Tell*, and an unnamed popular song accompanied by slides. While the audience remained silent during the popular song, the *Variety* reviewer did not dismiss this as an expected reaction (as he would a month later). Instead, he observed that "Crawford couldn't get 'em to sing here" and suggested that "it may have been too early in the morning for the vocal calisthenics."[98] It is clear that the position of the Paramount as a singing or nonsinging house was still in flux.

After an initial two-year period during which the Paramount established its reputation as a nonsinging house, its patrons suddenly began to vocalize in late 1928. An analysis of the trade press reveals a notable upward trend in audience participation at the Paramount between December 1928 and March 1929. During these months, Crawford's solos elicited singing more often than not, and in the following month, April, reviewers made a point of remarking upon the absence of singing. Why had the patrons at the Paramount suddenly taken to singing at the end of 1928? It would appear that the New York Paramount was being influenced by the newly opened Brooklyn Paramount and, more generally, by Brooklyn's burgeoning community singing culture. The Brooklyn Paramount opened in November 1928; it is unlikely to be coincidence that community singing began to surface at the New York Paramount in December. And yet, after March 1929, community singing was no longer a regular practice during Crawford's solos, and it had disappeared completely by early 1931.

Because it was not explicitly invited by Crawford, community singing at the New York Paramount was quite unlike that in Brooklyn. The low-key vocalisms that Crawford provoked were never described as energetic or raucous. In addition, this participation did not always constitute singing per se. In August 1928, for example, several months *before* the Brooklyn Paramount opened, the audience hummed along with a current waltz tune played by Crawford. The reviewer excused their lapse in behavior with the explanation that "the waltz and softer melodies are coming back."[99] This account also illustrates another element of participation at the New York Paramount: it almost only occurred during well-known musical numbers. In this case, the audience remained silent until the final tune, which they recognized and found irresistible. In January 1929, patrons sang another recent hit, "I Faw Down an' Go Boom" (1928). Popularized by the likes of Billy Murray and Eddie Cantor, this song was quickly becoming a favorite with singing audiences across the country; in the next two months it would appear with great success at the Brooklyn Paramount, the Chicago Oriental, and Lloyd's theater in Menominee, Michigan.[100] In all probability, many of the Paramount patrons would have already sung "I Faw Down an' Go Boom" in other New York City theaters.

When reviewers did not explain audience singing as a natural response to a familiar and beloved tune, they often suggested that it had been provoked by Crawford's exceptional musicianship. In November 1929, for example, the audience joined in with Crawford's performance of "Singin' in the Rain" (1929). The *Herald* reviewer, after dismissing the occasion as a fluke, attributed the unexpected participation to "Crawford's masterly playing," which "forced the audience to burst forth in song."[101] At the same time, other reviewers suggested that the Paramount audience did *not* sing for precisely the same reason: yet another reminder that trade professionals were often at a loss to explain audience behavior.[102]

In only one case did a reviewer suggest that singing at the Paramount was actually expected, though in this case Crawford worked explicitly to undermine its success. In December 1928, shortly *after* the Brooklyn Paramount had opened, Crawford offered a presentation that relied upon audience participation. The solo was entitled "Popular Song Parade." In it, Crawford played only the beginning of each song then quickly abandoned it for the next. In the words of the *Herald* reviewer, "the audience . . . had only time to begin to hum or sing one song when the organ started another."[103] It was surely not a coincidence that Crawford presented this unique solo soon after the opening of the Brooklyn Paramount. It might well have been a conscious jab at community singing culture, which Crawford disdained but could not ignore.

The most interesting aspect of this December 1928 solo, however, is the *Herald* review itself. Here we find the only mention of community singing at the New York Paramount in which the reviewer failed to exhibit surprise that it took place. Throughout the brief period in which community singing occurred regularly at the Paramount, the trade press critics did not document it as a regular part of the entertainment. When the audience hummed along with Crawford's program of waltz tunes, for example, the reviewer expressed shock and described the Paramount as "a house where they never open their mouths."[104] When the patrons joined in on the song "I Faw Down an' Go Boom," the reviewer noted that singing "is quite unusual for this house."[105] When Crawford played "All by Yourself in the Moonlight" (1928), the reviewer observed that "this audience sang, where they have never sung before."[106] But of course this was not true. Singing occurred almost every week at the Paramount in late 1928 and early 1929. The trade press simply refused to accept what was happening.

In a review of a solo from February 1929 that did not inspire singing, we read that "no one sings at the house, and Crawford does not try to make them."[107] While the latter statement was certainly true, the notion that "no one sings" at the Paramount was clearly false. More accurately, the review ought to have read, "no one *should* sing." Trade professionals and theatergoers alike understood the class connotations of community singing, but trade reviewers used their position to try to enforce normative behavior. Organists read these reviews, and they understood what exhibitors expected of them. The "class" audience was to remain silent.

THESE Maurice Workstel slides for the 1926 hit "On the Tamiami Trail" were recommended by organist Harry L. Wagner, who performed them at the Chicago Empress and who contributed regularly to the *Exhibitors Herald*. In a June 12 article titled "Solo Numbers That Scored with Chicago Audiences," Wagner proclaimed that this "special version," released by the publishing house of Remick, "should go over very good in any house." These are sixteen of the original thirty slides. Complete set in the author's collection.

Presenting an original
Version Entitled
'ON THE
TAMIAMI TRAIL'
or
"Florida, you owe me a lot"

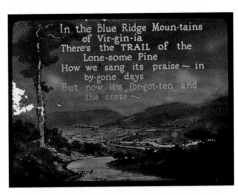

In the Blue Ridge Moun-tains
of Vir-gin-ia
There's the TRAIL of the
Lone-some Pine
How we sang its praise — in
by-gone days
But now it's for-got-ten and
the craze —

Is a long, long TRAIL that's wind-ing
Way down in Flo-ri-da State
I took a trip up-on that TRAIL
Of which I'm gon-na re-late.

There's a road
from Tam-pa to
Mi-a-mi town
Known as the
Ta-mi-am-i Trail.

In the Sea ~ In the Sea ~
In the beaut-i-ful Sea
Me Oh My! That's where I
found all my prop-er-ty

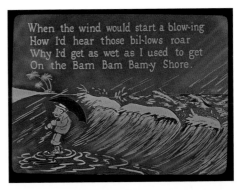

When the wind would start a blow-ing
How I'd hear those bil-lows roar
Why I'd get as wet as I used to get
On the Bam Bam Bam-y Shore.

When you wan-der down the
Tam-i-am-i Trail ~ Tam-i-am-i Trail
Pay us just a lit-tle call.

I am giv-ing you these in-vi-ta-tions
You will get a 'treat' for I'll have
you meet
All the lit-tle wife's
re-la-tions

Her Un-cle Joe and her Aunt Flo
the Ba-by and me
You'll find we'll all be glad
to greet you there with a smile

All I ask you now is let
your voic-es ring
And we all will sing
On the Tam-i-am-i Trail.

THIS unusual Maurice Workstel novelty uses an explanation of the process by which a song is published as an excuse to sing the 1927 number "I'm Back in Love Again." The set alternates between cartoon-style and photographic slides, and it introduces real celebrities from the music business. These are eighteen of the original thirty-three slides. Complete set in the author's collection.

The day that photo was taken Cliff had lost on the 'ponies' so he mused 'I'm back in debt again' which gave him the idea for his new song 'I'M BACK IN LOVE AGAIN'. Cliff says one is as bad as the other.

Next is the building of Jerome H. Remick & Co. Music Publishers,—Cliff is there next day with visions of plenty of advance royalty. Will he get it? We'll see! —

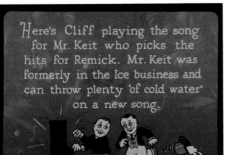

Here's Cliff playing the song for Mr. Keit who picks the hits for Remick. Mr. Keit was formerly in the Ice business and can throw plenty 'of cold water' on a new song.

Mr. Keit thinks the song great but tells Friend, 'It's fair, how much advance do you want?' Friend says '$3000'. Mr. Keit says 'I'll give you $150.' Friend says "Sold".

Now we'll see America's greatest song-demonstrator, Joe Santly playing the song for Helen Morgan of 'Night Club' fame.

By the look on Helen's face you'd think she didn't like the song. But that's not so. She's thinking of the income tax statement she has to pay.

And now you probably would like to hear the song, so Folks listen to — 'I'M BACK IN LOVE AGAIN'

THESE four slides belong to the sixteen-slide illustrated song set designed to accompany the 1913 song "Stick to Your Mother Mary." These slides were staged, photographed, and hand-colored by the New York firm of Scott & Van Altena—without question the finest producers of illustrated song slides. The final slide in the set contains the lyrics to the chorus. MarNan Collection.

5 COMMUNITY SINGING AND LOCAL OUTREACH

The previous chapters have introduced a number of organists. Each of these men and women had different performance styles, stage personas, and favored repertoires, and each suited his or her talents to the requirements of the theater that offered employment. However, all of them had one important factor in common: employment in a theater located centrally in a downtown area. Downtown theaters were conveniently situated amid shopping and dining destinations, and they were highly visible to out of towners. They were also likely to have the advantage of big-name performers, lavish stage shows, and first-run films, all of which made them attractive to a broad customer base. As a result, these theaters could rely on significant itinerant patronage. Any single patron might attend infrequently, but an "itinerant theater" (the trade press designation) could count on steady box office numbers all the same.[1] This had a profound effect on the presentation of entertainment. Since any individual patron might never return, exhibitors did not trouble to build a sense of geographic community or to link the theater with local interests. Instead, they focused only on satisfying the customers who appeared in the theater for each individual show. The sole duty of an organist at a downtown theater, therefore, was to entertain whoever happened to be in the house.

Organists in neighborhood theaters had other concerns, for they depended on community support and patronage. Exhibitors were eager to keep neighborhood residents from patronizing the flashier, better-appointed downtown theaters, for if locals stopped attending the local picture show, that theater would go bankrupt. As a consequence, exhibitors sought to secure local patronage by promoting community spirit and by joining forces with local businesses and organizations. Neighborhood organists played a particularly important role in attracting a local audience. Like their downtown counterparts, neighborhood organists were engaged to entertain the patrons sitting in the seats. They offered many of the same solos, used the same slides, and led community singing of the same songs. However, these organists presented their entertainment with a local flavor that appealed to neighborhood patrons, and they used gimmicks to encourage regular visits to the theater.

Exhibitors who catered to child audiences shared many concerns with the managers of neighborhood theaters. They too had to prioritize the values of the community, and they could not succeed without close ties to local special interest groups. While the neighborhood picture show was only expected to entertain, however, the children's matinee was additionally subject to close moral scrutiny. If an exhibitor misstepped, the penalty might be worse than a few lost patrons. Matinee exhibitors were also beholden to a nationwide consortium of organizations that policed children's programming and lobbied for censorship legislation. The exhibitor was concerned, therefore, both with her immediate community and with the powerful organizations that backed local reformers. Matinee exhibitors, as we shall see, were often organists. They used music to attract children to the show, during which they provided underscoring, played the children's favorites, and led community singing. This chapter will survey the role of organ music in matinee programming both before and after the advent of sound.

First, however, a case study will reveal the tactics that a neighborhood organist might employ to attract and maintain local patronage.[2] At the Chicago Harding, a large neighborhood theater in the Balaban and Katz chain, the organist, Edward Meikel, played an exceptional role in ensuring the success of his theater. Over the course of several years, Meikel developed a dedicated fan base, built enthusiasm for the Harding, and became a mainstay of the local business community. As a result, he became a much-praised model for neighborhood organists everywhere.

THE CHICAGO HARDING

The Harding Theatre, which no longer stands, was located in the Logan Square neighborhood of Chicago, a district some six miles to the northwest of the Loop. Construction began under the auspices of the Chicago exhibition firm Lubliner and Trinz, but, due to a merger, the Harding became the property of B&K three months before it opened on October 19, 1925.[3] The 2,962-seat Harding was designed in the Italian Renaissance and Neoclassical style by Freidstein and Company. It belonged to a trio of

The exterior of the Chicago Harding. Chicago Architectural Photographing Co.
Collection, Theatre Historical Society.

similar theaters that included the Congress and the Tower, but the Harding surpassed its siblings and was by all accounts among Chicago's "most elaborate" neighborhood houses.[4] It cost a fantastic $2 million to construct and, like most urban theaters, was installed in a large commercial structure that also contained offices and storefronts. While small compared to B&K theaters in the Loop, the Harding was among the largest theaters in the Logan Square neighborhood. It offered three complete shows each weekday and four on the weekend.[5]

A neighborhood theater of the 1920s and 1930s differed enormously from its downtown brethren. On paper, the Harding appears to have been quite similar to the B&K palaces found in the Loop. All B&K theaters showed the same films, presented the same stage acts, boasted the same standard of service, and used the same programming formula. The Harding, however, offered these entertainment features at a disadvantage. To begin with, the Harding was not among Chicago's first-run theaters, which at the time included only B&K's Chicago, Roosevelt, and McVickers, RKO's State-Lake, Warner's Orpheum, and the independent Monroe (all located in the Loop).[6] Instead, the Harding received films booked by the B&K chain only after they had completed runs in other palaces. A similar arrangement governed the stage at that theater. The Harding was able to book the same stage presentations that were seen at the Chicago but could only offer the shows some weeks later, after they had passed through the Uptown Theatre.[7] Moreover, the Harding did not get exclusive access to the outdated stage shows. When the presentation acts finally reached the neighborhood they were paired with a local twenty-four-piece orchestra directed by Benjamin Paley and then shared between the Harding and the Senate. The house temporarily without the stage show featured Art Kahn and his Ash-style stage band instead.[8] Finally, the Harding was denied access to the true superstars of the B&K chain. The resident musicians were highly capable, but they did not have the drawing power of Paul Ash at the McVickers or Jesse Crawford at the Chicago. Any Logan Square resident who wanted to hear the best stage band and see the latest acts could easily travel downtown for a show. A patron would only stay close to home if the Harding had something special to offer.

All neighborhood theaters faced this challenge, and they all responded with essentially the same strategy. To provide something that the downtown palaces could not, neighborhood theaters emphasized their local

The Harding's lobby. Chicago Architectural Photographing Co. Collection,
Theatre Historical Society.

connections. This entailed two different sorts of actions. Inside the theater, management offered entertainment uniquely suited to the interests of the local populace or even utilized the patrons' talents. They also promoted and celebrated local events. At the same time, patrons were on friendly terms with the manager and with one another and could expect to see familiar faces. In short, these theaters developed an atmosphere of camaraderie and neighborhood spirit. Outside the theater, the managers of neighborhood houses took a strong interest in community affairs. They supported local youth organizations, developed tie-ins with local merchants, donated tickets to the community's less fortunate, and operated benefit performances near holidays.[9] Often, the manager himself would be a prominent figure in community work, which would in turn generate good will and loyalty to the theater.[10] When a neighborhood theater was functioning properly, it was viewed not as an entertainment venue or a profit-driven business but as a community center. Local residents were encouraged to take pride in their theater, and the theater in turn was expected to make the community a better place in which to live and do business.[11]

The neighborhood theater of the mid-1920s also attracted a different demographic than did the downtown palace. While all classes attended—or were at least reputed to attend—the lavish downtown venues, the neighborhood theaters specifically attracted a working-class crowd. In practice, downtown theaters drew primarily middle- and upper-class patrons, while the working class stayed close to home so as to enjoy the convenience of proximity, the lower ticket prices, and the neighborhood culture.[12] African Americans usually patronized their own neighborhood theaters, where they could expect to be treated with dignity and entertained by their peers. In terms of character, the neighborhood theater was a hybrid between the contemporary picture palace and the early nickelodeon, an exhibition model that had thrived on local working-class attendance. Neighborhood theaters of the 1920s were larger than nickelodeons, usually seating between three hundred and one thousand patrons, and they offered an entertainment program based on that of the downtown palace, although budgetary constraints reduced the extravagance of the sets and the number of performers. Films were both selected and altered to suit the patrons, while stage shows and musical acts often reflected the ethnicity of the local populace. Lizabeth Cohen, a scholar of Chicago's neighborhood theaters, sums up their appeal to the local residents: "For much of the decade, working-class patrons found the neighborhood theater not only more affordable but more welcoming, as the spirit of the community carried over into the local movie hall. Chicago workers may have savored the exotic on the screen, but they preferred encountering it in familiar company."[13]

In many ways, though, the Harding was an atypical example of a neighborhood theater. To begin with, at nearly three thousand seats it was much larger than average. The Harding also offered a higher standard of musical entertainment than the typical neighborhood house, which could afford to employ only a keyboardist (piano or organ) or a small instrumental ensemble.[14] The Harding management had only limited control over the programming, since films, stage shows, and bandleaders were prescribed by B&K. Perhaps because of this arrangement, the Harding did not tailor its programming to reflect the cultural heritage of local residents. Logan Square was a predominantly Polish neighborhood, but any locals who desired ethnically flavored entertainment must have found it in other theaters.[15] We do know, however, that the Harding catered to a local, working-class clientele and that it fulfilled the same social role as other neighborhood houses.

The Harding is an attractive candidate for this case study because it belonged to the all-important B&K chain and it received significant trade-press coverage, which was unusual for a neighborhood theater. Even in the case of the Harding, there is a shortage of trade press accounts in comparison with downtown B&K houses. For example, there were 42 trade press reviews of organ solos at the Harding between 1925 and 1929, whereas there were 154 reviews for the Oriental between 1926 and 1932. In addition to these reviews, however, the *Exhibitors Herald* also published a number of articles specifically about the Harding, including an article and a letter written by the Harding's organist, Edward Meikel. Most of the trade press accounts describe the extraordinary success of Meikel's Organ Club, which generated a great deal of industry talk in the late 1920s.

The opening of the Harding on October 19, 1925, exemplifies many of the commercial strategies that allowed a neighborhood theater to succeed. That splendid affair is best captured in the words of the *Herald*:

> The pageant in celebration of the opening of the new theatre lasted eight days. On the night of the opening the streets of three locations were roped off for dancing. Bands played. A parade held the attention of a multitude. A public marriage was performed before the festal crowds. Each day differed from the other.

Friday was children's day. A special mardi gras was theirs.

October 19, the final day of the festivities, the girls living in the vicinity of the theatre took part in a beauty contest.[16]

The author noted that this wild celebration in the streets actually prevented people from entering the theater during its grand opening period, but he went on to praise the exhibitors for the clever marketing and foresight behind the public production. Even if money was lost, "the effect of the carnival was of great value to the establishment of an amiable spirit towards the Harding," and as a neighborhood theater, the Harding was to rely entirely on this "amiable spirit."[17]

The street festival was neither the beginning nor the end of the publicity put together for the Harding's opening week. The management of the theater arranged for a ten-page spread concerning the Harding to be issued as a supplement to the October 12 edition of the *Chicago Evening American*. From this feature, locals learned that on opening night their tickets were to be sold by Ziegfeld star Mary Eaton, a dancer, and collected by none other than comedian and singer Eddie Cantor. Reviewers gave these two celebrities some of the credit for the two-hundred-yard line that formed before the first performance at six o'clock in the evening.[18] Once inside the theater, patrons were treated to another surprise: the feature film, First National's *What Fools, Men*, had been shot in Chicago—and it appears that some footage of a monument in the Logan Square neighborhood was interpolated into the film especially for its run at the Harding. The familiar sight "drew thunderous applause when flashed on the screen."[19]

The Harding's first organist was Edward K. House, who had previously been at the Tivoli in Chicago.[20] He spent his career rotating among B&K houses and was to be found at the Oriental six years later. House was only reviewed once while at the Harding, a month after that theater opened, and he moved on soon thereafter. The reviewer did not find House's work to be exemplary. Although the solo in question lasted for only five minutes, it proved to be a disaster far beyond its modest proportions. House, who "has a bad conception of what audiences want," featured a pop number that had failed to make inroads with the public. After his straight version with slides met with an icy reception, House tried to engage the patrons in a song contest. No one sang, and his solo concluded in dead silence, all applause withheld.[21] A month later, House was replaced by Edward Meikel, although a reason for the substitution was never published in the trade press.

This photograph of Edward Meikel was published in *Exhibitors Herald* in November 1927. By that time, he was well known to exhibitors throughout the nation for his innovative community singing programs.

In Meikel's first week he offered a typical introductory solo, entitled "The Family Album," that featured a comedic survey of the organist's relatives. While the solo did not include community singing, it was a success, although the *Variety* reviewer observed that it had only passed muster because it "fitted the occasion" and that Meikel would have to do better if he wished to make a career for himself at the Harding.[22] After Meikel's installment, the trade press ignored the Harding entirely until April 1926, when the *Herald* published its first review of the theater. This was to be expected: the Harding was important because of its location (Chicago) and affiliation (B&K), but it offered very little unique entertainment and was not a leader in the exhibition industry. The *Herald* had published a full-page article on the theater's opening only because the management employed excellent promotional techniques that others might want to emulate—a high-priority concern for that publication. In the *Herald*'s belated review, however, Meikel did not fare well: "The only weak spot on the bill was that in which Edward Meikel, organist, sat."[23] It seems that Meikel had attempted to lead community singing with a set of humorous lyric slides, but very few patrons had joined in and "the whole affair was a dud."[24]

Given the extraordinary success that Meikel was about to achieve with community singing, this account is fascinating. It may be, of course, that the *Herald* reviewer considered the solo to be a bigger flop than it really was. The Chicago *Herald* reviewers, after all, were often critical of community singing. However, that same journal (and probably the same author) began to provide Meikel with very positive reviews one year later, while praise from *Variety* was forthcoming in only three weeks. In this short time, Meikel did not become a better organist or showman, nor did his patrons suddenly develop a taste for singing. The only change was in his approach to community singing.

For a neighborhood organist, Meikel attracted an extraordinary amount of attention from *Variety* beginning in April 1926. The first review of his new idea in organ presentations was short, but it effectively described the activities that had begun to take place at the Harding: "Edward Meikel's novel Organ Club is gaining in popularity. Meikel instituted in Chicago the novel stunt of using 'request' programs, and having the names of the requesters projected on the screen. The Harding fares take to it strongly."[25] While the Organ Club idea was still to develop further, this early account described the feature that would make Meikel's club a success.

Meikel observed that the Harding attracted an audience of neighborhood regulars: patrons who attended the theater every week and who were largely familiar with one another. Meikel himself was the only live performer present at every show; Art Kahn's stage band alternated with the Chicago Theatre presentation unit, such that Kahn was only at the Harding every other week. This arrangement offered Meikel the unique opportunity to connect with his audience on a personal level and to incorporate neighborhood patrons directly into the performance. He began with a simple plan. Regular patrons were invited to submit requests, a procedure that was not uncommon in picture theaters. During the organ solo, however, Meikel publicly displayed the name of each Harding patron who had made a request. This unusual (and possibly unprecedented) tactic had two effects. First, patrons were thrilled to see their own names and to feel that they were a part of both the show and the theater family. Second, patrons read the names of their friends and neighbors on the screen, which reinforced the notion that the Harding was truly a neighborhood institution. As one reviewer noted, the names were greeted by "exclamations of recognition from all portions of the house," an account that confirms the immediate impact of Meikel's request lists on his patrons.[26] Another observed that Meikel's "audiences enter with the hope of getting in some personal notes."[27] Audience members loved both to be publicly recognized and to recognize those around them, an experience that only a neighborhood theater could offer. The idea must have met with instant success, for the very next issue of *Variety* featured a paid advertisement for Edward Meikel and his Organ Club. B&K would not have invested in this sort of publicity unless they believed that Meikel's new idea had the potential for large box office returns.

One week later, *Variety* reviewed Meikel's work at the Harding again. This time, the reviewer made an explicit comparison with Henri Keates's community sings at the McVickers, pointing out that community singing was not new to Chicago and that singing served the same purpose at both the Harding and the McVickers: "It thaws out the audience" and prepared them to enjoy the stage show in good humor. However, the reviewer also noted that "Meikel has gone one better" than Keates with his Organ Club idea, which produced even more successful results. In the show observed, Meikel—to the delight of his enthusiastic club members—extended the period of community singing beyond the standard time allotment for an organ solo. In the view of the trade press, Meikel had latched onto something unique and highly lucrative.[28]

When *Variety* wished to feature an exceptional presentation whose basic idea others would be advised to consider, the journal extracted the offering from the Film House Review column, where entire programs were summarized, and instead printed an extended review under New Acts. Meikel achieved this honor in August 1926. The review was printed "by request," perhaps on behalf of the many readers who had inquired about Meikel's work. Near the top of the review, *Variety* included a warning to any who sought to imitate Meikel's strategy: "It must be remembered that the Harding is a neighborhood theatre and that portions of his stunt would not work in downtown or 'transient' houses."[29] Trade professionals recognized the difference between a neighborhood house like the Harding, which catered to a

"THE MEETING WILL PLEASE COME TO ORDER"

EDWARD MEIKEL
ORIGINATOR OF THE ORGAN CLUB
Assisted by
JIMMIE, Vice President

Harding Theatre
CHICAGO, ILL.

A *Variety* ad for Edward Meikel and his Organ Club, published in May 1926.

regular, local clientele, and a transient house like the McVickers or soon-to-open Oriental, which often entertained visitors to the city and could not risk alienating the out-of-town crowd. As a neighborhood organist, however, Meikel was positioned to take full advantage of his regular patronage.

Initially, membership in Meikel's Organ Club was not a formal affair. His patrons did not fill out applications or receive membership cards, although some of Meikel's imitators later used such devices. Instead, the original Organ Club was a vaguely defined and fluid institution to which all patrons belonged by merit of their attendance.[30] Later, Meikel accepted letters from his patrons in which they requested membership, and he assembled a mailing list of members to whom he sent updates in the form of "Club Letters."[31] With or without formal membership, the notion of a club was valuable, for it encouraged regular attendance and fostered a sense of belonging and civic pride.

Each meeting of the Organ Club opened with an official call to order, which set Meikel's feature apart from the rest of the program and indicated that this was not an ordinary organ solo.[32] The call to order also shifted the balance of power in the theater. The organist in every picture house was a hired performer and therefore could never achieve full equality with his patrons. In high-class theaters that featured artistic entertainment, this did not present a problem. In theaters that sought a more relaxed atmosphere, however, there was a variety of means by which an organist could bridge the gap between performer and audience. Meikel's call to order transformed the Harding's constituency from passive consumers into participating club members, and it transformed Meikel himself from theater employee to social club president—still in charge, but of a kind with his patrons.

The core feature of the club, as already mentioned, was Meikel's practice of displaying the names of all those who had submitted requests. After some months, though, Meikel had to discontinue this aspect of the program because his club had grown much too large, and "owing to the limitations of time," he could not possibly include every name.[33] Instead, Meikel incorporated the names of his club members into the program on a variety of other pretexts. First he began to list the names of local brides and grooms, accompanied by the community singing of comic parodies with which the patrons conveyed their best wishes.[34] Later, he listed the birthdays of club members each week. (This was only possible once patrons began to register their membership in 1927.) While the list of member birthdays was on display, Meikel led the singing of a special birthday song that he had composed himself and that all of the members had memorized.[35] Anniversaries, births, and any other cause for community celebration also found a place in Meikel's presentations, and the appropriate song for the occasion always made an appearance.[36] In his attempt to personally incorporate patrons into the program, Meikel did not limit himself to names: to celebrate Mother's Day in 1927, he projected photographs of local mothers onto the screen during a medley of mother songs. While a gimmick like this would have meant nothing in a downtown house, it had a tremendous effect on patrons at the Harding.[37]

Each club meeting was structured around such business items as might constitute any such gathering, although Meikel's agenda was always "entertainingly presented." For example, for "New Business" Meikel would introduce a tongue-in-cheek issue for his patrons to vote on, such as "should dresses be longer or shorter?"[38] The membership voted by singing specially written parodies on the topic at hand. Meikel also incorporated Logan Square happenings into the meetings whenever possible, so as to enhance his ties with the community and remind patrons that the Harding was there to serve their neighborhood. This last issue was near and dear to Meikel, who wanted patrons to embrace the Harding as their personal social club. "I keep reminding the members," he wrote in November 1927, "that the Harding theatre is *their* clubhouse, and that the 'Organ Club' is *their* club." At the time Meikel was writing, that club had reached a membership of five thousand patrons.[39]

Meikel may have initially won over his audience with the interactive and personalized Organ Club approach, but he sustained that loyal following on the basis of his skill as an organist and showman.[40] He offered excellent organ specialties that would have satisfied a singing audience anywhere, into which he integrated local touches and audience-request numbers. Meikel often abandoned any notion of a theme and simply led his patrons in singing their favorite songs. He also employed standard community singing strategies, such as an onstage thermometer that supposedly registered the volume of sound produced by the audience.[41] Some of his scripted solos, such as a school-day stunt from 1927, were found in singing houses everywhere.[42] However, Meikel's most innovative and fascinating solos fell into two distinct categories: presentations that celebrated the Harding's performers and staff members, and solos that incorporated the Harding's patrons beyond the listing of names and the projection of photographs. We shall look at each of these in turn.

ED MEIKEL'S
ORGAN CLUB
Conducted Each Week
at the
HARDING THEATRE, CHICAGO

This advertisement was published in *Exhibitors Herald* in February 1928. By that time, Meikel's Organ Club was heavily advertised across the trade press.

It was not unheard of for an organist to reference other theater performers in his solo. At the Oriental, for example, Henri Keates, Preston Sellers, and Milton Charles all presented solos in honor of Paul Ash.[43] These miniature celebrations served two purposes. First, they portrayed the Oriental performers and patrons as an affectionate family in order to promote community sentiment. Second, they boosted Ash, who was the theater's headliner and therefore indirectly responsible for the success of all those affiliated with the Oriental. Meikel presented similar tributes at the Harding, such as his solos celebrating the theater's master of ceremonies, Mark Fisher. Meikel, however, explored new territory when he featured members of the theater staff who never appeared in the spotlight. Finally, Meikel promoted various B&K stars, some of whom performed at the Harding and some of whom did not. It seems likely that these presentations were provided by B&K, although Meikel achieved excellent results with them.

Singer and master of ceremonies Mark Fisher had a successful career, but he was not a draw for the Harding like Ash was for the McVickers and the Oriental. Meikel was the bigger celebrity and therefore did not have the same relationship with Fisher that Keates and his associates had with Ash. All the same, Meikel featured Fisher in his organ solo on three occasions. One was a celebration of Fisher's first year, for which the Harding patrons sang the birthday song that Meikel had composed for them.[44] In the other two instances, Meikel led his patrons in a communal welcome to celebrate

Fisher's return following an absence. In July 1927, the club members sang a special version of "Hello, Aloha" (1926) that began, "Hello, Mark Fisher, we're glad you're back."[45] In January 1928, the solo was billed as "Welcome Mark" but consisted primarily of standard community singing numbers. At the conclusion of the singing Meikel "requested his members to give Mark the usual club cheer," which they did with gusto.[46] It is not clear whether Fisher was present to receive these accolades on any occasion, but of course the celebration was really for the patrons, not for the emcee. When Meikel and his followers welcomed Fisher back to the theater, they reaffirmed the notion that the Harding had become a family in which every member was important. Master of ceremonies was not just a position, and Fisher was not a mere employee. Instead, the patrons were inspired to feel a unique loyalty to Fisher and, by extension, to Meikel and to the theater. This model—theater as family—was anything but uncommon, but Meikel carried the idea further than had any other performer.

In March 1928, Meikel presented an unusual solo in which he introduced his audience to "every man and woman in the employ of the theatre." This included ushers, receptionists, doormen, projectionists, and stagehands—all of the picture palace functionaries that usually remained nameless and even invisible. The presentation featured a photograph of each employee, beside which was printed their position in the theater and "a clever little verse about them."[47] These verses would have been accompanied by a familiar tune, and they may even have been sung out loud.

On other occasions, Meikel incorporated the staff into his solos not as featured characters but as bit players. In early 1927, Meikel cast his organ solo as an argument between himself and the motion picture operators. The text of the argument, projected onto the screen, was set to the tunes of various Irish songs. Comedy slides featuring verses set to "Hello, Swanee, Hello" (1926) were interspersed throughout, and of course the program consisted primarily of community singing.[48] The contents of this argument have been lost, but the identity of the interlocutors is of great interest. In a downtown theater, patrons were encouraged to forget that motion picture operators existed at all. To contemplate the film projection equipment and the men who operated it was to tear down the traditional veil of illusion. Meikel, however, explicitly drew his patrons' attention to the projection booth and its occupants, thereby furnishing his audience with a glimpse into the "family" affairs of Harding employees: real people who had lives outside the show—and bickered like anyone else.

In other solos, Meikel featured his own patrons. Community singing always meant that the audience was the focus, but Meikel often took audience boosting to a new level. The Organ Club format was the perfect venue in which to feature the audience, for club members already possessed a form of recognition (their memberships) and already contributed to organ solo programming via weekly requests. Meikel took audience participation a step further by importing the atmosphere of a club meeting into his solos. His patrons exercised an active role in the organ solo, just as they would in the club room. Sometimes the patrons were featured as characters in the lantern slide narrative. On such occasions their influence on the solo, although predetermined, took center stage. Sometimes the patrons were allowed an active voice and had the power to change the presentation's outcome. And other times, the community singing feature itself was exaggerated until the patrons became stars in that activity.

While Meikel's audience-boosting organ solos were neither original nor unique—many of his tactics were employed in the downtown palaces as well—three things in his approach stand out: the context of the Harding as a neighborhood house, the frequency with which Meikel featured his audience, and the changes that Meikel made to the content and delivery of his solos. The simplest way for any organist to flatter his audience members was to present fan letters on the screen. This procedure indicated that audience opinions were taken seriously and that patrons had real influence over the entertainment. At the same time, a fan letter solo moved the spotlight onto the audience and could even turn some lucky patrons into celebrities—at least for a few minutes. In truth, though, the fan letters were usually faked to suit the organist's design. It may be that the patrons were fully aware of this, especially in a few outrageous cases. Nonetheless, Meikel's club members were still pleased to be the focal point of the solo, even if their on-screen ambassadors were fictional.

The fan letter solo was particularly popular, and it appeared in theaters across the country. In 1927, Bob West projected a fan letter at the Houston Metropolitan in which a young girl begged West to play a sad song so that the girl's sweetheart might take pity on her.[49] In 1930, Bill Meeder of the Richmond Hill RKO displayed a letter from a young man who wanted to know how to propose, while the next year Russ Henderson of the Worcester Plymouth presented handwritten letters full of "the oddest requests and 'lines' this audience has ever seen."[50] All of these letters, though, were obvious forgeries, designed to deliver humor or pathos and to introduce songs already selected by the organist. In the case of Meikel and his Organ Club, most of the letters at least took on the appearance of being genuine. That club members did in fact make requests on a regular basis made the stunt all the more believable.

The trade press was less trusting of the fan letter gimmick. In a *Herald* review from April 1927, we learn that Meikel projected onto the screen "an open letter supposedly written by one of his club members."[51] The reviewer presumed that the letter was not genuine, and he was probably right. However, he did not offer any justification for his doubt, and it appears that the letter was realistic (unlike those used by Henderson). Later in the same year Meikel offered a request solo that featured a series of fan letters, each of which introduced a community singing number. Again, there is no indication that these letters were not genuine.[52] Their authenticity, however, is less important than how Meikel employed such fan letters. Organists in other theaters used them to put across gags or frame the community singing. At the Harding, fan letters were an extension of the fleeting celebrity already granted to patrons who submitted requests. Meikel's fan letter solos featured the patrons, if only through a surrogate, and emphasized the spotlighted role of the club member.

Fan letters allowed patrons to control their entertainment but only in a delayed and indirect manner. Vocalisms and other noises made during the performance could allow the audience to exert an immediate influence over the course of events. The most basic manifestation of this power was applause, which audiences everywhere used to express their satisfaction and thereby assure the continuation of desired entertainment. (Negative counterparts to applause, such as boos and physical attacks, were nonexistent in picture palaces. At worst, an audience would respond with silence.) Every picture palace audience was explicitly invited to contribute to the entertainment via applause, but organists who featured community singing often invited their patrons to contribute more actively.

In one common stunt, anything but unique to the Harding, the organist would invite his patrons to decide a question by means of vocal response. This opportunity to participate beyond the usual singing allowed an audience to express its feelings on an issue and, in some cases, actually determine the program. The voting element in a solo also encouraged more enthusiastic singing, since each patron was eager to voice his opinion. The sorts of questions put to the audience were often intended to have a single right answer, and the resulting agreement among the patrons reinforced their ties both to one another and to the theater. In 1930, for example, Fred Kinsley at the New York Hippodrome asked his patrons to express their opinions on Prohibition. He provided three songs—one for enforcement, one for reform, and one for repeal—and invited each patron to sing the song that corresponded with her position. To the surprise of no one, those in favor of repeal produced the loudest singing. The patrons were then rewarded with another chorus of the song that had represented their vote, "Happy Days Are Here Again" (1929).[53]

Two of Meikel's voting-style solos were reviewed in the trade press. Neither of these presentations was particularly original, but both were well suited to the patronage and met with great success. Shortly after he created the Organ Club in 1926, Meikel offered a solo in which he asked the audience to help him decide whether to get married or not. To facilitate the vote, Meikel provided specially composed lyrics with which the patrons could express their opinions for or against. After the patrons had taken sides, Meikel projected a slide which read, "I will be married in October." Then, as half of the audience burst into applause, he changed to a slide that read "1982." This howl-inducing gag was followed by a short session of community singing, for which "so much good feeling had been worked up ... that the choruses were practically shouted."[54] In this solo, Meikel demonstrated the organist's power to encourage partisanship among his patrons, only to diffuse the tension with humor and reunite the disparate elements of his patronage with community singing. Patrons became invested in the presentation because they were asked to express an opinion, but this also created the possibility of division and discomfort. No one wanted to be on the losing side. The introduction of a humorous punch line assured universal goodwill at the end, and each participant was able to hold onto his point of view without threatening the harmony within the theater community.

One year after Meikel asked his patrons to vote on the subject of marriage, another important Chicago organist offered a very similar solo. Albert F. Brown, famous for his unique stage presentation solos, queried audiences about marriage at the Granada and Marbro Theatres, two Marks Brothers houses located in the Rogers Park and Garfield Park neighborhoods respectively. The premise of Brown's solo was identical to that of Meikel's, but its execution followed quite a different path. The text was given the rare honor of reproduction in the trade press. Because it was published in *Exhibitors Herald* as a fine example of an organ solo that others might want to emulate, I will reproduce the solo here in its entirety:

TITLE—THE MARRIAGE RIDDLE (Burlesque).
(Play Mendelssohn's "Wedding March.")
Opening (the following to melody, "Marching through Georgia"):
    Folks, I've got a problem that I wish you'd solve for me,
    For a year I've been keeping steady company,
    But I don't know just how happy I am going to be,
    If I go out and get married—
        Oh gee—you see, I need your good advice,
    Do you believe that married life is nice?
    Please don't make a joke of this, but answer truthfully,
    Do you think that I should get married?
    Looks like you are all afraid to tell me anything,
    But I heard when folks are happy that they always sing,
    So I'll flash a song and if I hear your voices ring
    I'll know that I should get married—
        Before I start I warn you once again
        This song is for the happy married men
    So if you've not lived your married life successfully
    Don't sing the words of this chorus.
(Insert chorus of popular song.)
        I thought all the happy married men would sing right out
    But there's no such animal I've learned without a doubt,
    If there's any HAPPY married WOMEN let them shout
    Loud as they can in this chorus.
(Insert Chorus—"Always.")
        That proves there's few happy married women—don't forget
    But I haven't heard from all you single people yet
    Those of you who wouldn't dare get married on a bet
    All join in on this chorus—
(Insert chorus of popular song.)
        Now let's hear from both the married WOMEN and the MEN
    And the ones that wish that they were single once again
    and the SINGLE ones that wish that they were soon to wed
    All join in this chorus—
(Insert chorus—"Russian Lullaby.")
(The following to melody "Here Comes the Bride.")

> By all advice, marriage is nice,
> If first you don't succeed, just try it over twice—
> Love dreams come true, I'll prove to you
> Don't say I'm wrong till you hear this sweet song—
> TITLE SLIDE—BABY FEET GO PITTER PATTER

While Brown's text did play on a cynical view of marriage, he steered clear of almost all humor and chose a serious conclusion: a "human-interest presentation" on the stage that featured a man, woman, and baby in a portrayal of domestic bliss.[55] This serious note suited Brown, who had made his name with artistic and sentimental stage productions that accompanied his organ solos.[56]

So far, we have observed that Meikel and his colleagues featured the names, photos, letters, requests, and opinions of their patrons. In addition, the singing of an individual patron was sometimes singled out for its quality or volume, and that patron was rewarded with special recognition from the organist and fellow audience members. For example, at the turn of the decade both Adolph Goebel of the Yonkers Loew's and Preston Sellers of the Chicago Oriental offered similar solos intended to seek out vocal talent for the newly emerging talkies.[57] To conduct the search, an assistant moved up and down the aisles with a portable microphone and invited patrons to sing one at a time. The sound was projected through amplification horns hidden backstage. Sellers's audience "applauded enthusiastically" after each person had completed the test, but Goebel found it necessary to minimize the embarrassment that some of his patrons experienced with a hearty round of community singing at the conclusion.[58] In both cases, however, the solo was a great success.

The first time that Meikel singled out a patron for exceptional vocalizing, he took the idea in quite a different direction, for the patron in question was in fact a song plugger planted in the audience by Meikel. After Meikel called his plant up onto the stage, he presented him with a "mammoth cigar" (proportioned so as to let the audience in on the joke) and then invited the plugger, Jack Perry, to sing a number.[59] Pluggers did not appear regularly in Meikel's solos; in fact, this early example was never duplicated. While there is no indication that the appearance of the plugger provoked a negative reaction, the club idea was inimical to outside performers, and Meikel began soon thereafter to focus on the relationship between himself and his patrons. Over time, Meikel developed a reputation for his avoidance of "out and out plugging"—quite the opposite of many other organists, including some as renowned as Jesse Crawford, who plugged songs ostentatiously at the Paramount.[60] A neighborhood organist like Meikel had to take care not to offend his audience, for his patrons all lived locally and all attended on a weekly basis. Most likely, he concluded that if he annoyed his club members with constant plugging, they would defect to another theater.

A year later Meikel featured the voices of his patrons in a more conventional manner, although the innovative details of the solo were unique to the Harding. Meikel informed his audience that during the community singing he would "auction off" sheet music to the loudest singers. Two ushers passed out music to members of the audience while he played, and at one point Meikel himself climbed onto the stage in order to throw rolled-up music into the balcony. It was not uncommon for Meikel to leave his console to encourage the audience in their vocalizing, a "cheer-leading" practice that was widely decried in the trade press because it meant that the organ—an instrument of great dignity—was abandoned midperformance. Meikel's 1927 auction solo was a smashing success and required an encore.[61] Although the featured patrons were tangibly rewarded for their exuberance, none of them were actually invited to show off for their peers. In this sense, Meikel's auction solo was similar to other presentations in which he used gimmicks to encourage wholehearted participation. Just one month earlier, for example, Meikel had led a community singing session in which his console began to sink back into the orchestra pit whenever participation flagged.[62] This stunt, used by many organists, kept the energy up and introduced an element of humor. The auction, organ lift, and thermometer gags all introduced a reason to sing and helped participants to overcome self-conscious tendencies. However, one of Meikel's audience-centered solos stands out as uniquely suited to the neighborhood house.

To celebrate the third anniversary of the theater, Meikel projected the name and birthday of every member of his organ club onto the screen. Then he led the club members in singing the official songs of the Rotary, Lions, Kiwanis, and American Legion clubs—all organizations to which patrons belonged.[63] This program achieved a number of Meikel's objectives as a neighborhood theater musician. First, the singing of club songs demonstrated that patrons were not only moviegoers but active members of the Logan Square community as well. We have seen a number of examples in which organists humanized themselves or their fellow performers, but in this case Meikel humanized his patrons. He permitted each of them to transcend the role of entertainee and to express deeply held commitments within the context of the picture theater. Second, the singing of club songs spotlighted the role played by community organizations, which in turn validated the Organ Club as a legitimate body of civic-minded locals. Finally, in order to celebrate the theater, Meikel wisely chose to celebrate the community. Because the Harding, like all neighborhood theaters, relied on its ties to the community, any endorsement of that community could only strengthen the theater.

This style of presentation was probably commonplace in many other neighborhood theaters, even though no accounts of them exist in the trade press (few neighborhood theaters were reviewed at all). In any event, this solo would not have been appropriate for a downtown house. A downtown palace would have nothing to gain from the singing of club songs other than their pure entertainment value, which could be derived more easily from the catalog of recent hits. In addition, downtown palaces sought to homogenize their audiences, the members of which came from varied backgrounds and social classes.[64] It was not in the exhibitor's interest for patrons to identify with clubs or other social organizations. In a neighborhood house, the patrons had a great deal more in common and could therefore express a greater degree of individuality without the threat of disharmony. Instead, the theater community thrived on personalized contributions and on the notion that the theater itself had now become an important community center, belonging to the whole neighborhood.

This notion—that the Harding belonged to the residents and merchants of Logan Square—was never better expressed than on the occasion of Meikel's five-thousandth performance at the Harding, which took place in November 1929. To celebrate his extraordinary success, local merchants came together to launch a newspaper-based exploitation scheme that would solidify Meikel's position as a community institution and boost their own enterprises in the process. The *Logan Square Life*, a community newspaper that enjoyed high circulation in the neighborhood, dedicated an entire issue to the celebration of Meikel's five-thousandth performance.[65] A cover story featured Meikel's Organ Club and described the success and notoriety he had achieved with it over the years. The highlight of the issue was a series of congratulatory advertisements placed by local businesses, many of which included photographs of Meikel patronizing their neighborhood stores.

In addition, a specially commissioned drawing of Meikel was cut up and inserted into advertisements throughout the paper. Readers were invited to find and cut out each of the pieces, and local merchants offered a prize to the reader who could best fit the pieces together.

This newspaper extravaganza, while inspired by Meikel's contributions to the community, greatly benefited all of those involved. In a single stroke, *Logan Square Life* generated goodwill among its readership, most of whom were enthusiastic members of the Organ Club, and increased advertising revenue due to the congratulatory notices inserted by local merchants. The merchants themselves benefited by being associated with a neighborhood favorite, as well as from their puzzle-piece promotion. The Harding received an enormous volume of free publicity of a kind far more effective than any paid advertisement. And, of course, Meikel himself basked in this "testimony to the friendship and esteem which he has merited for his faithful and completely successful work at the Harding."[66]

This celebration of Meikel's five-thousandth performance bears witness to two important points about the Harding and its position as a neighborhood theater. First, it substantiates reports of Meikel's enormous success with the Organ Club idea. Positive reviews and trade press articles tell us a great deal about an organist's reception and influence, but the fact that the Logan Square business community invested time and money into a promotion of Meikel is a solid affirmation of the organist's effective performance style. In fact, the trade press coverage of this event indicates that Meikel and his Organ Club contributed more to the Harding's success than any other employee or program feature. Second, the business community's investment in their local organist illuminates the unique position of a neighborhood theater. All of the Logan Square businesses, including the Harding, relied overwhelmingly on local patronage. The larger the volume of potential patrons who visited the neighborhood business district, the more successful all the businesses could be. By 1929 the Harding had become a significant boon to the other businesses, which could rely on their local theater to attract a steady flow of patrons to the area. It was therefore worthwhile for the entire business community to promote the success of its biggest draw. This prestigious position was hard won, for the Harding initially had to prove its value to the community—both on a social and a commercial level—in order to succeed. Here we might recall the expensive street festival that celebrated the theater's opening in 1925, an investment on the part of the Harding to ensure the goodwill of the Logan Square neighborhood. Only with persistent attention to the needs and values of the neighborhood, boosted by the invaluable contributions of Meikel, could the Harding have achieved its enviable position in the local economy.

In a 1928 article titled "Organ Clubs Draw Good Patronage," *Herald* commentator A. Raymond Gallo lamented that, despite the many advantages they afforded, "there are not many organ clubs."[67] Gallo, who was in an excellent position to survey the field, was doubtless correct in his observation. At the same time, it seems that a few organists began to imitate Meikel's Organ Club idea almost immediately. It is clear that he inspired imitators within the first year of his experiment and that these imitators generally met with a great deal of success.

Among the first to jump on this bandwagon was Clark Fiers of the West Side, a neighborhood theater in Scranton, Pennsylvania. In early 1927, Fiers published an article in which he offered advice on how to conduct community singing. Among his recommended tactics was the "community singing school," an organized approach to singing during the exhibition program that was clearly modeled on Meikel's club.[68] Fiers had recently started his own West Side Singing School, an effort that he expected to pay off in the near future even though his patrons were not "singing so loudly and lustily yet."[69] Although Fiers does not mention Meikel by name, he does pay him an obvious tribute: "One familiar Chicago organist has every audience at his feet, literally, and how they sing with him."[70] Any *Herald* reader would have immediately recognized Meikel as the originator of the club idea, and this description of his success rings true with other published accounts.

One year later, the Organ Club idea resurfaced in Chicago with Chauncey Haines of the B&K Norshore, another neighborhood house. Via slide, Haines invited patrons to become official members of his new organ club and to submit requests each week. He then proceeded to demonstrate the importance of community spirit to the neighborhood theater by conducting a singing contest between the two neighborhoods represented by the Norshore patronage: Evanston and Rogers Park. This good-natured exhibition of community spirit resulted in an encore and much good cheer.[71] Contests were a staple in all singing houses, but only a neighborhood theater could reliably assign teams based on local residence instead of, say, gender or hair color. Neighborhood loyalty doubtless inspired the patrons to greater effort as well.

The Organ Club idea took root not only in neighborhood houses but also in small-town theaters. Exhibitors in both of these situations faced the same problems and met with the same opportunities, since in each case they catered to a local population. Few small-town organists were granted coverage by the trade press, but in 1928 Charles Kusserow was acknowledged for his success with an organ club. Kusserow was the organist at the Adler Theatre in Marshfield, Wisconsin, a rural town located some distance from any major city center. Kusserow's strategy was to mail a letter to every patron of the theater, in which he invited the recipient to fill out the attached membership card and join his organ club. Kusserow named his club the "I Scream Club" (a play on words already employed by the ice cream industry) so as to clearly indicate its primary function: community singing.[72] The following year another small-town organ club cropped up in Lockport, New York, at the Palace Theatre. There, organist E. B. Davis adopted the slogan "All for Fun and Fun for All" to characterize his organization.[73]

In later years the organ club became a lifeline for console artists who struggled to retain a theater post. The introduction of film sound threatened theater musicians everywhere, and those in neighborhood and small-town houses were the first to go. In 1929, Paul H. Forster, organist at the Syracuse Eckel, developed a Meikel-style organ club in order to prove his value to the management. Forster's club revolved around audience requests. To facilitate these, he installed a box in the lobby and invited theatergoers to submit requests on special cards that included blanks for a name and address. An average of four thousand requests were submitted each week. Forster would then choose which numbers he wished to play and decide in which week each number would be performed. Once a schedule had been drawn up, Forster would send a printed card to each patron who had successfully submitted a request. His cards read: "Dear Patron: I thank you for your request. . . . will be played for you in my Novelty during the week of. . . . I hope you will be here to sing with the Organ. Cordially yours, Paul H. Forster, Organist."[74] Forster would then project the names of every patron whose request was to be played at the beginning of the organ solo, at which point those patrons became official members of the Eckel Organ Club. As the idea developed, the community newspaper provided assistance by printing regular notices about Forster's work. The management observed that the box office receipts were up, since every patron who had a request accepted was sure to attend the theater during the week in question. It was in this way that Forster was able to secure his position for quite some time.[75]

While a Meikel-style organ club never found a home in the downtown theaters, some of the flagship houses did develop similar strategies in their effort to secure regular local patronage. This is not surprising, for, like neighborhood theaters, downtown houses primarily attracted locals, and the locals responded well to community tie-ins at the picture show. However, these palaces also catered to itinerant audiences, and for this reason could not tailor their shows to suit the locals exclusively. The introduction of a once weekly club was an excellent solution to this dilemma. Club membership gave the locals a sense of community and belonging, while limited meetings prevented the alienation of visitors. These clubs could also be used to attract a specialized audience during the slowest part of the week.

One such club was developed under band leader Paul Ash at the McVickers in 1925, even before Meikel established his Organ Club at the Harding, and the idea (along with the members) moved with him to the Oriental in 1926. In the 1920s, regulations prohibited picture palace stage shows on Sunday mornings. This legislation eliminated the biggest appeal of houses like the McVickers and Oriental, and almost eradicated interest in the show. The Paul Ash Sunday Morning Club sought to mitigate this problem by using local talent instead. This ingenious solution provided stage entertainment, attracted a loyal patronage, and appealed to the community spirit of the locals, all while adhering to the letter of the law, if not the spirit. The primary object of the club was to supply between ten and fifteen acts for the Sunday morning picture show. The club, however, also took on a striking social dimension. Officers were elected from the body of members and the club met regularly outside of the picture show, "sometimes after the theatre in the rehearsal halls, or at the homes of some of the members, who arrange get-together parties and little social affairs for dances and so forth."[76] The appearance of locals onstage also attracted unprecedented crowds to the Sunday morning show, when all 2,500 of the Oriental's club members regularly appeared. Such a club provided a sense of community and intimacy to the middle-class locals, who might otherwise have felt lost in the cavernous auditorium of this busy itinerant theater. The *Herald* columnist noted that this idea, like that of the organ club, spread quickly to other downtown theaters. He observed that it was not appropriate for the neighborhood house, presumably because smaller theaters could not draw enough business on Sunday morning to justify the cost of operation.[77]

CHILDREN'S MATINEES

Meikel relied upon community support because the Harding could not offer first-run films or top-tier stage entertainment. Patrons would only visit, therefore, if he could provide a unique experience that was not available in downtown houses. The other type of exhibitor to require community backing was the manager or organist who offered children's programming. The matinee exhibitor, however, usually exceeded Meikel's efforts in catering to the local population and securing the active participation of community members. This is because matinee exhibitors needed not only to provide quality entertainment and to engage with local businesses and community organizations—obligations that also fell to the neighborhood exhibitor—but also to assuage a wide variety of fears concerning motion picture entertainment and to guarantee that the program on offer would educate and uplift.

The period of the 1920s and 1930s was characterized both by broad efforts to spread middle-class childrearing values and by growing anxiety over the influence of motion pictures.[78] Concerns about the dangers of the picture theater—whether these were moral, intellectual, or sanitary—were hardly new, of course, and had in fact contributed to the emergence of palace-style entertainment. In the early 1910s, exhibitor Samuel L. "Roxy" Rothafel had struggled to win over skeptical citizenry; many of his innovations, which later became industry standards, were originally intended to satisfy social reformers, women, and religious leaders.[79] In order to survive, the 1920s matinee exhibitors had to convince local representatives of interest groups—including the General Federation of Women's Clubs, the Parent Teacher Association, Daughters of the American Revolution, the Women's Christian Temperance Union, the International Federation of Catholic Alumnae, the Better Films Council, and many more—that children's matinees were wholesome and educational. The matinee exhibitor, therefore, had to function on two levels: she had to entertain the children who appeared at the theater while simultaneously assuaging the moral concerns of parents and reformers.

The matinee of the 1920s was a complete picture show, usually presented each Saturday morning or afternoon, when children were free from school and church. Some matinees were scheduled for Sunday afternoons, but this depended on local opinion and law; in many regions, movie theaters were prohibited from operating on Sundays. Like the regular shows, these matinees featured a combination of films and stage entertainment, all of which had been designated suitable for a young audience. Unlike the regular shows, children's matinees were more ideological than commercial. They highlighted moral uprightness, educational values, and civic responsibility—and they did so to cultivate local favor for the theater. As one columnist put it, the matinee "builds prestige through discussion of the theatre's interest in the young folks."[80] To emphasize this angle, managers always invited extensive community involvement and sought actively to secure local support for the weekly show.

Because of the matinee's emphasis on education and civic values, the community singing experiences designed for children differed significantly from those offered to adult theater patrons during the organ solo. These divergences applied to both repertoire and presentation. The music was carefully selected, of course; no exhibitor would run the risk of offending community watchdogs with risqué lyrics or dangerous rhythms. The singing of ephemeral popular songs was generally discouraged, and many exhibitors programmed nineteenth-century classics in their place. Patriotic numbers featured in most matinees and were usually accompanied by a flag ceremony or pledge. The format of the sings was highly varied. Although organists often led the singing, either as part of an integrated matinee or in a stand-alone club format, it was also common practice for a song leader to direct participation from the stage. This aligned matinee practice with the civic-minded community singing that took place outside of the theater and further enhanced the prestige and "uplift" value of these programs.

Children's matinees provided a unique opportunity for women to take leadership roles in the planning and staging of picture shows. Women were offered few opportunities in the motion picture exhibition industry, and more often than not they were confined to managing ticket sales at the box office.[81] Because children's matinees required the approval of local mothers and members of the Parent Teacher Association (PTA), female community leaders were invited to assist with the matinees and to keep a watchful eye on the program contents. Film companies hired women to head their national-level public relations departments, while individual theaters employed female organists and chaperones. Women also monopolized the trade press discussion of entertainment for children. They published frequently on the topic of children's matinees, and exhibitors willingly yielded to their authority.

A great deal of ink was spilled over children's matinees in the trade press—out of concern not for children but rather for the picture industry. Film exhibition itself was in a state of flux and controversy in the mid-1920s, and exhibitors were searching for a way to redeem their trade. In 1922, William H. Hays became president of the Motion Picture Producers and Distributors of America (MPPDA), a fledgling organization convened by the heads of several prominent film production companies. The purpose of the MPPDA was to clean up the motion picture industry. A major scandal the year before, in which Roscoe "Fatty" Arbuckle was accused of raping and murdering a young actress, had tarnished the industry's reputation. In reality, the scandal had nothing to do with the pictures exhibited in theaters, and Arbuckle himself was acquitted with a written apology from the court. All the same, the incident distressed a faction of conservative citizens who were concerned about motion picture entertainment, and religious groups began to call for federal censorship of the movies; in most regions, local censorship was already in place, although rules and enforcement standards were highly variable. The efforts of the MPPDA during the 1920s culminated in the Motion Picture Production Code of 1930, a tool for moral censorship known popularly as the Hays Code. While the MPPDA monitored all motion pictures, those intended for children came under especially close scrutiny. The Hays administration also policed the exhibition of films for children to ensure that questionable elements were not introduced into the program. In concerning itself so intimately with young people's exposure to film, the MPPDA sought both to redeem the image of the motion picture industry and to appease the public.[82] The children's matinee was the perfect venue for this work, for it allowed exhibitors, according to *Film Daily*, "to create good-will with the vast army of parents throughout the country whose chief duty is to protect the influences surrounding their children."[83]

The Public Relations Department of West Coast Theatres—which was later to merge with Fox and become a leader in matinee programming—offers a good example of how exhibition corporations addressed concerns about children and film. The department was founded in 1925 and placed under the leadership of a woman, Regge Doran. Although Doran pursued the broadly stated ideal of "better pictures for larger audiences," she was particularly concerned with the children's matinee.[84] Shortly thereafter, a division was created within the department to oversee the presentation of what West Coast termed "Junior Matinees," and yet another woman, Ryllis Hemington, was appointed to supervise that initiative. She would later become head of Public Relations for all of Fox West Coast Theatres. In 1926, the current head of Public Relations, Jack Retlaw, published a formal statement concerning his intent to "protect these future fathers and mothers from anything coarse, crude, suggestive or demoralizing in the slightest degree." Retlaw outlined his procedure for winning the support of local organizations concerned with child welfare:

> Prior to its general release, arrangements are made whereby a special preview of a picture to be shown in one of our theaters is given for mothers, teachers, women's clubs or any recognized organization which cares to send a representative. The film is carefully studied and later discussed for the purpose of deciding whether any scene or bit of action would be likely to have any other than a most helpful influence on the minds of children. If any question does arise on this angle notes are made and the questionable parts of the film are cut for the showing at the Junior Matinees. All the objections are carefully tabulated on cards, and these cuts are made every time the film is shown at a Junior Matinee in any West Coast theater.[85]

This was a typical policy for matinee exhibition and was intended to allay growing fears that films were harmful to children.

Because the primary purpose of the matinee was to win public support, such programs were usually not expected to turn a profit. It is true that some exhibitors found the children's matinee to promise significant box office benefits, and its potential as a moneymaker would be heavily exploited in the 1930s.[86] At first, however, the matinee was designed to build goodwill, not cash flow. In the extreme case of the UC Theatre in Berkeley, California, where community singing featured in every program, the meager profits were not even funneled back into the matinee but rather handed over to "some worthy charitable organization" chosen by a committee of PTA members.[87] In this way, the UC Theatre guaranteed the allegiance of the Berkeley PTA and the goodwill of the entire community. Industry insiders concurred that this approach would best serve a theater in the long run, and in 1925, Harold B. Franklin, general manager for Paramount, encouraged exhibitors to consider the value of children's matinees "not in dollars and cents but in the far-reaching goodwill they create."[88] In a *Film Daily* article, Franklin told exhibitors to expect a number of benefits from the children's matinee, all of which transcended immediate concerns about profit. First, children would develop a moviegoing habit that would last into adulthood and ensure the future success of the industry. Second, children would spread the love of movies to their parents, who would in turn become supporters and patrons. Third, the matinee would establish the theater as a community institution and thereby quell moral objections to the film industry. Finally, children's matinees would forestall any move toward widespread censorship of films. Franklin hoped that exhibitors could stave off wider MPPDA interference if they voluntarily segregated and monitored films that were shown to children. He also predicted the additional benefit that children would develop a better taste in films than that of their parents and would thereby encourage the long-term uplift of the industry.[89] While voluntary censorship of children's matinees may have delayed the imposition of widespread censorship, Franklin's hopes on this count were not realized; beginning in 1934, the Hays Code was heavily enforced across the film industry.[90]

In pursuit of these goals, the Committee for Public Relations of the MPPDA launched a major campaign for Saturday children's programming in 1925.[91] The editors of *Film Daily*, who were equally invested in preventing censorship and winning support for the industry, put up the Crandall chain of theaters in Washington, D.C., as "one of the outstanding examples of exactly what can be accomplished" in the line of children's matinees; they would remain a model for all children's matinees throughout the 1920s.[92] The Crandall chain—which would merge with Philadelphia's Stanley chain later in 1925 to form the Stanley-Crandall Company—was founded in the late nickelodeon era by Harry Crandall and in the 1920s was the preeminent chain in the D. C. area.[93] Matinees at Crandall theaters were overseen by the chain's Public Service and Educational Department, which was established a few months after the MPPDA itself. The head of the department, Harriet Hawley Locher, was another reform-minded woman who plunged into the task of ensuring child welfare: she served prominently alongside other women on national committees dedicated to improving films for children, offered advice to women's clubs and other community organizations, and became a noted speaker on the topic of children's matinees throughout the nation.[94]

Even before she helped Crandall to develop a model children's matinee, Locher had been at the forefront of children's motion picture reform for most of a decade. She had previously served as Chairman of the Motion Picture Department of the District of Columbia Federation of Women's Clubs, and in 1917 a columnist for the *Social Service Review* colorfully described her mission with that organization as follows:

Mrs. Locher is seeking better pictures for Washington children, supervised attendance with chaperonage at the picture theatres, moving pictures on the playgrounds and instead of the vulgar, sensational, sensual and tragic, she would have the films give forth the best of the human emotions, rouse the dormant fires of loyalty and patriotism, stir up the lofty ideals of honor and justice, and withal let them give forth wholesome fun and humor to dissipate the tug of pathos and the gloom of horror and depression which some of the blood curdling exhibitions on the screen leave in their wake.[95]

Locher also served in leadership positions with the League of American Pen Women, a society founded by progressive journalists in 1897 and dedicated to the furtherance of professional female writers and artists; she was invited to become a member because she authored devotional poetry and composed hymns, for which she provided both text and music.[96] As this biography indicates, Locher was a dedicated progressive who must be numbered among the most ardent reformers of the early picture theater.

Crandall and Locher were both committed to the notion that a picture theater should also serve as a community center. This position had implications both for the use of the theater building itself and for the theatrical organization's level of engagement with the local community. Concerning the physical theaters, Crandall desired that all of his houses should be used for educational, cultural, and religious activities whenever possible. Locher was involved in several ambitious educational outreach programs that took place in Crandall theaters.[97] In 1924, she invited congressmen and members of President Coolidge's cabinet to the Ambassador Theatre to participate in a demonstration of "visual-instruction" that presented movies as alternatives to textbooks. She also offered programs of films and lectures on various topics to local schoolteachers, who were invited to the screening room at Crandall's Metropolitan Theatre.[98] The best opportunity for enhancing the community value of a theater, however, was the children's matinee, which Crandall inaugurated in the early 1920s. Crandall also provided equipment for four boys' baseball teams (named after four of his houses) and oversaw league competition.[99]

Although Locher claimed that the Crandall matinees were the first to become a regular feature, the Children's Motion Picture League had in fact organized matinees in New York City by 1913; closer in time and place to Locher, the Wells Theater Syndicate of Richmond, Virginia, was giving free children's matinees, complete with community singing, in 1917.[100] All

Harriet Hawley Locher,
as pictured in the July
1917 edition of the *Social
Service Review*.

the same, Locher was among the first to respond to the MPPDA's call for comprehensive children's programming, and her matinees may indeed have been the first to employ the up-to-date model for which the Committee for Public Relations advocated. Although it is difficult to say whether Locher can claim precedence for various aspects of her matinee design, all of which were broadly repeated throughout the industry, her detailed trade press reports make her matinees exemplary.

The first Saturday matinee under Locher's supervision took place on October 11, 1924, at the Tivoli Theatre. It began at ten fifteen in the morning with an organ recital, "bright and pleasing without jazz." The program was introduced at ten thirty with a bugle call, after which all of the Boy and Girl Scouts proceeded onto the stage while the organist played a lively march. The prominent role given to the Scouts was central to Locher's design, for by inviting children's organizations to become involved she secured broad community support. This move also allowed Locher to imply that her children's matinee was an activity comparable to the Scouts, and therefore beneficial to local youth. Next in the program came the only trace of community singing: one verse of "America," under the direction of a song leader. This was followed by another participatory act, the Scouts' pledge to the flag said by all. The remainder of the program was usually dedicated to films, although a popular storyteller from the radio, Peggy Albion, replaced two of the reels for some time.[101]

The exhibitors who staged children's matinees at the aforementioned UC Theatre in Berkeley echoed many of Locher's concerns and shared her programming decisions. For example, the UC declared that "no element of jazz is allowed to creep into any part of the program"—a mandate, so the exhibitors claimed, of the "mothers and educators" who monitored the show. So as to best capitalize on this fear-assuaging move, both Locher and the UC took care to prominently advertise the musical purity of their children's programming.[102] Both theaters also invited censorship by the appropriate community organizations. In Berkeley, the PTA was permitted to legislate "that only such films be run as are educational and produce the proper emotional reaction; preferably films that send the youngsters home with new ideas and thoughts."[103] Regular selections included historical films, such as Yale University's "Chronicles of America"; educational animal films, which were a favorite with the children; and the occasional story film, "when the subject is suitable for children."[104] Locher's openness to censorship is particularly significant in light of Crandall's staunch opposition to the practice, which he had been combating for the previous decade. It is clear that Locher, Crandall, and others hoped that, by cooperating with the censors where children were concerned, they might win greater freedom for general programming.[105] Finally, Locher's use of a song leader appears to have been typical of the matinee; the UC Theatre featured a song leader known as Big Brother, who spoke directly to the youngsters in an informal manner and served an educational function.[106]

Under Locher, community singing did not play a large role in the children's matinee. This, however, was soon to change. In 1927, organist Irene Juno was assigned to the Saturday morning children's matinees at the Chevy Chase Theatre, which had recently been acquired by Stanley-Crandall.[107] Juno had been employed by Crandall since at least 1924, and she had already developed a national reputation both as an arranger for theater organ and as a trade press contributor.[108] She shared Locher's commitment to education and collaborated regularly with Ludwig E. Manoly, the director of instrumental music for Washington high schools, to bring music education to the city's youth. In her capacity as a columnist for the *Herald*, Juno advocated for music in the public schools and described the significance of music education to the motion picture community. Among other things, she observed that rising musical standards in the schools meant that she and other organists had to offer high-quality performances of the numbers selected for children's matinees, for "if they are played in a careless, sloppy fashion the organist will come in for comparison and criticism."[109] As a matinee organist, Juno developed relationships with local music students and carefully monitored their reactions to music in the theater. She then used her deep understanding of children and music to craft advice for her readers and to improve her own effectiveness.

In collaboration with Locher and Gladys Mills, the supervisor for the matinees, Juno inaugurated a series of musical experiments that took place in the Crandall children's matinees during 1927. Juno published extensively on her work in the *Herald*, and she served as a model for other organists in her position. Juno also reminds us that children's matinees offered a unique opportunity for women to become prominent in the film exhibition industry. Indeed, Juno was posted as a matinee organist precisely because of her sex: her peers generally considered a woman to have natural authority on the topic of children's entertainment. At the same time, her position created the opportunity for Juno to contribute regularly to the national trade journals. She also worked as a community liaison for the matinees and was required by her post to interact with local reformers—tasks that would not fall to a regular organist.

At the Crandall theaters, Juno sought to discover what impact music had on children and how music could be used to improve their experience and to better satisfy the requirements of reformers and parents. With the assistance of Locher and Mills, she set out to informally study the children's responses to music during the show. The results of their investigation were conclusive: "We found out that musical reaction with children was 100 percent."[110] By this, Juno meant that the children were highly sensitive to the music they heard during the film, quick to associate a tune with a situation, and easily distracted by well-placed musical excerpts.

Juno used this knowledge to "censor" distressing scenes that were integral to the plots of films and could therefore not be cut, although she made it

This photograph of Irene Juno was published in *Exhibitors Herald* in September 1927. She was well-known to *Herald* readers as a columnist: she not only wrote extended articles about children's matinees but also published a regular feature titled New Songs Reviewed by Irene Juno.

clear in her report that the films were heavily censored: "All gruesome matter is chopped, also drinking or drunken scenes unless direct comedy." For example, she distracted her patrons from an all-too-realistic fight scene by interpolating popular numbers that the children knew. This "started them singing and whistling," and it was duly noted that not one child had to be carried from the theater in hysterics.[111] (This had happened once, it seems, when a guest organist failed to dampen the terror of a gruesome scene with music.[112]) On the occasion described, Juno had invited a group of skeptical community members to attend the show and watch the children's reactions. By her account, "they all threw up their hands" in amazement at what they had witnessed. "Well," said one witness, "I guess you women without any children know more about them than some of the mothers."[113] Juno was convinced that she had proven that engagement with participatory singing was more powerful than the image on the screen.

Juno's success with the use of community singing to control the matinee experience was echoed by other exhibitors, who employed the practice to police juvenile conduct. In 1926, theater manager H. E. Wilton noted that participation was the perfect antidote to restless behavior: "After the community singing the kiddies give undivided attention to the program."[114]

He found that the activity provided release for pent-up energy and consequently helped children to enjoy the show. Cliff F. Chellew, manager of the Alexander Theatre in Glendale, California, and inventor in 1929 of the popular Brownie Club model for matinee exhibition, also exploited community singing to control behavior. In order to prevent questionable interactions between "adolescent youngsters with slightly perverted twists to their minds," Chellew segregated his audience, seating girls in the middle and boys on either side.[115] Although there was potential for resistance to this arrangement, the organist, Herb Kern, was able to secure cooperation by conducting regular singing contests between the boys and girls. Each child gleefully joined in with others of his or her gender to secure a victory, and the contest gained in popularity until "neither the girls or boys would think of sitting in the others' sections."[116] Chellew and Kern also used the club model itself to police behavior; children guilty of pulling hair, fighting, or disrupting the film had their memberships suspended.

Despite Juno's efforts to manage her patrons' engagement, she observed that children could not be kept from singing during the film when the mood took them. To capitalize on this tendency, she offered a session of community singing from ten to ten thirty. Juno remarked that the children "like something with rhythm," and we can see from her sample song list that musical guidelines for children's matinees had become less stringent than in previous years (although Juno's songs tended to be well worn and hardly constituted "jazz").[117] She listed the following songs as being among the "most popular" with her patrons in 1927: "Bye Bye Blackbird" (1926), "For My Sweetheart" (1926), "Collegiate" (1925), "Show Me the Way to Go Home" (1925), "Mary Lou" (1926), "Barney Google" (1923), "California, Here I Come" (1924), "Over There" (1917), "Keep the Home Fires Burning" (1914), "The Battle Hymn of the Republic" (1862), and (for one young boy in particular) "Sweet Adeline" (1903). Juno also accepted on-the-fly requests from her patrons, who left their seats and crowded around the organ console during the singing. Although it appears that the children knew the songs well, she still arranged to have the lyrics of programmed songs projected via slide.

Children sang during other parts of the show as well. In one reported incident, a child cried out "there goes Barney Google" upon seeing a character in the film. In response, Juno began to play "Barney Google" on the spot, and all of the children sang. She also noted that "Show Me the Way to Go

Home" had become indelibly connected in the minds of the children with any drunkard who appeared on screen. Hoping to eradicate this association, she once refrained from playing the song. Despite her efforts, however, the children launched into the chorus, and she was forced to find the key and provide an accompaniment. Juno noted that such impromptu interpolations "would have been unbelievable in correct scoring of the picture, but there were no musical critics in the house, and what is more to the point, no one would have cared if there had been."[118]

All of this was in addition to the community singing component that had predated Juno's tenure. The opening ceremony, which had not changed much from the first days of the matinee under Locher, was still followed by one verse of "America," led by Gladys Mills. Under Juno's leadership, a bugler called the show to order at ten thirty sharp, at which point the boys processed down the aisles, bearing the Scout flag and a pair of American flags. They marched to the strains of Sousa's "The Stars and Stripes Forever," which Juno had determined gave the most "pep" to the children's steps. Boy Scouts, Girl Scouts, and Campfire Girls continued to participate actively in the show; a selected Boy Scout, for instance, was assigned to monitor each exit door from the moment the house opened, and he remained "on guard" until the last child had left. Civic-minded adults were incorporated into the show as well: prominent club women, (female) teachers, and (female) members of the PTA acted as hostesses each week.[119]

Although Crandall matinees dominated the trade press discussion between 1924 and 1927, there were many other approaches to programming and marketing children's matinees. In the final years of the decade, a wide variety of matinees were described in the trade press as models for imitation. While some of these echoed the values and practices of Crandall, Locher, and Juno, others took on quite a different form. In particular, a number of exhibitors used community singing as the main draw for the matinee—a practice that only grew in popularity as sound films began to drive live performers from the theaters in 1928. This activity was often organized using a club model borrowed from mainstream exhibitors.

It was typical in the late 1920s for a children's matinee to open with a period of community singing. The Empire Theatre in New Bedford, Massachusetts, and the Seattle Theatre in Seattle, Washington, both offered an entire hour of singing before the exhibition of films each Saturday morning. In Seattle, the accompaniment was provided by the famous organ-playing team of Ron

Baggot and Don Moore; they would later lead community singing at the Brooklyn Fox, opposite Merle Clark and Elsie Thompson at the Brooklyn Paramount.[120] In 1929, Baggot and Moore became national leaders in children's matinee development with the extraordinary success of their Ron and Don Organ Club. The club met between ten thirty and eleven thirty every Saturday morning for community singing and solo performances by club members, who could win prizes donated by local businesses. The theater issued membership cards to local children and charged ten cents at the door, with every sixth admission free. After just one month, attendance had reached six hundred children and seventy-three adults; the latter paid the full fifty-cent admission fee. Baggot and Moore's success was all the more significant because the Seattle had been wired for sound in September 1928, six months after opening as a silent house.[121] The Paramount Publix organization had reason to ensure that the magnificent Wurlitzer organ—an organ advertised to resemble that played by Jesse Crawford at the New York Paramount—they had installed in their new 3,049-seat theater was put to good use, but it was up to the organists to devise new ways of turning the organ into a draw for the Seattle.[122] Although the pair offered community singing with lyric slides during every program, the Ron and Don Organ Club was widely touted as their most profitable innovation.[123] The Empire Theatre also reported great success with its hour-long prematinee sing; the weekly event, which was widely advertised and also relied on lyric slides, attracted SRO (standing room only) audiences on a regular basis.[124]

Also in 1929, Harold Daniels of the Chicago Buckingham—a 965-seat neighborhood theater—launched his own Saturday sing-along program for children: the Kid's Glee Club. Although the trade press published only a single review of Daniels's matinee work, the reviewer waxed rhapsodic about the organist's success and encouraged adults in the area who were "looking for a thrill of an unexpected nature" to visit a session. "What they do with a popular song," the reviewer wrote, "is startling."[125] For each of his club meetings, Daniels wrote a story to tie the songs together. His narrative was then read into the microphone by the theater manager, Charles Ryan, who was known in this role as the "Big Voice of the 'Kid's Glee Club.'" Ryan also delivered instructions to the children, such as "girls only" or "real soft," which Daniels believed was necessary so as to include children who could not read instructions from slides.[126] When the *Herald* reviewer visited Daniels's matinee, he reported that "East Side, West Side" (1894), "The Man I Love"

(1927), and "Mississippi Mud" (1927) were requested by the club members, while "My Ohio Home" (1927), "Just Once Again" (1927), "Dolores" (1928), "Ramona" (1927), "Sunshine" (1928), and "Highways" (probably the 1927 song "Highways Are Happy Ways") rounded out the program. The singing was presumably followed by an appropriate selection of films.[127] Like Baggot and Moore, Daniels was deeply concerned about his position after the introduction of sound technology. On October 20, 1928, the Buckingham became the first neighborhood theater in Chicago to be wired for sound. In response, Daniels appointed himself "a committee of one to further our [organists'] best interest when ever possible" and began developing a higher grade of organ novelty that would appeal to all of his patrons.[128] The "Kid's Glee Club" was but one of his inventions, introduced to protect his position in the changing motion picture industry.

In 1930 and 1931, the entire picture palace industry—and with it, the children's matinee—found itself radically transformed. Sound technology had already been chipping away at the job security of organists and theater musicians for some years, but the onset of the Great Depression proved a catastrophe for everyone involved with motion picture exhibition. Across the board, attendance plummeted and ticket prices had to be slashed; even theater design was reformed to reflect the new economic situation, as cheaper art deco theaters were erected in place of outmoded, glamorous palaces.[129] In the final month of 1930, theater managers began to report steeply declining attendance at children's matinees. "Where are the kiddies who used to pack our theatres in the days gone by?" mused one columnist.[130] There was general consensus that children simply did not like talking pictures, although it is hard to believe that the economic conditions did not contribute.[131] Exhibitors became increasingly preoccupied with attracting young people to their theaters by any means. This change in circumstances had an influence, therefore, both on matinee programming and on the discourse that surrounded it.

In an influential article on the subject, published in *Motion Picture News* in August 1930, Madaline Woods of the Publix Indiana Circuit signaled the change in thinking when she stated that the goal of children's programming should be to "directly or indirectly [stimulate] adult attendance."[132] Although this purpose had always lurked in the background of matinee theorizing, Woods was the first prominent commentator to make it a top priority. She suggested a laundry list of tactics, many of which echoed the work of Crandall and Locher. These included the programming of PTA-ap-proved films, regular collaboration with the schools for promotions and contests, the incorporation of Boy Scout representatives, and the inclusion of educational lectures by librarians and city officials. Woods also described talent contests, dance recitals, games, and prize giveaways that would attract children, and suggested a model for an organist-led Kiddies' Club. (She did not mention community singing, but most exhibitors made the activity a feature of the matinee, as we shall see.) In short, Woods concurred with the matinee pioneers that community support was essential to the success of the program and the theater, but she did not suggest that the matinee should exist primarily to educate and improve local youth. Instead, she por-trayed it as a means to increase box office receipts and secure long-term patronage.[133]

Several exhibitors pursued the Kiddies' Club model, which was pro-moted by Woods and had already proven successful. As the economy took a turn for the worse, however, exhibitors displayed remarkable ingenuity in their quest to attract patrons to the theater. At the Fox Theatre in North Platte, Nebraska, manager Chet Miller collaborated with organist Eddie Stone to develop the Fox Theatre–Eddie Stone Organ Club, which met every Saturday at one thirty. In an attempt to reach as broad an audience as possible, Miller made the unusual decision to extend formal membership to adults, to whom he issued special membership cards. He also admitted members at the low cost of five cents for children and ten cents for adults, a move that he claimed brought in so many new patrons that it did not dam-age the theater's bottom line; indeed, in the first year of the club he was able to boast that four thousand of the town's twelve thousand residents held membership cards. To further encourage membership (and stem competi-tion from other leisure providers), Miller arranged a discount at the local miniature golf course for all card holders. This meant that cash-strapped locals could visit the Saturday matinee and then play a round of golf for less than the regular cost of either activity. Inside the theater, Miller offered prizes to club members that ranged from a week of free admission to live rabbits and puppies, and he held a weekly drawing that allowed twenty members to get their matinee and golf at no charge. Outside of the theater, he staged public events to promote films, such as a parade for children and their pet dogs an hour before the matinee screening of the MGM comedy *Hot Dog*, and he cultivated personal relationships with club members and their parents. Miller also arranged to have the club meetings broadcast on the local radio station.

Of course, all of this marketing would be for nothing if the show itself were not entertaining. Stone directed the actual club meetings from his place at the organ console, although Miller was always present. Each meeting began with a cheery greeting from Stone: "Hi, Gang!" He then explained the club proceedings for the benefit of new members and listeners at home before launching into a ten-minute period of community singing. Stone selected his songs from requests that the children submitted by letter, and he used slides to project the lyrics. Next, Stone would conduct solo singing contests for girls, boys, and adults, with the winners selected by applause and rewarded with passes to the theater. Finally, all members would sing the club song, "Sunny Side Up" (1929), and give the club yell. "We have found this to be a wonderful good-will builder for the theatre," reported Stone, using language that echoes that of his reform-minded predecessors in the field of matinee development.[134] When Stone referred to "good-will," however, he meant local appreciation for the Fox's efforts to provide excellent entertainment at a low price—not its role in educating or protecting children. (Indeed, he reported without a shade of remorse that a large number of the dogs that marched in the promotional parade had been stolen the night before.) Miller and Stone's only ambition was, without a doubt, "cornering the Saturday afternoon trade of both kiddies and adults."[135]

When discussing his Kiddies' Club at the State Theatre in Stoughton, Massachusetts, manager Paul W. Kunze also repeatedly invoked the value of goodwill, although he made it clear that his purpose in founding the club in early 1930 was to bring back "the once lucrative and valuable patronage" of local children. Like Miller and Stone, Kunze reported great success, which he attributed to the child-friendly atmosphere of his theater, the entertaining program, and the candy and other prizes that he solicited from local merchants. Kunze employed a young female kindergarten teacher known as Big Sister to issue membership cards, chaperone the show, and serve as a much-loved confidant to the club members. The club meetings, which took place after the Saturday matinees, were conducted by a male master of ceremonies, while the theater organist played request numbers in the lobby before the show, led the singing, and accompanied the stage acts. Although community singing did not occupy a large portion of Kunze's program, he reported that "it plays an important part of every meeting, with very enthusiastic response." Each program opened with the singing of "America" while

children in "patriotic costume" displayed the colors on stage. This was followed by a specially written club song set to a popular melody and finally
the Kiddies' Club cheer. In late 1930, Kunze capitalized on widespread interest in community singing by starting a Kiddies' Glee Club of thirty children,
which rehearsed under the direction of a public school music teacher.[136]
He noted that the close supervision, stage coaching from Big Sister, and
opportunities for musical training all served to attract the support of local
parents.[137]

   Other Depression-era matinees were less ambitious, but it was common
for exhibitors to offer a brief period of community singing before the matinee in order to attract patrons and make use of the expensive organ. At
the Colonial Theater in Hartford, Connecticut, for example, manager and
organist C. M. Maxfield opened his Saturday program with fifteen minutes
of singing accompanied by homemade, typewritten slides of popular choruses. Maxfield reported that the sessions had a greater positive effect on
attendance than anything else he had tried, with the added benefit that the
sing-along kept the children from running around the theater and caus-
ing trouble before the films began.[138] Bob Soffer, another manager-organist,
reported his intent to lead matinee singing at the Hollywood Theatre in
Manhattan—a house constructed in 1930 by Warner Brothers to showcase
talking pictures and therefore wired for sound from the start. "From past
experience," Soffer wrote of his plan, "I know that they [the children] just
love to sing out loud."[139] He also incorporated a talent show for children who
could sing, dance, or recite.

   Maxfield and Soffer only controlled one theater each, but their strategy
was repeated on a grand scale in 1931. With the object of increasing revenue in a difficult time, Warner Brothers opened children's matinees in about
forty-five theaters in and around Pittsburgh. These shows also provided
employment for out-of-work theater organists, who accompanied the singing and acted as masters of ceremony. *Variety* reported that these Warner
Brothers matinees "are staged with the express intention of bringing the kids
to the theatre through community singing"—a departure, once more, from
the high moral tone that characterized the work of Crandall and Locher.[140]

   Although many exhibitors were eager to share their ideas for promotions
and community tie-ins, the most detailed information that we have about
Depression-era matinees themselves comes from a series of suggested programs published in *Motion Picture News* in 1930. The series was authored
by Ryllis Hemington, director of public relations for Fox West Coast

Theatres, and it described real shows that were being staged in Fox theaters. Hemington's stated purpose was to help exhibitors avoid common pitfalls "in their campaign to build up goodwill in their community" by offering a children's matinee.[141] Unlike Woods, Hemington heavily promoted community singing as a useful tool for the matinee exhibitor; in her words, the practice "should be encouraged at all children's performances to build goodwill for neighborhood theatres."[142]

The children's matinee had the potential to generate much-desired goodwill in the community, but it was also dangerous ground for many exhibitors. If the children's matinee happened to produce controversy or outrage instead of support, it became a serious liability. The *Motion Picture News* noted the challenge of staging these matinees: "With Saturday kiddie shows now in full swing throughout the country, exhibitors find themselves in a ticklish spot where screen material is concerned, especially with women's clubs and parent-teachers' associations throwing a spotlight on the suitability of programs offered."[143] For this reason, the *News* provided complete program recommendations, including ideas for feature films, short subjects, guests of honor (including Scout leaders), lecturers, displays, contests, community tie-ins, and any number of other appropriate program elements. Each of the programs was organized around a historical personage or event that was suitable for the Saturday in question, and they all emphasized educational elements.

Community singing did not appear in every recommended program, but it did constitute a regular presence, and it was to be found in several different forms. Hemington regularly suggested that a local music educator or glee club be brought in to lead the singing of a suitable number. To celebrate the birthday of Theodore Roosevelt, for example, she recommended a selection of navy songs under the direction of a music teacher.[144] To celebrate Lincoln's Gettysburg Address, "Tenting Tonight on the Old Camp Ground" (1863) and "Marching through Georgia" (1865) were indicated.[145] The birthday of Joseph Conrad called for the "singing of songs of the sea, such as, 'Over the Bounding Main'" (1880), while that of Jakob Ludwig Karl Grimm suggested (with notable lack of inspiration) the "singing of American and German songs."[146] Hemington did not frequently make specific recommendations for community singing numbers, but her endorsement of the practice featured in headlines for the series, such as the unambiguous "Community Songs at Kiddie Shows Boost Business."[147]

Hemington also encouraged exhibitors to get children singing in more formal settings. She suggested a variety of activities that involved a children's chorus, including performances, song leading, and even a tableaux for Armistice Day, complete with costumes and flags representing the Allied nations and a performance of "The Star-Spangled Banner."[148] Hemington always indicated that the children were to be rehearsed and directed by their music teacher, with the implication that these choruses were made up of school children who prepared their performances during class time—yet another example of collaboration between matinee exhibitors and educators. Apart from her frequent call for a "Glee Club or chorus" to lead community singing, Hemington made several specific recommendations.[149] To celebrate the birthday of Robert Louis Stevenson, for example, she suggested that a children's chorus perform some of his poems set to music, while the occasion of an Indian summer evoked a call for "autumn songs."[150]

While Hemington recommended community singing frequently throughout her series in the *News*, she also suggested in her final two installments that exhibitors program an alternative variety of sung participation: the sing-along film. All of the films listed by Hemington were either silent Ko-Ko Song Car-Tunes, released by Red Seal in the mid-1920s, or the newer Screen Songs, released by Paramount with soundtracks.[151] Both series were created by the Fleischer brothers in their New York studio, and their presence on Hemington's lists attests to the enormous popularity of sing-along films by the beginning of the 1930s. While the Fleischer sing-along films certainly appealed to children, they were in fact intended for a broad audience and were consumed primarily by adults. In recommending these films, Hemington continued to align her selections with the matinee theme. The birthday of Joseph Conrad suggested to her the Song Car-Tune *Sailing, Sailing* (1925), while three films struck her as suitable for the birthday of Eli Whitney: *Dixie* (1925), *Swanee River* (1925), and *Old Black Joe* (1926).[152] She also recommended the 1929 Screen Song version of this last song both for Whitney's birthday and for the anniversary of the Emancipation Proclamation.[153] The fact that Hemington included Song Car-Tunes in her sample programs is interesting not only because they were community singing tools but because the films she listed were mostly five years out of date—an indication that they were popular enough to still be in circulation.

Although Hemington's program recommendations were not published after December 1930, the idea was almost immediately taken up by Rita

McGoldrick, who wrote several regular columns in *Motion Picture Herald* in 1931 and 1932, including Your Public, The Junior Show, School and Screen, and Selections, the last of which listed her film recommendations for both adult and family audiences. At the same time, she also began broadcasting radio lectures on the subject of children and film; her program was widely lauded and picked up by a number of stations. McGoldrick had been a vocal matinee reformer for nearly a decade, and her views had appeared regularly in the trade press since 1924.[154] She was a member of the first MPPDA Public Relations Committee, which convened in 1922, and in 1927 she established the Motion Picture Bureau of the International Federation of Catholic Alumnae, for which she served as chair. In 1930, McGoldrick joined other leaders of religious and civic organizations in supporting the Hays Code, and in 1932 she embarked on a lecture tour that saw her discussing children's programming with club women and community organizations across the Midwest.[155] All of this contributed to McGoldrick's unique position in the Depression-era conversation about children's matinees, for she represented both the concerns of the exhibitor and the concerns of the community: she *was* the woman that theaters wanted to please.

McGoldrick's philosophy might best be summed up by a quote from the Bronxville Women's Club that she incorporated into one of her early columns about children's programming: "We have found that we must intelligently consider *the box office* if we are to have that cooperation that spells success."[156] Later, McGoldrick saw fit to sum up her position in three points and position it prominently alongside her reports on successful children's matinees:

RITA C. McGOLDRICK BELIEVES:

1. That well exploited Junior Shows and Junior Motion Picture Clubs are a community success and a box office gold mine.
2. That cooperation with leaders in the community is the important element, the organized local women's clubs being the basic factor for Junior Show success.
3. That the proper handling of entertainment for young people is the safest antidote for censorship.[157]

Informed by her experiences and convictions, McGoldrick set out to preserve a high moral standard in children's programming by helping exhibitors to make it pay.

McGoldrick was overwhelmingly concerned with the films themselves. Beginning in August 1931, the *Herald* regularly published her reviews as "Mrs. Rita C. McGoldrick's selection of specially approved motion pictures classified according to her opinion of their merit and the special fitness for the two principal audience classifications: the family audience including grown-ups and children, and, the strictly adult audience." She also compiled data on film suitability that had been provided by the General Federation of Women's Clubs, the International Federation of Catholic Alumnae, the Daughters of the American Revolution, the Los Angeles Women's University Club, and the Young Men's Christian Association, all of which accounted for over three hundred features and six hundred short subjects each year; approval rates hovered around 75 percent.[158]

Among the short subjects that McGoldrick personally approved for family consumption were a number of Screen Songs, including *Betty Co-Ed* (1931), *Kitty from Kansas City* (1931), *By the Light of the Silvery Moon* (1931), and *Oh! How I Hate to Get Up in the Morning* (1932). She also recommended Screen Songs in her sample programs, which were explicitly based on those created by Hemington.[159] These recommendations included *Come Take a Trip in My Airship* (1930) to celebrate the birthday of pioneering aviator Richard E. Byrd, *In the Shade of the Old Apple Tree* (1930) to celebrate the Harvest Festival, and *And the Green Grass Grew All Around* (1931) to celebrate National Garden Week.[160] McGoldrick also continued to advocate for traditional community singing in conjunction with holiday celebrations. For Mother's Day, for example, she recommended "Mother Machree" (1910) and "Mother of Mine" (1927), while for Flag Day she listed "The Star-Spangled Banner," "Battle Hymn of the Republic," "Hail Columbia," "Tenting Tonight on the Old Camp Ground," and "America."[161]

McGoldrick also took an active role in founding and directing matinee programs, and an examination of her on-the-ground work further illuminates the central role of community singing in matinee exhibition. In May 1932, for example, McGoldrick hosted the inaugural matinee at the Carlton Theatre in Brooklyn, where she resided. The program consisted of "a newsreel, a short of an educational nature, two features selected from the approved lists of club reviewing groups, and community songs," including "The Star-Spangled Banner," sung standing while a waving flag was projected onto the screen.[162] The matinee attracted so many children, eager to pay the fifteen-cent admission fee, that police were required to halt traffic and keep the crowds in order. Immediately thereafter, the Randforce Amusement Company announced that it would expand matinee programming to all forty of its Brooklyn houses.

McGoldrick also regularly reported the activities of theaters and oversight committees around the country, many of which also incorporated community singing into their matinee programs. In her column from October 3, 1931, for example, McGoldrick published accounts of matinees conducted by a variety of theaters and women's clubs, several of which indicated reliance on community singing. The manager of the Florida Theatre in Jacksonville, Florida, reported that "community singing, with popular song slides projected on the screen, is another medium which we use to advantage"; the chair for motion pictures of the Delaware State Federation of Women's Clubs reported that the local public school music supervisor led a program of community songs, including a national anthem and "Delaware, My Delaware!," at their matinees; and the Better Films Council of Birmingham, Alabama, reported that their programs opened with community singing under "a competent leader."[163]

⑥ THE ADVENT OF SOUND

It is traditional for film history narratives to credit *The Jazz Singer*, which premiered on October 6, 1927, with popularizing sound technology and prompting the industry-wide conversion to sound. This, of course, oversimplifies the process through which sound film emerged. Sound technology —a collection of competing innovations developed over a decade—faced the challenges of monopolistic distribution practices, limited equipment availability, and deep-rooted industry prejudices. Even after it had become clear that sound was the future of film production, silent and sound films coexisted for years while theaters were slowly wired by Western Electric.[1] In fact, the enormous revenues reported for *The Jazz Singer*, which even in its own time was heralded as an epoch bringer, were secured primarily by the silent version of the film.[2]

While *The Jazz Singer* did not independently bring about the sound revolution, it provides an excellent case study for the development—practical, social, and economical—of sound technology. The film was produced by Warner Brothers, a struggling production company that was willing to take risks in order to survive in the competitive film market. Warner Brothers, a "minor" in the industry, did not control large chains of theaters and therefore did not have a guaranteed outlet for its product. In the late 1920s, the production of sound films was indeed a risk—one that the profitable "majors" were not willing to take. At the same time, it was not a new idea. Inventors and film producers had been experimenting with sound technology since before 1924, when Max Fleischer released sound versions of his Song Car-Tune shorts using Lee de Forest's Phonofilm process.[3] Despite Fleischer Studio's commitment to the exploitation and popularization of sound technology, however, de Forest's system never caught on and the Song Car-Tunes were exhibited with sound in only a few Manhattan theaters.[4] Another major innovation came in 1927, when Fox—seeking entry to a larger number of theaters—began to produce sound newsreels. Fox's Movietone Newsreels accelerated the installation of Western Electric sound equipment and were well received by audiences, but their popularity still failed to convince the film industry that sound was anything other than a passing curiosity.[5] Thomas Edison himself did not believe that sound technology would have a lasting impact. In 1927, *Film Daily* quoted the skeptical film pioneer: "Yes, there will be a novelty to it for a little while, but the glitter will soon wear off and the movie fans will cry for silence or a little orchestra music."[6]

During the late 1920s, Warner Brothers found a niche producing sound shorts. They released their films under the Vitaphone label and utilized a sound-on-disc technology, although a 1927 licensing agreement meant that the films could be exhibited using the same Western Electric equipment that brought Fox's optical soundtracks to life.[7] Warner Brothers boasted that their Vitaphone films would bring big-name performers into small theaters that could not afford the best in live entertainment. At first, Warner Brothers had no plans to expand into the production of sound features. Although their musical shorts were successful, most industry professionals agreed that sound technology should be employed only for the reproduction of music, not dialogue.

In 1927, however, Warner Brothers embarked on a new kind of project: a feature film that would itself be silent but that would tie together a series of musical performances recorded for the Vitaphone system. Early advertisements for *The Jazz Singer*, which was to star George Jessel, emphasized the film's novel use of sound technology. After a contract dispute, Jessel was replaced by Al Jolson, one of Warner Brothers' most successful Vitaphone acts.[8] Although the dialogue in *The Jazz Singer* was to be conveyed exclusively by intertitles, Jolson famously charted a new course for motion picture production when he extemporized a few spoken lines after performing one of his sung numbers—a practice carried over from his theatrical experience. *The Jazz Singer* was followed by another highly successful Jolson vehicle, *The Singing Fool*, which premiered September 20, 1928.[9] By this point, the Big Five producers could no longer ignore the impending domination of sound technology. Warner Brothers had demonstrated that sound was more than a passing fad, and the industry responded by equipping all production studios—and eventually theaters—to handle sound technology.[10]

SOUND AND THE THEATER MUSICIAN

It is easy to guess the impact of sound technology on theater musicians: as theaters were wired, the musicians—no longer needed to accompany the films—would be dismissed. In the long run, this is exactly what happened. The specific course of events in the late 1920s and early 1930s, however, was more complicated.

In the early days of the sound era, the American Federation of Musicians (AFM) was not willing to allow tens of thousands of jobs to disappear without a fight. By the late 1920s, the film exhibition industry was the top employer of musicians; theater orchestras provided jobs for more players than all other orchestras combined. At the same time, organists were leaving church positions to take lucrative picture palace posts—an irrevocable career move, since many churches were unwilling to take these corrupted players back after the theaters were wired for sound.[11] By the summer of 1928, the AFM was fighting on all fronts to preserve jobs for its members. The union's biggest stand took place in Chicago at the end of the summer, when 750 musicians walked out after a failed contract negotiation. While this impressive show of force won headlines, all of the two hundred theaters affected were able to remain open; most turned to "mechanical devices" to provide music, while those that still relied entirely on live performers simply went without.[12] In the end, the efforts of the AFM were doomed, and the coming year saw evaporating jobs and dwindling salaries.[13]

The AFM failed to keep live music in the theaters, but—at least for a time—public opinion succeeded. Theater operators were much more concerned about the demands of their patrons than those of union bosses, and the influence of picture audiences can be seen in a wave of rehirings at the turn of the decade. Audiences enjoyed talking pictures, but they were dissatisfied with the impersonal character that wired theaters had assumed. They missed the human touch. After all, regular stage performers, like Paul Ash at the Oriental, had been the leading attraction at many picture palaces. These gracious hosts struck up a jovial repartee with the audience, cultivated a sense of community, and brought personality to a mass-produced program. Patrons still wanted to make personal connections in the picture theater, and they were not yet ready to give up that element of motion picture entertainment.

For this reason, the predictable trade press headlines about dismissals, which first appeared in the summer of 1928, were soon joined by headlines proclaiming the return of musicians to the theaters—and the cheapest way to satisfy audiences was to hire an organist.[14] Paramount Publix took the lead in reinstating organists and expanding the use of organ music in its theaters. Only months after fighting with the musicians' local in Dallas over the dismissal of organists in late 1929, Paramount Publix reversed its policy and installed fifteen Wurlitzers into theaters that were under construction, the plans for which had not originally included organs.[15] A few months later, Paramount further expanded its program of new organ installations. As *Variety* observed, "This is a reversal of some of Publix's last year's plans when new theatres were proposed to be not only minus organs but also stages. The trend of things has been such since that not only were stages ordered back, but remodifications [*sic*] also made provisions for the organists, heretofore an important integral factor in Publix theatres."[16] Paramount completed its revival of organ entertainment in 1931 with the establishment of a "special organ services department." This new branch of the Paramount Publix music department was dedicated to the development of novelties for Paramount organists. The slide solos created by the department—most of which featured community singing—were efficiently distributed to the growing force of Paramount organists across the country.[17]

Paramount Publix was not the only exhibition chain to return live music to its theaters after the advent of sound. All of the major exhibitors followed suit, although this musical renaissance was confined to large urban palaces; small-town and neighborhood houses usually pursued a sound-only policy for financial reasons and did not reinstate live musicians. Instead, the combination of talking pictures and the Great Depression put the vast majority of theater musicians permanently out of work.[18] A 1929 survey conducted by the *Herald* found that among exhibitors "the organ is considered an indispensable factor in building theatre patronage."[19] But why did exhibitors recommit to the substantial expense of performers and organ maintenance after their theaters had been wired for sound? Fortunately, a sophisticated trade press narrative exists to account for the shifting fortunes of live music in the picture theater.

As early as the summer of 1928, trade professionals were diagnosing the problem with all-sound programs: there was no "flesh" element.[20] The idea of a missing flesh element dominated the discussion of picture theater entertainment for the next two years.[21] This notion encompassed a diverse selection of attributes that were absent in the new, wired theaters: human connection, personalized entertainment, high-quality sound production, performer-patron interaction, musical variety, and a "tangible" quality that only live music could supply.[22] "In many cases," wrote Chicago organist Albert F. Brown, "the personal contact, the followers that many soloists have, is one of the most important factors in the success of the theatre."[23] Columnist W. S. Russell agreed: "This personal element can no more be eliminated from the theatre than the picture itself."[24] In addition, trade professionals agreed that an organist must be kept on hand in case the sound system failed.[25] Columnists had different ideas about what was missing, but they all agreed that talking pictures alone were not entirely satisfactory. This consensus produced two immediate outcomes. On the practical front, described above, exhibitors returned live performers to the theater—at least for a time. On the theoretical front, trade professionals discussed the role of live entertainment in motion picture exhibition and collectively imagined the future of the picture show.

The *Herald* was the only journal to publish long commentaries on this issue, and it quickly became the platform for the discussion of flesh in motion picture entertainment. This discussion centered primarily on the organist. If theaters were to retain a flesh element, the organist was the obvious choice: the organist drew only one salary but could create the effect of an entire orchestra. In addition to this, exhibitors had already installed organs at great expense. Trade commentators argued that it was foolish to let this investment go to waste when the cost of the upkeep and the organist was comparatively low.[26]

Without an exception *Herald* contributors were optimistic about the future of live entertainment. Brown published the first article on the subject, titled "Why Be ALARMED!," in July 1928.[27] Journalist A. Raymond Gallo followed this up the next month with "Organists! Do Not Fear Talkies."[28] Both writers were responding to the Vitaphone (Warner Brothers) and Movietone (Fox) reels that were becoming popular in houses across the country. Although Brown and Gallo understood that talking pictures had come to stay, they did not see them as a threat to organ entertainment. Instead, Brown and Gallo predicted that talking pictures would transform the role of the organist. "He is now a feature," wrote Brown, "a definite attraction, drawing people into the theater to the same extent that some of the other attractions do—even as talking pictures themselves do."[29] Brown's new breed of feature organist might present community singing or classical music, depending upon the tastes of the audience.

Brown and Gallo's predictions did come to pass, if only temporarily. In 1930, New York organist Louise M. Roesch published an account of her experience during the transition to talking films. Like many organists of the time, her initial reaction was one of fear: "I well remember the panic I felt as I watched the theatres in our city being wired for sound. Each one seeming to me like another nail in my musical coffin."[30] Before long, however, Roesch realized that the new technology was instead "a blessing in disguise."[31] Her long hours of film accompanying were replaced by three or four six-minute features per day, and her high-profile appearances garnered twice the salary. Roesch offered community singing, during which she used a public address system both to sing and to speak familiarly.[32] Entertainment such as this provided the flesh element in all of its dimensions. Indeed, Roesch was the postsound organist that optimistic commentators had envisioned: a featured artist who would remain secure in her position for many years to come. Unfortunately, positions such as hers were hard to come by. By 1933, the last optimistic headline had been printed, and industry professionals reluctantly concluded that the theater organ was all but a thing of the past.[33]

SING-ALONG FILMS IN THE SOUND ERA

In 1928 Albert F. Brown published a litany of reasons for which the organist could never be eliminated. Among them: "Then too, in community sings the mechanical organ solo is entirely out of the question for it would be merely a stiff routine and not flexible and adaptable enough to be successful."[34] As it turned out, however, community singing was to remain popular in theaters long after the organs had fallen silent. Throughout the 1930s, singing was directed not from the console but from the screen.

Sing-along films were not an innovation of the post-1927 sound era. Two series of silent sing-along films—Sing Them Again (1923–24) and Ko-Ko Song Car-Tunes (1924–27)—had already met with success. In terms of tone and repertoire, these series provided a model for the sing-along films of the sound era. Sing Them Again inspired later nostalgic films that strove to capture the spirit of the community singing movement. One example was The Harmony Club, a two-reel sound short released by Columbia in

January 1930. In it Geoffrey O'Hara, a well-known figure in the community singing movement, who had served under the Commission for Training Camp Activities and "built a reputation as an instructor of music and song leader at public gatherings," led the singing from a stage.[35] He was aided by the Victor Male Chorus, which rendered old-time numbers (unnamed in the trade press) in four-part harmony.[36]

The popularity of the 1924–27 Song Car-Tunes, on the other hand, led to a second animated series from the same studio: Max Fleischer's Screen Songs (1929–38).[37] These films were comical instead of sentimental, and they conveyed the urban aesthetic for which Fleischer was known.[38] Screen Songs was by far the most popular and well-documented sing-along series of the sound era, and it is also the only series from which a large number of films are still available.

In the 1930s, a third category of sing-along film arose as well. These were organ-replacement shorts: films that featured notable organists on the screen. Warner Brothers had already demonstrated in the 1920s that sound technology made it possible for a film to replace a musical act. Indeed, it was their original vision that sound films would bring high-end talent into every theater. As live organ solos were discontinued, film producers began to release organ solos for the screen—and, naturally enough, many of these films featured community singing, such as the Master Art Organlogues (1932–35).[39] Before considering the important Fleischer films themselves, therefore, we will survey the Organlogues, which document the disappearance of the organist from American picture palaces.

Although Master Art Products Inc. did not have a monopoly on the organ replacement short feature, their Organlogue series was the most important to feature community singing. These films—a few of which have survived—presented famous console artists performing popular numbers, often with the assistance of a celebrity vocalist, and they met with a great deal of critical acclaim. The organists who appeared in these films had all occupied important consoles in the 1920s, although most had fully transitioned to radio and film work by this time. Two of these organists had been affiliated with theaters examined earlier in this volume: Jesse Crawford, the New York Paramount's "Poet of the Organ," and Dick Leibert, who "had no difficulty in having the audience sing" at the Brooklyn Paramount.[40] (Leibert left the Brooklyn Paramount in 1932 to become chief organist at Radio City Music Hall, a position that he held for forty years.) While in their respective

Paramount theaters, Leibert had led community singing every week, while Crawford had never invited participation. The 1930s represented a different era in movie theater entertainment, however, and musicians everywhere were forced to modify their practices.

The screen action in these films generally consisted of two elements: lyrics and simple images. Scenic views that had "no connection, as a rule, with the words" served as background material for the text of each song, which was presented in synchronization with the organ music.[41] The songs were tied together by short pantomime scenes intended to illustrate the overall theme of the musical selections.[42] The organist or singer did not often appear on screen, although there were notable exceptions. These included the films *Four Star Broadcast*, in which a still photograph of each singer was "flashed on screen" ahead of his performance, and *America's Celebrated Young Organist Don Baker Playing the Mighty Organ of the Paramount Theatre, New York*, which, naturally enough, featured Don Baker onscreen throughout.[43] Instead, the audience was asked to focus entirely on the words.

A number of the Organlogue shorts replicated popular organ solos. Two of the shorts were stylized as travel solos, in which the organist conducted his patrons on a virtual tour. *Round the World in Song*, for example, took viewers on a musical trip from Broadway to France, Spain, Germany, Russia, Japan, Hawaii, and California. This film featured Don Wallace at the organ, Sid Gary and the High Hatters quartet on vocals, and Norman Brokenshire as narrator.[44] Another film, titled *Melody Tour*, conducted the audience on a journey through U.S. cities, including Chicago, Saint Louis, San Francisco, New Orleans, and New York. According to the review, this release stressed "the sentimental angle for those who come from these cities"—a tactic that no doubt helped the film to succeed locally.[45]

Many of these films were structured around simple thematic ideas, as had long been the practice of picture palace organists. In *Oriental Fantasy*, for example, Lew White and Charles Carlisle performed a program of thematically suitable ballads. The words were displayed against a backdrop of "beautiful girls in Oriental dances and some silhouettes of desert riders."[46] In another film, White teamed up with the Eton Boys for *What's in a Name*, which featured a selection of "pop songs named after girls."[47] Incidentally, White had not been associated with community singing during his picture palace career. He was featured at the New York Roxy, a theater famed for exclusive, highbrow entertainment.

Other films in the series relied on familiar community singing tactics—the sorts of stunts that had once been used by live theater organists everywhere. *Tongue Twisters* featured the classic gag in which an organist asked patrons to sing difficult lyrics set to familiar tunes. The film was primarily illustrated with static cartoon images that functioned exactly like slides; indeed, the animators even introduced motion by moving all or part of a given image while it was being filmed—a technique introduced by lantern slide pioneers in the previous century. This film is a distortion, however, of historical organ solo practice: tongue twisters, while often incorporated into the organ solo, never constituted an entire solo on their own. In *Tongue Twisters*, as in all of the films in this series, the organist remained silent, while the vocalist took on the master-of-ceremonies role and invited the audience to sing.[48] This represents a curious aspect to these films. They had originally been intended to feature the organist and replace the organ solo—hence the title Organlogues—but at the same time, they routinely diminished the role of the organist. The console artist, who had once been a complete entertainer in the picture palace, one who had spoken and joked via slide, and who had even sung, was now responsible only for the instrumental soundtrack. When the Organlogue series drew to a close in 1935, the era of the theater organist was truly over.[49]

While many different production companies experimented with sing-along films in the sound era, Fleischer was both the first to do so and the most successful. In addition to its role in the history of picture palace community singing, the Screen Song series is generally important to music historians, film historians, and scholars of popular culture. Today the series is best remembered for introducing Betty Boop to the American public. Even her name is derived from a Screen Song: she kept it after an appearance in the 1931 film *Betty Co-Ed*. The series also preserves filmed performances by some of the most important entertainers of the decade, including Rudy Vallée, Ethel Merman, Arthur Tracy, the Mills Brothers, Lillian Roth, the Boswell Sisters, Jimmy Dorsey, and dozens of other top performers. Over the course of its nine years in production, the Screen Song series became a remarkable repository of popular music documentation, and it deserves a great deal of further study.

Since the Fleischer brothers had been at the frontier of sound innovation for five years, it was natural that they should be the first to take advantage of sound technology in the production of sing-along films. Their position

This advertisement for Paramount Screen Songs appeared in a June 1929 issue of *Exhibitors Herald-World*. The accompanying text reads, "No short subject in sound during the current season leaped to more universal popularity than Paramount Screen Songs. Scores of theatres of all classes voluntarily wrote wires and letters of enthusiastic praise for these novelties. The words of the songs appear in unique and humorous style on the screen, with the celebrated 'bouncing ball' to keep time. With instrumental and vocal accompaniment. The entire audience joins in singing—and signifies its approval at the end by thunderous applause. Prove this for yourself!"

in the industry, however, had changed significantly since their early experiments. The Song Car-Tunes, launched in 1924, had originally been distributed by Red Seal, Fleischer's own company, but accumulating financial troubles meant that Red Seal had to be abandoned in 1926. The Fleischers' production company, Out of the Inkwell Films, was taken over by Alfred Weiss, who renamed it Inkwell Studios and negotiated a new distribution contract with Paramount.[50] Weiss soon declared bankruptcy and disappeared, and his brief tenure at the helm of Inkwell Studios produced some confusing late releases of Song Car-Tunes under his own name.[51] A 1929 reorganization created Fleischer Studios, and Paramount would continue to distribute all Fleischer products until it absorbed the studio in 1941. Between 1947 and 1951, Famous Studios—later renamed Paramount Cartoon Studios—created new animated Screen Songs for distribution by Paramount. These shorts all featured classic songs.

When the Screen Song series premiered in 1929, the role played by sing-along films in the picture program was as yet poorly defined. Organists still used sing-along films as community singing aids: in March 1929, for example, organist Arthur Gutow used the 1926 Song Car-Tune *East Side, West Side* in his solo at the Michigan Theatre in Detroit.[52] At the same time, Screen Songs were being presented elsewhere as stand-alone short films. During this period of transition, the film industry in general demonstrated uncertainty about the role of sound shorts. As late as November 1929, *Exhibitors Herald-World* still had two separate categories for sound short listings: Sound Act Releases and Short Features with Sound.[53] The former were intended to replace live acts on the bill, while the latter were short features (mostly comedies) with soundtracks. Critics might assign the Screen Songs to either category, depending on how they perceived the film to have been used. Both functions were built into the films themselves: the sing-along element and the appearance of celebrity performers positioned the Screen Songs as "sound acts," while the comical animation and rudimentary story lines indicated that the films were "short features." This confusion resonated for years as reviewers criticized the films for falling short in one category or the other.

Two *Film Daily* reviews illustrate the two attitudes that a contemporary observer might take toward a Screen Song. The first concerns *Old Black Joe* (1929), one of the earliest releases: "This subject is best when the cartoon master of ceremonies, so to speak, does his funny antics and drops when the words only appear on the screen."[54] In other words, *Old Black Joe* was an excellent short feature but a mediocre sound act. Another *Film Daily* reviewer relied on a different set of values when he assessed *That Old Gang of Mine* (1931). After describing the film, he observed, "They have a very fine quartette singing this, which makes it an entertaining number."[55] This reviewer considered the film to be first and foremost a sound act. Other commentators agreed that the primary function of these films was to replace stage acts in theaters that no longer employed live performers. "Paramount," observed one reviewer, "seemingly is the only company to appreciate the possible need of a musical interlude such as this for the houses which can neither afford an organist nor an orchestra."[56] On occasion, a Screen Song was exhibited in a manner that transcended all genres of motion picture entertainment. The Paramount Theatre in Los Angeles borrowed an idea from the silent era and staged a full-scale burlesque of Fleischer's famous bouncing ball as part of a stage presentation. After patrons had watched and presumably sung with one of the films earlier in the show, they witnessed a live reenactment of the sing-along stunt in which an actor in a white sailor suit was "jerked from word to word on a large screen by wires from the flies."[57]

Reviewers also differed in their opinions as to whether it was necessary for the audience to join in for a Screen Song to be a success. Many reviewers recommended the films for any type of theater—including, presumably, those in which the patrons did not sing. Evaluations such as "will provide several minutes of pleasant amusement for any class of folks," "can be chalked up as a bracer for any program," "will find gleeful acceptance anywhere," "will make any audience go in for chuckling on a wholesale scale," and "*For any bill*" abound in the trade press.[58] Although most reviewers concluded that the films were best suited to singing houses, contemporary accounts make it clear that the Fleischer shorts had a great deal to offer beyond the participatory experience. One *Variety* reviewer observed that the films could be entirely successful without participation: "[Urging the audience to sing is] an idea, though it doesn't seem necessary with these cartoons as either a house will sing or it won't and no amount of persuasion can entice them into it if they're not so inclined. Rather a shame to break up the antics of the animals here to insert the worded audience guide. . . . They didn't sing at this house but they liked it."[59] This reviewer concluded that the animation was entertaining enough to put the film over with any audience; he even suggested that the sing-along was an unwanted distraction. His assessment, however, was challenged by another *Variety* reviewer, who proclaimed that the cartoons were only of value in theaters that featured community singing: "Okay for nabe houses, where the gang can be coaxed to join."[60] A third *Variety* reviewer found that the cartoons had the power to inspire singing even in a "Broadway de luxer where the mob doesn't commonly join in."[61] He was supported in this observation by numerous colleagues, some of whom exhibited displeasure at the development. While a *Film Daily* reviewer was able to report neutrally that a Screen Song "had a Broadway audience humming out loud—which is quite a record in itself,"[62] another *Variety* reviewer was both surprised and, it seems, unimpressed when the audience at a different Broadway theater burst into song: "At the Rialto Thursday night, opening of 'Cocoanuts,' with a $3 premiere scale, many of the audience joined in the chorus without invitation. That was much funnier than the cartoon."[63] His specific mention of the occasion—a major film opening—and the high price of admission, combined with the dismissive final remark, make it clear that this reviewer did not smile upon community singing's invasion of the class house.

Fleischer picked up the new Screen Song series right where he had left off with the Song Car-Tunes, and the early films in the series echo their predecessors in terms of style and repertoire. Over the course of the Screen Songs series, however, Max Fleischer—influenced by his distributor, Paramount—significantly changed his approach to crafting the films. These changes concerned song repertoire, the method of song performance, and his treatment of the verse.

The Screen Songs, which ran until 1938, can be divided into three distinct periods based on form and content. Cartoons belonging to the first period (1929–32) did not feature a performer. These early cartoons had a basic format that was always recognizable. This description applies into 1932, even though the first cartoons featuring filmed performers had appeared by that time. First, the chorus of the song played during the opening title. This was followed by an introductory cartoon, which usually suited the subject matter of the song and might incorporate the chorus in the soundtrack, although most of the time the music consisted solely of quotes from other songs that were appropriate to the on-screen action. At the end of the cartoon, some form of oscillating motion transformed into the bouncing ball, the rest of the screen went black, and a voice invited the audience to sing along. The bouncing-ball portion of the sing-along consisted primarily of words, while motionless cartoon drawings provided humorous commentary on the bottom of the screen. The tempos for the sing-along were invariably very slow, as would be appropriate for a group of amateurs joining together in song. After a verse and chorus in this format, a second verse was provided beneath a full-screen animation, usually of a character playing the music on one or more instruments. A final chorus was provided in the characteristic mode of transforming words, which assumed the forms and actions of whatever they described. At the very end, a comic outro unified the subject matter and brought the story to a close.

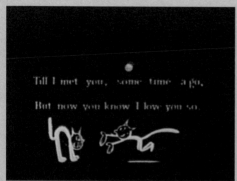

The first verse of "Oh, You Beautiful Doll," as
presented in the 1929 Screen Song of the same
name. The bouncing ball indicates the syllable
to be sung.

The second verse of "Oh, You Beautiful Doll."

In the middle period (1932–34), an on-screen performer led the singing. (This technique was pioneered in 1930 but did not become standard until nearly two years later.) The form of these cartoons was similar to those treated above, although they were less consistent. Sometimes segments were abandoned, such as the second verse with animation or the final transforming chorus, and eventually a closing cartoon replaced all of the singalong after the bouncing-ball portion. Every one of the films in this period featured individual singers or small vocal groups. The performer(s) occasionally provided a solo chorus before the audience was invited to join in, although this was not the norm. Verses, especially second verses, were generally excised in these middle cartoons, and some of the presentations were medleys of different popular choruses. The songs were often fairly recent, and in some cases closely associated with the person who appeared in the cartoon to sing them, such as Rudy Vallée in *Betty Co-Ed*.

In the final years (1935–38), an on-screen performer provided a nonparticipatory rendition of the song before the audience was invited to join in. These cartoons featured dance bands with unnamed vocal soloists instead of star singers with anonymous accompaniment, a reflection of changing tastes in music. Each Screen Song opened with a cartoon in the form of a series of news shorts, each a comical play on words or perceptions. Eventually one of the shorts introduced the band, which usually performed an instrumental chorus before the vocalist came on stage to sing a chorus. Tempos were set to suit the on-screen performers, not the in-house participants. The band leader then invited the audience to join in, and the band played a final chorus without the vocalist while the words and bouncing ball were superimposed on the scene. This was followed by a final cartoon short that brought the entire presentation to a satisfying close. While the cartoon portion of the early Screen Songs was usually based on the topic of the song, such was no longer the case in the final years. The central focus of the film as a whole, however, was always the song, and the treatment of the song determined the form of the cartoon.

In terms of repertoire, the early Screen Songs favored Tin Pan Alley classics from the first decade of the century. The trade press continued to have doubts about the entertainment value of old songs and remained skeptical about popular interest in musical nostalgia. When the Fleischers released *After the Ball* in 1929, for example, the *Variety* reviewer wrote, "Reminiscent to the oldtimers; what it means to the flaps questionable. But a nice little interlude, for that 'After the Ball' gurgle may still hold up."[64] What the reviewer fails to mention is that the short offered a startlingly modern ending to the song's well-worn sentimental narrative: a cartoon dog, having returned home drunk "after the ball," is booted down the stairs by his angry wife and carted away by the dog catcher.[65] Other films in the series similarly combined nostalgia and humor. A *Variety* reviewer, for example, credited the entertainment value of the 1934 film *This Little Piggie Went to Market* to "a gay spirit of satire" that pervaded the short, while countless observers noted that it was "the eccentricities of the drawing" that made these cartoons stand apart.[66] A *Motion Picture News* reviewer recommended the 1931 film *A Hot Time in the Old Town Tonight* "for any program and any audience, the harder-boiled, the better."[67] The featured number—a ragtime song written for the minstrel stage in 1896—was hardly up to date, but the reviewer concluded that the treatment it received at the hands of Max Fleischer effectively endeared it to the young, modern theatergoer. In this way, the Fleischers successfully appealed to the tastes and interests of a heterogenous audience.

Contemporary songs entered the repertoire in 1931 and dominated it from 1933. By 1934 the Screen Song repertoire had been transformed to feature brand-new numbers exclusively. However, we will never know what the film trade professionals thought about this move, for the trade press appears to have lost interest in Fleischer's sing-along films. No reviews of the final four years of Screen Songs were published in any national journal.

The change in repertoire was initiated by Paramount. In 1929, Paramount announced that it intended to introduce "prominent entertainment personalities" into the company's lineup of short subjects, and Fleischer began to feature live performers in his animated films in 1930.[68] Cartoon scholar Christopher Lehman describes the unique relationship that the Fleischer brothers had with the performing artists who appeared in their cartoons: "Studio employees visited jazz clubs in New York and chose the acts they wanted for the cartoons. If a musician agreed to star in and sing for a cartoon, Paramount Pictures would promise to release the film to the theater where he was scheduled to appear. Former Fleischer animator Myron Waldman remembered, 'The performers jumped at the chance to appear on screens all over—coverage they could not get before.'"[69] While Lehman's research does not focus on the sing-along cartoons, he suggests that the Fleischers would have treated their musicians for the Screen Song series the same as for any other.[70] Daniel Goldmark adds that Paramount permitted the Fleischers to use their newsreel recording facilities and "to film famous performers scheduled to appear in Paramount shorts and films."[71] This created remarkable opportunities for the Fleischers to capture performances by the best-known musicians of the day.

The on-screen appearance of a star performer could draw patrons to a theater in a region where that performer was popular, but it could also damage box office receipts if the performer was unknown. Trade press reviewers were concerned about regional inconsistencies in the popularity of certain Screen Song stars and warned theater managers to choose their films with care. For example, reviewers for two separate publications advised discretion in booking *I Ain't Got Nobody*, a 1932 film that featured the Mills Brothers, an African American vocal harmony group that had gained fame through radio broadcasts. Both agreed that the film was excellent, but they recommended that exhibitors tailor the film's promotion to local tastes. "Managers will be the best judges of what [the Mills Brothers] mean on the radio in various communities," advised the *Variety* reviewer, "and how much they're worth on the marquee and billing. Where strong, Mills boys should be given display type in ads."[72] "Whether or not the Mills Brothers of current radio popularity are well enough known in your community to be worth something as a name draw," agreed the *Film Daily* reviewer, "the fact remains that their work in this short ought to prove plenty satisfying to almost any audience."[73] It is easy to imagine that the reviewers' ambivalence stemmed from pervasive racism, but this does not seem to have been the case, for other radio personalities were given identical treatment. When Alice Joy appeared in the 1932 film *Shine On Harvest Moon*, for example, she was hesitantly recommended as a celebrity whose name might serve as "a fairly good draw in most sections."[74] And when Arthur Tracy, known to radio audiences as The Street Singer, appeared in the 1933 film *Romantic Melodies*, he was savaged as "one of those individuals who listens better in the abstract than he appears in likeness." The reviewer concluded that the film would prove a "liability" to his career and that Tracy would have been better served to resist the temptation of film and stage engagements.[75] The introduction of celebrity performers into the Screen Songs changed the way in which theaters used these films. Previously, exhibitors had been concerned only with the catchiness of the song and the cleverness of the animation. Now they had to consider the star power of the film's headliner.

Reviewers often suggested that the incorporation of celebrity song leaders enhanced the shorts with "added entertainment values," but they usually divided credit for a film's success between the singer, the clever animation, and the humorous gags.[76] One *Variety* reviewer, for example, concluded that the 1932 film *Let Me Call You Sweetheart*, starring Ethel Merman, was a "winner" due to the "combination of a personality and the humor of the animated drawings."[77] In an extreme case, a *Motion Picture News* reviewer considered the animated material in the 1930 film *Stein Song* to save the short from what he described as a number that "has been over-plugged by every jazz band in the country" and a performer—the generally beloved Rudy Vallée—whom he clearly regarded with some distaste: "Despite Rudy Valee and 'The Stein Song' this 'Bouncing Ball' cartoon of the Max Fleischer series is a laugh riot. The audience watching Fleischer's clever pen-and-ink characters burlesque Rudy's favorite just howled during the entire reel."[78] For this reviewer, Fleischer took a tired song that would have bored most audiences and put it over with his brilliant animation.

The introduction of an on-screen performer into the sing-along also transformed the audience experience. In the early Screen Songs, which incorporated either disembodied voices or none at all, patrons were invited to focus on their own participation. These films featured the act of community singing itself, and in most houses the enjoyment derived from participation was the primary object. Beginning with the 1931 Screen Songs, the focus was split: an on-screen celebrity encouraged participation, yet continued to perform throughout the sing-along while the text and bouncing ball occupied the bottom third of the screen. The split-focus format, in which live-action shots were integrated into animated sequences, was introduced to plug stage acts. Because celebrity performers preferred to sing numbers for which they were known, this new approach eventually necessitated a shift in repertoire. At first—perhaps out of concern for the audience's ability to join in—the songs were divided evenly between recent hits and established classics; a 1932 reviewer was still able to question "whether it's smart using nine-year-old songs for these items."[79] After 1933, however, the songs were always brand new. (Unlike the lasting hits used in earlier films, most of these have been forgotten today.) Patrons could not sing songs they did not know, and it therefore became necessary—not just entertaining—for the on-screen performer(s) to introduce the number first. The late Screen Songs presented the chorus twice before the audience joined in, once in instrumental form and once sung. The verses were usually omitted. Consequentially, these films heightened the focus on performance and formalized the division between presentation and participation.

The exclusion of verses was a gradual process. The producers of sing-along films used three techniques: sometimes they incorporated both verses, sometimes they repeated the first verse in place of the second verse, and sometimes they presented only the more tuneful refrain. In cartoons featuring old songs, Fleischer tended to incorporate one or both verses. In just a few cases, such as *After the Ball* and *Little Annie Rooney* (1931), only the refrain was used. These are some of the oldest songs to appear in the Screen Songs series, and Fleischer reduced them to their most memorable component. At the same time, Fleischer sometimes presented new songs complete with verses. The decision seems to have been made on a song-by-song basis.

It is not clear that audience participation was important in the presentation of a Screen Song. As already noted, reviewers did not always consider participation to be necessary for the success of a sing-along film. In addition, from time to time there are indications in the films themselves that participation was not required or perhaps not even advisable.[80] In the early cartoons, for example, recorded voices played an unusual role. The very first Screen Songs had included only a spoken introduction to the sing-along. In this respect, these cartoons emulated the organ-based community sing: the cartoon's spoken invitation to sing recalled the similar invitation delivered by an organist via a public address system. This was followed in both cases by an instrumental presentation of the song. Early in the run of the Screen Songs, however, singing voices began to be heard—first just on the final chorus, and finally in all portions of the sing-along. These voices were always anonymous and did not usually draw undue attention to themselves.

In some cases, however, the voices stood out from the cartoon's soundscape. In the bouncing-ball portion of *Put On Your Old Grey Bonnet* (1929), for example, Fleischer provided comic voices for the lines of the song spoken by Silas and Miranda. By casting characters and including a separate narrator, Fleischer dramatized the song and provided an unusual comic detail. This, in turn, presumably discouraged audience participation, for if the audience were singing full force, they could not appreciate the film's special effects. It seems as if Fleischer, at least in this short, was expecting the patrons to listen instead of to sing. This is only one of many examples in which either the voices or instrumentation were treated in such a way as to imply that they were to be listened to—that they were more than a backdrop for community singing. The second verse of "Oh, You Beautiful Doll," in another 1929 cartoon, for example, is provided with a flute obbligato played by an on-screen character. The audience did not need to stop singing in order to be amused by this, but they would have at least divided their attention between participation and appreciation.

There are additional reasons to question the role of audience participation during these films. Over the course of six to eleven minutes, each cartoon presented an increasingly complex participatory environment; each segment of the film furnished the audience with more and more visual and auditory stimulation. At the beginning, the first verse and chorus appeared with the bouncing ball against a simple background. Here, clearly, the focus was on participatory singing. A full-screen animation, however, typically accompanied the second verse. Could a participant have read the lyrics to the second verse (probably unfamiliar) at the bottom of the screen while also appreciating the animated antics? Additionally, this is the point where recorded voices regularly joined in if they were not already present. Did

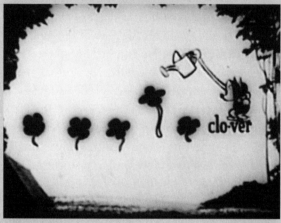

These three screen shots from the final chorus of "Put On Your Old Grey Bonnet" (from a 1929 film of the same name) illustrate the transforming words that were the hallmark of Fleischer sing-along cartoons.

some of the patrons stop to look and listen? Trade press accounts suggest that they did; a *Film Daily* reviewer cited earlier, for example, concluded that the 1931 film *That Old Gang Of Mine* was an "entertaining number" *because* it featured the voices of "a very fine quartette"—an element that patrons could not appreciate if they were busy drowning out the soundtrack.[81] Finally, the last chorus was always ornamented with transforming words—a subtle and clever effect that demands the viewer's attention even today. Were patrons tempted to drop out and enjoy the animation?

The second wave of Screen Songs began with the appearance of Rudy Vallée in the 1930 *Stein Song*. This innovation was "so successful ... in inducing audiences to follow the Bouncing Ball and sing with the characters on the screen" that it revolutionized the series, and a number of performing artists were immediately signed by Paramount to appear in one-reelers. Vallée himself committed to appear in several more Screen Songs, always performing a number that he had made famous.[82] But again we must ask, how much did people sing along? Would a fan of Rudy Vallée want to sing with him or listen to him? Often sing-along and audience performance blended effortlessly into one another, as when the Mills Brothers scatted a conclusion to two bouncing-ball choruses in *Dinah* (1933). The patron in this case transitioned instantly from noisy participant to silent listener. A more subtle case appeared in *Sleepy Time Down South* (1932), when the Boswell Sisters provided sophisticated vocal harmonies for a second chorus. Clearly they were performing, showing off their vocal prowess above and beyond that of the audience. At the same time, participation was still welcome. In *The Peanut Vendor* (1933), featuring Armida, the bouncing-ball sing-along was interrupted by a dance interlude at two different points; in a 1932 film, Irene Bordoni mimed dramatically to a second sing-along chorus of "Just a Gigolo." Both of these women expected to be watched and appreciated, not just sung with.

That border between sing-along and performance finally became impregnable in the late Screen Songs, starting with *I Wished on the Moon* in 1935 (this film followed a year-long gap in production). Overall, these shorts built in far less singing time than had the first Screen Songs. In fact, many of the prints that I obtained in 2009 from animation historian Jerry Beck have been edited to remove the performance and sing-along entirely, implying that they continued to be exhibited in theaters as animated shorts long after the community singing craze had died out. Unlike the middle-period cartoons, in which performance and sing-along blended into one another, these final cartoons made the role of the viewer clear at all times: first the band and singer performed, then the audience got to sing.

The Screen Song series transitioned from a focus on participation to a focus on spectatorship. Instead of providing old favorites that the audience wanted to *sing*, the final films provided star performers whom that audience wanted to *see*. A song was featured because it was in the performer's repertoire, it was appropriate for a contemporary dance ensemble, and it would benefit the band if turned into a popular hit. These films, however, represent more than shallow music-marketing strategy. The final Screen Songs also exhibit the decline of participatory music culture in the movie theater. After years of exposure to the new sound technology, audiences were finally being trained to sit quietly and to view films as passive consumers. The flesh element, which had been so prized at the turn of the decade, was almost entirely gone, and with it the opportunity to interact with theater performers. The final Screen Songs seem to retain the sing-along form only out of habit. The patrons, however, were not necessarily accustomed to joining in. Although sing-along films would continue to be produced for another decade, the heyday of picture palace community singing was well and truly over.

EPILOGUE

While community singing ceased to be a typical component of the movie-going experience in the 1930s, it never completely disappeared from mass media entertainment in particular or from American popular culture in general. Over time, however, the practice—at least in those forms directly descended from the picture palace sing-along—became increasingly associated with children and families. Children had been exposed to picture theater community singing since the mid-1920s, and in the 1930s exhibitors incorporated the practice into new strategies they developed to confront the dual challenges of sound technology and economic depression. Matinee clubs increased their focus on community singing just as it was beginning to disappear from the regular program, and producers began to explicitly target children with sing-along films. Perhaps the earliest example is Disney's *Minnie's Yoo-Hoo* (1930), which led Mickey Mouse Club members in singing their theme song. Many theaters continued to incorporate community singing into matinee programs well past 1950; today, it is not difficult to find a baby boomer who remembers participating in a Saturday afternoon sing-along at the movies.

Beginning in the early 1930s, community singing also shifted to other media. Sing-along radio programs flourished throughout the decade. These were usually sponsored by major brands that provided complimentary song pamphlets to customers, a gimmick that served both to increase store traffic and to further advertise their products. One early example was *Safeway Square*, which aired in Los Angeles in 1933. Listeners could pick up a complimentary song sheet at their local store, with the added incentive of a chance to win free groceries.[1] The most successful of these programs was Gillete's *Community Sing*, which ran from 1936 to 1937. While most radio sing-alongs were conducted by an emcee and chorus housed in a studio, *Community Sing* was actually a broadcast of a live sing-along that took place at the Repertory Theatre in Boston.[2] Gillette issued two editions of a songbook, each of which contained profiles of the program's star performers, photographs from a *Community Sing* broadcast, advertisements for Gillette razors, and the lyrics to over a hundred favorite old songs.[3] *Community Sing* was also the basis for a sing-along film of the same name— dismissed in *Variety* as "not very good"—that was released by Columbia in 1937.[4] Many of these radio programs were explicitly associated with the practice of picture palace community singing, which—despite the continued presence of sing-along films on motion picture bills—had already assumed a nostalgic value. One review described the 1936 New York–based *Come On, Let's Sing*, sponsored by Colgate-Palmolive-Peet, as an "attempt to transpose the oldtime mass vocalizing of the Wurlitzer-cinema days"— forgetting, perhaps, that the Wurlitzer and its associated entertainment practices had been ubiquitous only a few years before.[5] Many displaced theater organists took to the airwaves in this period, although they tended to offer recitals of light classics and popular songs instead of community singing.

The production of sing-along films continued into the 1940s. Columbia launched its Community Sing series of one-reel shorts in 1937 and continued production until 1949, while Warner Brothers issued a short-lived series entitled Let's Sing (1947–48). Both of these series featured nostalgic presentations of old songs selected to suit a theme. Warner Brothers offered miniature dramatizations of the lyrics, while Columbia recruited some of the most famous theater organists—including Don Baker, Dick Leibert, and Lew White—to provide accompaniment while a vocal ensemble led the singing. Max Fleischer abandoned commercial sing-along films after the conclusion of the Screen Songs series in 1938, but during World War II he employed his copyrighted bouncing ball for the benefit of American soldiers fighting overseas. These sing-along shorts, which were included in the Army-Navy Screen Magazine between 1943 and 1946, featured major stars leading the audience in live-action renditions of popular songs. Back home, the Screen Song series was resurrected by Famous Studios, the animation division that Paramount created after taking over Fleischer Studios in 1941. Famous began production in 1947 and carried on the tradition of old favorites framed by humorous animated antics. When Fleischer sued over Famous Studios' use of the Screen Songs name and his bouncing ball, the series was renamed Kartunes (a blatant reference to the first Fleischer sing-along series) and continued until 1953.

In the 1960s, community singing found its way yet again to the latest entertainment medium: television. NBC's *Sing Along with Mitch* (1961–64), hosted by recording industry executive Mitch Miller, catered to a segment of the American public that sought to retreat from the modern world by indulging in community singing as a nostalgic practice. Miller and his all-male chorus invited the home viewer to join in the singing of family-friendly songs from before the war. Lyrics were provided at the bottom of the screen, while the action might consist of costumed dramatizations, dancing, solo spots, or Miller's ebullient conducting. Miller attempted to resurrect his series in 1981 with a focus on repertoire that, by then, had become classic: he programmed some Beatles tunes for the pilot episode.[6] Community singing can also be found on LPs of the era, including a large number featuring "Mitch Miller and the Gang." Other releases included *Sing Along with the Mighty Wurlitzer* (1959), with Dick Scott at the organ, and *Community Sing: Follow the Bouncing Ball* (1960), which contained a selection of Norman Leyden's arrangements for Famous Studios performed by an orchestra and chorus. The text on the jackets of both LPs recalled the bygone days of picture palace sing-alongs.

Although nostalgic community singing programs aimed at adults enjoyed considerable popularity in the 1950s and 1960s, the vast majority of sing-along materials produced in the past half-century have been designed for children. When *The Mickey Mouse Club* became a television program in 1955, it featured a new sing-along club theme: the "Mickey Mouse March," composed by the show's host, Jimmie Dodd. For the most part, however, children's sing-alongs have thrived on the home entertainment media of VHS and DVD (and, more recently, streaming services). Examples include sing-along films by Disney, based either on their animated features or classic cartoon characters; sing-alongs based on the Dr. Seuss books and films; an Animaniacs sing-along based on the Warner Brothers series; Alvin and the Chipmunks sing-alongs; and sing-along segments of the Barney television series. The recent success of Disney's sing-along version of *Frozen* (2013) indicates that interest in this genre has not waned.[7] At the same time, film-based community singing has never completely disappeared from the world inhabited by adults. Sing-along screenings of *The Rocky Horror Picture Show*, *The Sound of Music*, and other films have attracted fanatic audiences for decades, while karaoke has maintained a base of enthusiastic participants since it came to the United States in the early 1990s.[8]

As the preceding summary suggests, there is much work to be done on the topic of sing-alongs in American culture throughout the twentieth century and into the present day. But this summary also reveals something about my own perspective: I see the present volume primarily as an investigation of the sing-along as a means of entertainment, expression, and community building. At the same time, of course, this is a study of early film exhibition practices, and I hope that interested parties will pursue the lines of inquiry I have laid out. Film scholars Malcolm Cook and Nicholas Sammond have already contributed to the literature on sing-along cartoons, but there is still much to be learned about community singing as an element of the motion picture program. Indeed, I hope that this volume invites as many questions as it answers. How frequently was community singing practiced in rural theaters, and what was it like? Was community singing also popular in theaters that attracted African American or immigrant clienteles? How did song repertoires vary geographically? It is likely that regional and local news sources house insight into nonmainstream exhibition practices that would greatly enrich our understanding of community singing in the picture house. At the same time, there is still more information to be mined from the national trade press. Additional case studies might be performed on urban theaters reviewed in *Variety* and the *Herald* or on organists who practiced community singing extensively yet were passed over for inclusion in this volume (for example, Rosa Rio, who led singing at the Brooklyn Fox and gazes at you from the cover). A rigorous study of song slides is sorely needed. Thomas J. Mathiesen has carefully cataloged the two collections held at the Embassy Theatre in Fort Wayne, Indiana, but other collections still require a great deal of labor to be properly organized and documented, and there is no comprehensive published source of information about the slides or slide makers. Finally, there is much to discover about community singing in theaters beyond the borders of the United States—not just in the United Kingdom, where Cook has documented the use of sing-along films, but in Latin America and continental Europe as well.[9]

My interests, however, lie in the direction of community singing as both a historical and living practice—whether it takes place in the movie theater or not. Sheryl Kaskowitz made an important contribution in 2013 with her study *God Bless America: The Surprising History of an Iconic Song*, which documents the community singing of Irving Berlin's 1939 hit at baseball games, political events, social gatherings, and memorials. Others have examined sing-along practices in the contemporary movie theater: film scholar Desirée J. Garcia dedicated a chapter of her 2014 monograph *The Migration of Musical Film: From Ethnic Margins to American Mainstream* to the present-day community singing of musical films. Additional volumes, such as the well-regarded *Chorus and Community*, have examined the impact of collective singing from an ethnographic perspective. At the same time, voices from beyond the fields of film studies, musicology, and ethnomusicology have much to teach us about community singing. Music educators such as Lee Higgins have written about current innovations and challenges in the field of community music from a practical perspective, while music therapists and cognition researchers have conducted clinical studies to determine the impact of contemporary group singing practices on health, affective engagement, relationship building, and worker productivity. Although I have not engaged directly with the data-driven scholarship on community singing, it might be fruitfully applied to this and other historical studies. Musicologist Kay Norton has begun this work with her 2006 volume, *Singing and Wellbeing: Ancient Wisdom, Modern Proof.* I would like to see more dialogue between the quantitative, qualitative, and historical approaches to community music studies—a subject, I hope, that remains relevant to American society for generations to come.

NOTES

INTRODUCTION

1. Naylor, *American Picture Palaces*, 40.

2. Hall, *Best Remaining Seats*, 30–35. For a detailed exploration of Rothafel's exhibition philosophy and techniques, see Ross Melnick's *American Showman*.

3. Doherty, "This Is Where," 147.

4. Melnick and Fuchs, *Cinema Treasures*, 70.

5. Carbine, "Finest outside the Loop," 243.

6. Maltby, "Sticks, Hicks and Flaps," 23.

7. Koszarski, *Evening's Entertainment*, 25–26.

8. Thomas H. Dickinson, "Movies Changing Life of the Nation," *New York Times*, July 1, 1923, xx1.

9. Koszarski, *Evening's Entertainment*, 28–29.

10. Ibid., 26.

11. Ibid., 34–35; Dickinson, "Movies Changing Life," xx1.

12. S. L. Rothapfel interview in *Green Book* magazine (1941), cited in Hall, *Best Remaining Seats*, 37.

13. Harold J. Lyon, "Variety Is Needed Element in Success of Solo Work," *Exhibitors Herald*, July 9, 1927, 17.

14. Edward Meikel, "Community Sings Passing? Not Yet, Says Organist," ibid., November 26, 1927, 25.

15. Breitenfeld, "Our Friend the Audience," 209.

16. Koszarski, *Evening's Entertainment*, 197.

17. Ibid., 195, 197.

18. Ibid., 197.

CHAPTER 1. A VISIT TO THE ORIENTAL

1. Gomery, "Coming of Sound," 181–83; Koszarski, *Evening's Entertainment*, 164–66.

2. Melnick, *American Showman*, 14.

3. Gomery, *Shared Pleasures*, 55.

4. Ibid., 41.

5. Merritt, "Nickelodeon Theater," 25–27.

6. Bowser, *Transformation of Cinema*, 121–23.

7. Gomery, *Shared Pleasures*, 44–45.

8. Ibid., 49–50.

9. Balaban, *Chicago Movie Palaces*, 45.

10. Gomery, *Shared Pleasures*, 53–54.

11. Koszarski, *Evening's Entertainment*, 89–90.

12. Ibid., 80–83.

13. Balio, *Grand Design*, 7.

14. Gomery, *Shared Pleasures*, 50–53.

15. A. Raymond Gallo, "Ash Policy Has Hold on Theatres," *Exhibitors Herald*, August 20, 1927, 33.

16. Levin, *Oriental Theatre*, 7.

17. Balaban, *Chicago Movie Palaces*, 97.

18. "The Nickelodeon," *Moving Picture World*, May 4, 1907, 140.

19. Gomery, *Shared Pleasures*, 48–49.

20. Doherty, "This Is Where," 145.

21. Hall, *Best Remaining Seats*, 16–17.

22. Carbine, "Finest outside the Loop," 242–44.

23. Semmes, *Regal Theater and Black Culture*, 4.

24. Ibid., 61

25. Levin, *Oriental Theatre*, 3–6.

26. Hall, *Best Remaining Seats*, 142.

27. Balaban, *Chicago Movie Palaces*, 62.

28. Naylor, *American Picture Palaces*, 103.

29. Levin, *Oriental Theatre*, 2–3.

30. Ibid., 3–6.

31. Loop, "Oriental (Chicago)," *Variety*, October 26, 1927, 26. "Loop" was this reviewer's trade press signature.

32. Levin, *Oriental Theatre*, 8–17.

33. Ibid., 13.

34. "—and Now It's Oriental," *Exhibitors Herald*, May 15, 1926, 53

35. Naylor, *American Picture Palaces*, 40.

36. Levin, *Oriental Theatre*, 2.

37. Ibid., 8–12.

38. Gomery, *Shared Pleasures*, 49.

39. Levin, *Oriental Theatre*, 19.

40. Ibid., 26.

41. Ibid., 19.

42. Ibid., 34.

43. "Magic of Partington's Flying Stages Explained," *Exhibitors Herald*, August 7, 1926, 14.

44. "New Policy Framed for McVickers," ibid., May 8, 1926, 114, 118.

45. Gomery, *Shared Pleasures*, 49, 53–54.

46. "Pre-Opening Old Master's Day of Days," *Exhibitors Herald*, May 15, 1926, 122.

47. Gomery, *Shared Pleasures*, 48.

48. Levin, *Oriental Theatre*, 25.

49. "Spring Fever," *Variety*, October 19, 1927, 29; "Spring Fever," *Film Daily*, October 23, 1927, 6; "Spring Fever," *Motion Picture News*, October 28, 1927, 1344.

50. Mae Tinee, "Gold Fans, Attention! Here's Your Photoplay," *Chicago Daily Tribune*, October 16, 1927, B1.

51. Loop, "Oriental (Chicago)," 26.

52. "Chi's New Policy Slow, $48,000; Ash Up $4,000, and Mindlin $4,750," *Variety*, October 26, 1927, 8.

53. Loop, "Oriental (Chicago)," 26.

54. Ibid., 26.

55. "Ukulele Vocalists, Spanish Dancers, in N.Y. Rialto Show," *Exhibitors Herald*, January 23, 1926, 49.

56. "Program Layouts," *Variety*, March 12, 1930, 21.

57. Hal, "Oriental (Chicago)," ibid., May 26, 1926, 24. "Hal" was this reviewer's trade press signature.

58. Loop, "Oriental (Chicago)," 26.

59. "Organ Solos: Henri Keates," *Exhibitors Herald*, October 22, 1927, 37.

60. "Chicago: Circa 1926," 15.

61. "Organ Solos: Albert F. Brown," *Exhibitors Herald and Moving Picture World*, January 18, 1928, 50.

62. Assorted programs (in American Theatre Organ Society Archives: Part 18—Organists: Keates, Henri).

63. "Paul Ash Triumphs," *Exhibitors Herald*, May 15, 1926, 123.

64. Balaban, *Continuous Performance*, 82.

65. "Paul Ash Triumphs," 123.

66. Balaban, *Continuous Performance*, 81–83.

67. Ibid., 84.

68. "$700 for Ash—3 Years," *Variety*, July 15, 1925, 38.

69. "Paul Ash Promoted," ibid., May 5, 1926, 48.

70. "McVickers (Chicago)," ibid., May 5, 1926, 24.

71. Ibid.

72. "Chicago," *Motion Picture News*, October 14, 1927, 1192.

73. Clark Fiers, "Theatre Organist and Showmanship," *Exhibitors Herald*, October 1, 1927, 17.

74. Gallo, "Ash Policy," 33–34.

75. "Chicago Oriental," *Exhibitors Herald*, October 29, 1927, 40.

76. "Advertisement," *Variety*, October 26, 1927, 18.

77. Loop, "Oriental (Chicago)," 26.

78. Hal, "Oriental (Chicago)," 24.

79. Loop, "Oriental (Chicago)," 26.

80. Balaban, *Continuous Performance*, 84.

81. Loop, "Oriental (Chicago)," 26.

82. Ibid.

83. "Chicago Oriental," 40.

84. Ibid.

85. "Organ Solos: Henry Keates," *Exhibitors Herald*, October 15, 1927, 58.

86. "Chicago Oriental," 40.

87. Loop, "Oriental (Chicago)," 26.

88. "Chicago Oriental," 40.

89. Ibid., 40.

CHAPTER 2. THE SING-ALONG TRADITION

1. Suisman, *Selling Sounds*, 79; Lethbridge, "History from below," 71.

2. Altman, *Silent Film Sound*, color plates.

3. Mooney, "All Join in the Chorus," 49.

4. Harry S. Marion, "Illustrated Songs," *Moving Picture World*, March 26, 1927, 331.

5. H. S. Sanderson, "The History of Song Slides," ibid., May 29, 1909, 716–17.

6. Marion, "Illustrated Songs," 331.

7. Ibid.

8. Mooney, "All Join in the Chorus," 51, 73.

9. Altman, *Silent Film Sound*, 190; "The Value of Lantern Slides as Advertisements for Sheet Music," *Moving Picture World*, May 15, 1909, 633.

10. Mooney, "All Join in the Chorus," 48.

11. "What Is a Nickelodeon?," *Moving Picture World*, October 1, 1910, 742.

12. "The Nickelodeon," ibid., May 4, 1907, 140.

13. Joseph Mendill Patterson, "The Nickelodeons," ibid., January 11, 1908, 21.

14. Altman, *Silent Film Sound*, 119–20.

15. Patterson, "Nickelodeons," 21; Merritt, "Nickelodeon Theater," 21–22.

16. Abel, "That Most American of Attractions," 149.

17. Ibid., 150.

18. Mooney, "All Join in the Chorus," 162.

19. Abel, "That Most American of Attractions," 143–44.

20. Altman, *Silent Film Sound*, 185.

21. Ibid., 182.

22. Abel, "That Most American of Attractions," 145–46.

23. Mooney, "All Join in the Chorus," 54, 68, 124, 183–84.

24. "Not a Song Hit on the Market," *Moving Picture World*, July 4, 1908, 6.

25. "The Picture Show Singer," ibid., December 12, 1908, 475; "Watch Your Illustrations," ibid., December 19, 1908, 499; "Moving Picture Shows Using Copied Lantern Slides," ibid., June 13, 1908, 514; "Anent Slide Copying," ibid., August 15, 1908, 124; "Illicit Trading in Song Slides," ibid., May 9, 1908, 419; "Among the Slide Makers," ibid., October 31, 1908, 337; Mooney, "All Join in the Chorus," 199, 202.

26. "Illustrated Song Men Want More Pay and Shorter Hours," *Moving Picture World*, May 23, 1908, 459; "Nickelodeon Employees Threaten to Strike in Chicago," ibid., September 19, 1908, 217.

27. Mooney, "All Join in the Chorus," 189–90; W. Stephen Bush, "Hints to Exhibitors," *Moving Picture World*, October 24, 1908, 317.

28. Mooney, "All Join in the Chorus," 244.

29. Altman, *Silent Film Sound*, 190; Mooney, "All Join in the Chorus," 226–27.

30. Altman, *Silent Film Sound*, 191.

31. Muri, "Silent Movies Weren't Silent," 19.

32. "State," *Variety*, February 9, 1927, 18.

33. "Inside Stuff on Music," ibid., October 7, 1925, 49; "Organ Solos: Preston Sellers," *Exhibitors Herald*, August 20, 1927, 41.

34. "The Old and the New," *Motion Picture News*, October 31, 1925, 2041; "A Moving Picture World Presentation," ibid., July 25, 1925, 427; "New Acts This Week," *Variety*, May 5, 1926, 22.

35. Abel, "Talking Shorts: 'Admission 5c,'" *Variety*, October 17, 1933, 19. "Abel" was this reviewer's trade press signature.

36. Campbell, "Higher Mission," 262–63.

37. K. Miller, *Segregating Sound*, 160.

38. Dykema, "Community Music Idea," 336.

39. Dykema, "Some Essential Passing-Tones," 184.

40. Ibid.

41. Gordon, "Community Music," 22.

42. Dykema, "Some Essential Passing-Tones," 184.

43. Dykema, "Community Music Idea," 339.

44. Bornschein, "Community Singing at Baltimore, MD," 436.

45. Campbell, "Higher Mission," 262.

46. Ibid., 259; Dykema, "Relation of School and Community Music," 86.

47. Lee, "Music Education and Rural Reform," 308–9.

48. Massey, "Organic Architecture and Direct Democracy," 594.

49. Ibid., 593.

50. Dykema, "Community Music Idea," 336.

51. Dykema, "Community Music and Spirit of Democracy," 376.

52. Freund, "Musical Alliance," 24.

53. Ibid.

54. Dykema, "Community Music Idea," 343.

55. Dykema, "Report of Committee," 103.

56. Unmarked article, *Baltimore Evening Sun*, February 10, 1915 (in Archives of the Peabody Institute: Record Group VII, Subgroup 1: Preparatory Department: Preparatory Scrapbook: Extension Courses, 1907–8; 1915–16).

57. Freund, " Musical Alliance," 24.

58. Katz, "Making America More Musical," 449.

59. Dykema, "More Life in the Open," MF8.

60. Miller, *Segregating Sound*, 85.

61. Birge, "Music Supervisors National Conference," 19.

62. "She Puts Life in Community Singers," *Baltimore Evening Sun*, May 1915 (in Archives of the Peabody Institute: Record Group VII, Subgroup 1: Preparatory Department: Preparatory Scrapbook: Extension Courses, 1907–8; 1915–16); Low, "Rural Life Betterment thru Music," 143.

63. Low, "Definition of Community Singing," 29.

64. "Explanatory Note," *18 Songs for Community Singing*.

65. Dykema, "Report of Committee," 103; Foy, "Brief Look," 26–27.

66. "Explanatory Note," *18 Songs for Community Singing*.

67. Converse, "Future of Music in America," 55.

68. Dykema, "Some Essential Passing-Tones," 185.

69. Bornschein, "How Baltimore Has Responded to the Community Music Idea," *Musical America*, August 25, 1917 (in Archives of the Peabody Institute: Record Group VII, Subgroup 1: Preparatory Department: Preparatory Clippings).

70. Massey, "Organic Architecture and Direct Democracy," 594.

71. Dykema, "Relation of School and Community Music," 85; "Community Singing in Baltimore," *Musical America*, May 22, 1915 (in Archives of the Peabody Institute: Record Group VII, Subgroup 1: Preparatory Department: Preparatory Scrapbook: Extension Courses, 1907–8; 1915–16).

72. May Garrettson Evans, letter to M. Alice Mackenzie, October 14, 1915 (in Archives of the Peabody Institute: Record Group VII, Subgroup 1: Preparatory Department: Preparatory Correspondence, 1903–17); "She Puts Life in Community Singers."

73. "Old Songs Sung at Peabody," *Baltimore Sun*, March 6, 1915 (in Archives of the Peabody Institute: Record Group VII, Subgroup 1: Preparatory Department: Preparatory Scrapbook: Extension Courses, 1907–8; 1915–16).

74. "Park Cornetist to Lead Singing," *Baltimore Evening Sun*, April 24, 1915; "All Like the Singing," *Baltimore Sun*, April 28, 1915; M. Alice Mackenzie, letter to Evans, October 18, 1915 (all in Archives of the Peabody Institute: Record Group VII, Subgroup 1: Preparatory Department: Preparatory Scrapbook: Extension Courses, 1907–8; 1915–16).

75. Chang, "Singing Program," 19–20.

76. Fosdick, "Commission on Training Camp Activities," 163–64; Bristow, *Making Men Moral*, 6.

77. Green, "Art for Life's Sake," 198.

78. Addams, *Spirit of Youth*, 102–3.

79. Woodrow Wilson, "Special Statement," preface to Fosdick and Allen, *Keeping Our Fighters Fit*.

80. Emery-Jones, "Community Development," 158.

81. Bristow, *Making Men Moral*, 1–2.

82. Fosdick, "War and Navy Departments Commissions," 131; Bristow, *Making Men Moral*, 98–112.

83. Fosdick, *Chronicle of a Generation*, 154.

84. Chang, "Singing Program," 20–21; Brundage, *Music in the Camps*, 26–27.

85. Fosdick and Allen, *Keeping Our Fighters Fit*, 67.

86. Ibid., 23–24.

87. *Commission on Training Camp Activities*, 21; Brown, *War Camp Community Service Calls*, 39–40.

88. I have published a case study in the *Journal of Historical Research in Music Education* under the title "Warren Kimsey and Community Singing at Camp Gordon, 1917–1918."

89. Brundage, *Music in the Camps*, 12; Chang, "Singing Program," 36–38.

90. "Community Singing Today at Piedmont and at Grant Park," *Atlanta Constitution*, July 14, 1918, B8.

91. Fosdick and Allen, *Keeping Our Fighters Fit*, 107–8; "Fine Program at the Auditorium Today," *Atlanta Constitution*, March 10, 1918.

92. "Atlanta Theatrical Benefits for Red Cross a Big Success," *Atlanta Constitution*, December 8, 1917; "Community Singing at Theaters," *Moving Picture World*, May 18, 1918, 1031.

93. "Slides," 26; "Mr. Hipple Makes a Suggestion," *Moving Picture World*, May 18, 1918, 992.

94. "Community Singing," *Atlanta Constitution*, July 28, 1918, B9.

95. Koch, "Cooperative Promotional Efforts," 269.

96. "Executives of Piano Manufacturers' Association Meet," *Music Trade Review*, January 27, 1917, 25.

97. Tremaine, *History of National Music Week*, 12.

98. "Editorial," *Music Trade Review*, February 24, 1917, 22.

99. Tremaine, *History of National Music Week*, 18.

100. "Wisconsin Association of Music Industries Meets," *Music Trade Review*, September 20, 1919, 23.

101. "Music Campaign in Arkansas Starts Auspiciously," ibid., October 9, 1920, 5.

102. "Great Music Week Celebration in Little Rock," ibid., November 27, 1920, 29.

103. Tremaine, *History of National Music Week*, 14.

104. Ibid., 19–20.

105. Carberry, "All Ready? Let's Go!," 25.

106. Harbin, *Parodology*, 5.

107. Davison, "Good Music for Community Singing," 455.

108. Hall, *Best Remaining Seats*, 17.

109. George W. Beynon, "Let's Sing!," *Moving Picture World*, August 3, 1918, 677.

110. "Latest News of Chicago," *Motography*, June 29, 1918, 1230.

111. "Half of Chicago's 400 Theatres Now Feature Community Singing," *Exhibitors Herald and Motography*, October 19, 1918, 27; DeBauche, "Reminiscences of the Past," 131.

112. Joseph A. McGuire, "Can Picture Shows Use Community Song?," *Moving Picture World*, March 24, 1917, 1965.

113. "Buffalo Manager Humanizes His Theatre and Finds New Patronage Is Drawn to His House," *Motion Picture News*, February 8, 1919, 862.

114. "Community Singing Scores Big Hit in Buffalo Neighborhood House," ibid., August 17, 1918, 1058.

115. "Community Singing Ruffner's Plan," *Motion Picture News*, December 29, 1917, 2.

116. "Community Singing Made Popular," *Moving Picture World*, September 7, 1918, 1405.

117. "Half of Chicago's 400 Theatres," 27.

118. "The Periscope," *Exhibitors Herald and Motography*, August 31, 1918, 35.

119. Klos, "Ted Meyn Story," 9.

120. Bettie Watford, "'Is Everything Alright?' You Bet for Earl Abel!," *Chuck Wagon*, 20, Archives of the American Theatre Organ Society: Part 18—Organists: Abel, Earl.

121. Annette Richardson, "Remember Earl Abel, THE ORGANIST?," *San Antonio* (May 1969), 17, ibid.

122. A. Raymond Gallo, "Novelties Are the Vogue," *Exhibitors Herald-World*,

March 16, 1929, 69. "The Saga of a Silent Theatre Organist," Archives of the American Theatre Organ Society: Part 18—Organists: Abel, Earl.

123. "Feature Song on Film," *Music Trade Review*, November 12, 1921, 47.

CHAPTER 3. PRACTICES AND TOOLS

1. Clark Fiers, "Playing the Organ Solo," *Exhibitors Herald*, February 19, 1927, 30; Harry L. Wagner, "Free Music Slides and Music Store Tie-Ups Are Available in Putting Over Organ Solos," ibid., January 23, 1926, 10.

2. "The Picture House Organist," *Variety*, October 6, 1928, 34.

3. Wagner, "Free Music Slides," 10.

4. "Eddie Peabody's First Granada Show Is Well Received; Finale Novel," *Exhibitors Herald*, March 13, 1926, 51; "Song Plug Hits American," ibid., September 25, 1926, 52.

5. "Norshore," *Variety*, September 8, 1926, 22; "State," ibid., February 23, 1927, 22; "Embassy, Chicago," ibid., November 17, 1931, 37; "Academy," ibid., March 23, 1927, 23; "Film House Reviews: State," ibid., May 25, 1927, 24.

6. W. S. Russell, "'Orchestral Vogue' Proves Big Bet," *Exhibitors Herald-World*, September 21, 1929, 58.

7. "Fox, Detroit," *Variety*, October 16, 1935, 23.

8. Tootell, "Cinema Aspect," 326–28.

9. Whitworth, *Cinema and Theatre Organ*, 104–5.

10. Ibid., 1–4.

11. "Double Console Organ Music Featured at Decatur Theatre," *Exhibitors Herald*, May 3, 1924, 98; "Installs Hydraulic Lift for the Organ," ibid., March 1, 1924, xxix.

12. For an example see "Organ Solos: Cornelius Maffie," ibid., April 30, 1927, 49.

13. Clark Fiers, "Light Values in Organ Solos," ibid., September 3, 1927, 17; Will Whitmore, "Brown Tells 'Herald' Readers How to Use Scrimaphone," ibid., August 6, 1927, 9.

14. Harry L. Wagner, "Solo Numbers That Scored with Chicago Audiences," ibid., June 12, 1926, 42.

15. King, *Framing the Cinema*, 9–10.

16. E. E. Bair, "Bair Makes Suggestion for Organists' Idea Exchange Column," *Exhibitors Herald*, October 3, 1925, 63; Presentation Acts, ibid., November 28, 1925, 56.

17. Hall, *Best Remaining Seats*, 184.

18. Wagner, "Free Music Slides," 10.

19. "Organ Solos: Don Isham," *Exhibitors Herald*, October 1, 1927, 41.

20. Wagner, "Free Music Slides," 10.

21. "Has Anybody Here Seen Kelly?," *Film Daily*, February 21, 1926, 8.

22. William R. Weaver, "Why Not Play the Organs?," *Exhibitors Herald*, July 24, 1926, 42.

23. Denzel Piercy, "PUBLICITY!—for the theatre ORGANIST," ibid., October 27, 1928, 32.

24. "Organ Solos: Henri A. Keates," *Exhibitors Herald and Moving Picture World*, June 23, 1928, 48.

25. Fiers, "Playing the Organ Solo," 23.

26. Malotte, "Stanleigh Malotte," 13.

27. Mathiesen, *Catalogue of Brenograph and Lantern Slides*, iv.

28. Lew White, "What Price Organists?," *Exhibitors Herald and Moving Picture World*, January 18, 1928, 29.

29. Muri, "Song Slides and Theatre Organists," 13.

30. American Theatre Organ Society Archives: Part 24—Glass Song Slides: GS 0179.

31. Muri, "Song Slides and Theatre Organists," 13.

32. Ibid.

33. American Theatre Organ Society Archives: Part 24—Glass Song Slides: GS 0246.

34. Ibid.: GS 0245.

35. "Organ Solos: Bill Meeder," *Exhibitors Herald-World*, April 26, 1930, 50; "Organ Solos: Henrietta Kamern," *Motion Picture Herald*, February 7, 1931, 61; "Organ Solos: William (Bill) Meeder," *Exhibitors Herald-World*, August 3, 1929, 65.

36. "The Picture House Organist," *Variety*, October 6, 1926, 34.

37. Ibid.

38. "Plans Community Song Fest," *Exhibitors Herald*, June 21, 1924, xxvi; Wagner, "Free Music Slides," 10.

39. "Music Men Seek Fair Treatment," *Exhibitors Herald*, February 4, 1928, 47.

40. Wagner, "Free Song Slides," 10.

41. "Slides Increase in Exhibitors Favor as Exploitation Force," *Exhibitors Herald*, February 12, 1927, 41.

42. "Presentation—One Year's Record," ibid., December 25, 1926, 81.

43. Wagner, "Free Song Slides," 10.

44. "Advertisement," *Exhibitors Herald-World*, June 8, 1929, 50; February 9, 1929, 58; March 9, 1929, 44.

45. "Inside Stuff," *Variety*, September 29, 1926, 51.

46. Wagner, "Free Music Slides," 10.

47. Wagner, "Solo Numbers That Scored," 41.

48. Jay M. Shreck, "What'll I Do Next?," *Exhibitors Herald*, September 3, 1927, 40.

49. American Theatre Organ Society Archives: Part 24—Glass Song Slides: GS 0232.

50. "Organ Solos: Henry B. Murtagh," *Exhibitors Herald*, April 30, 1927, 49.

51. "Screen Slide Plugging Out!," *Variety*, March 19, 1930, 65.

52. Muri, "Song Slides and Theatre Organists," 13.

53. "Talkers Stand 1st as Song Plug, Acts Now Rank Nearly Last; Radio 2d, With Reservation," *Variety*, November 27, 1929.

54. Dan Parker, "Preparing Organ Solos for the Circuit," *Motion Picture Herald*, February 13, 1932, 28.

55. Ed Dawson, "Publix Has Organist Service Station," ibid., March 28, 1931, 61.

56. American Theatre Organ Society Archives: Part 24—Glass Song Slides: GS 0200.

57. "Organ Solos: Don Williams," *Exhibitors Herald-World*, July 5, 1930, 51; "Organ Solos: Dougherty," *Motion Picture Herald*, March 28, 1931, 65; "Organ Solos: Arlo Hults," *Motion Picture Herald*, May 9, 1931, 50.

58. Shreck, "What'll I Do Next?," 40.

59. "Kahn's Varied Act Is Best in Months; All Supports Score High," *Exhibitors Herald*, December 25, 1925, 129.

60. Fox Theatre Historic Collections.

61. "Organ Solos: Earl and Elsie," *Exhibitors Herald*, August 9, 1930, 53.

62. American Theatre Organ Society Archives: Part 24—Glass Song Slides.

63. "Pennsylvanians End Successful 7-Week Chicago B. & K. Run," *Exhibitors Herald*, February 27, 1926, 62.

64. "Organ Solos: Henri A. Keates," ibid., April 2, 1927, 46.

65. American Theatre Organ Society Archives: Part 24—Glass Song Slides: Incomplete Sets.

66. Fox Theatre Historic Collections.

67. Loop, "Film House Reviews: Oriental (Chicago)," *Variety*, November 24, 1926, 23.

68. Ted Meyn, "The Vocal Lesson," *Exhibitors Herald*, January 22, 1927, 17.

69. "Organ Solos: Merle Clark and Elsie Thompson," *Motion Picture Herald*, September 19, 1931, 66.

70. Fox Theatre Historic Collections.

71. "Organ Solos: Harold Rieder," *Exhibitors Herald*, March 30, 1929, 55.

72. "Organ Solos: Edmund C. Fitch," ibid., June 25, 1927, 41.

73. "Organ Solos: Adolph Goebel," *Exhibitors Herald-World*, December 7, 1929, 60.

74. "Organ Solos: Melvin Peacock," *Exhibitors Herald*, April 14, 1928, 36.

75. "Organ Solos: Preston Sellers," ibid., July 16, 1927, 42; "Organ Solos: Bob West," *Exhibitors Herald-World*, September 14, 1929, 53.

76. "Organ Solos: Leo Weber," *Exhibitors Herald-World*, April 5, 1930, 51. Fox Theatre Historic Collections.

77. Fox Theatre Historic Collections.

78. American Theatre Organ Society Archives: Part 24—Glass Song Slides: GS 0069.

79. Meyn, "Vocal Lesson," 17.

80. Ibid.

81. Malotte, "Stanleigh Malotte," 13.

82. Albert F. Brown, "Field Open to Organist with Ideas," *Exhibitors Herald*, January 29, 1927, 33.

83. Edward Meikel, "Community Sings Passing? Not Yet, Says Organist," ibid., November 26, 1927, 25.

84. All of these practices are well represented in the Fox Theatre Historic Collections.

85. "Organ Solos: Art Thompson," *Exhibitors Herald-World*, April 26, 1930, 50.

86. For another version of the same solo, see: "Organ Solos: Herbie Koch," ibid., April 12, 1930, 67.

87. "Organ Solos: 'Guss' Farney," *Motion Picture Herald*, January 23, 1932, 69.

88. Ted Meyn, "Organist Appears on Screen in Ted Meyn's Latest 'Surprise Novelty' Titled 'Down and Out,'" *Exhibitors Herald*, February 19, 1927, 19.

89. Ted Crawford, "The Organ Solo As An Interlude," *Motion Picture Herald*, October 22, 1932, 10, 28.

90. Fiers, "Playing the Organ Solo," 30.

91. Ibid.

92. For the first mention of an organist speaking with the aid of a public address system, see "Organ Solos: Don Isham," *Exhibitors Herald*, August 6, 1927, 49. For another early account, see: "New Device Invented for Organists by Anthony," *Exhibitors Herald and Moving Picture World*, October 13, 1928, 45.

93. Crawford, "Organ Solo As An Interlude," 10, 28.

94. These included the pioneer Emil Velazco ("Novel Organ Solo Work," *Motion Picture News*, February 14, 1925, 693), "Symphonic" Hawley ("Organ Solos: Symphonic Hawley," *Exhibitors Herald*, March 19, 1927, 36), Elsie Thompson ("Organ Solos: Elsie Thompson," *Motion Picture Herald*, March 21, 1931, 62), and Milton Charles ("Stanley, J. C.," *Variety*, December 1, 1931, 33).

95. Dawson, "Publix Has Organist Service Station," 61.

96. "Ruth Brewer Flops; Western Quartette Hits," *Exhibitors Herald*, February 27, 1926, 60.

97. "Chicago *Oriental*," ibid., September 25, 1926, 53

98. "Well, Organists, What About It?," ibid., October 9, 1926, 54.

99. Ed Dawson, "Loew Organists Given Big Billing," *Motion Picture Herald*, October 10, 1931, 75.

100. "Organs and Courtesy," *Exhibitors Herald-World*, November 22, 1930, 18.

101. W. S. Russell, "Singing Popular with Audiences," ibid., September 13, 1930, 58, 61.

102. "Organ Solos: Dale Young," ibid., December 20, 1930, 57.

103. "Well, Organists, What About It?," 54.

104. W. J. Kress, "Untitled Letter," *Exhibitors Herald*, February 6, 1926, 64.

105. Russell, "Singing Popular with Audiences," 61.

106. Wagner, "Free Music Slides," 10.

107. "Feature Song on Film," *Music Trade Review*, November 12, 1921, 47.

108. Wagner, "Solo Numbers That Scored," 42.

109. Perhaps the first series of sing-along films was Imperial's *Animated Songs* (1914), but it is not likely that these films would have remained in circulation (Cook, "Sing Them Again.").

110. Cook, "Sing Them Again."

111. Cook, "Animating the Audience," 226.

112. Edwin Miles Fadman, "Music and Shorts," *Film Daily*, September 20, 1925, 35; "Advertisement," *Exhibitors Herald*, November 7, 1925, 47; "Organ Solos: Milton Charles," *Exhibitors Herald and Moving Picture World*, March 3, 1928, 45.

113. "'Close Harmony'—Sing Them Again Series—Educ'l," *Film Daily*, July 22, 1923, 5.

114. "'Sing Them Again' Authors Supplies Holiday List," *Exhibitors Herald*, January 17, 1925, 33; Cook, "Sing Them Again."

115. "Short Reel Releases June 1 to September 1, 1923," *Film Daily*, September 2, 1923, 23.

116. "'Close Harmony,'" 5.

117. "'Sing Them Again' Author Supplies Holiday List," 33.

118. Averill, *Four Parts, No Waiting*, 79–80.

119. "'Lest We Forget'—'Sing Them Again'—Educational," *Film Daily*, January 13, 1924, 9.

120. Ibid.

121. "'Heart Throbs'—Sing Them Again—Educational," ibid., April 13, 1924, 12.

122. "Nation-Wide Canvass of Exhibitors' Treatment of Short Subjects," ibid., May 11, 1924, 23.

123. "'Memories'—Sing Them Again Series—Educ'l," ibid., November 18, 1923, 12; "'Old Friends'—Sing Them Again Series—Educ'l," ibid., February 10, 1924, 8.

124. "Waiting for You," *Variety*, February 11, 1925, 31.

125. Cook, "Sing Them Again."

126. Ibid.

127. "Novelties," *Film Daily*, June 21, 1925, 26.

128. Goldmark, *Tunes for 'Toons*, 84.

129. Cook, "Animating the Audience," 222–23.

130. "Red Seal Growth Seen in Figures Furnished Showing Distribution," *Exhibitors Herald*, December 26, 1925, 47.

131. Pointer, *Max Fleischer's* Ko-Ko Song Car-Tunes, DVD; Jenkins, "The Saga of Koko," 9.

132. Jenkins, "The Saga of Koko," 7.

133. Fleischer, *Out of the Inkwell*, 36–37.

134. "Song Cartoons," *Film Daily*, January 20, 1924, 32.

135. "'Song Cartoons'—Charles K. Harris and Max Fleischer," ibid., March 9, 1924, 11.

136. Sammond, *Birth of an Industry*, 152.

137. Advertisement, *Exhibitors Herald*, February 27, 1926, 45.

138. "'Has Anybody Here Seen Kelly?'—Ko-Ko Song Cartune—Red Seal," *Film Daily*, February 21, 1926, 9.

139. "'Sweet Adeline'—Song-Car-Tune," ibid., July 11, 1926, 11.

140. "'The Children's Hour' at the Plaza Theatre," *New York Times*, December 26, 1926, x7; cited in Sammond, *Birth of an Industry*, 153.

141. "Ko-Ko Song Car-Tunes and Inkwell Get Radio Praise," *Exhibitors Trade Review*, August 22, 1925, 16.

142. "January, 1926, Designated 'Laugh Month'; Funds Are Being Raised to Aid Exhibitors," *Exhibitors Herald*, November 28, 1925, 54; "Red Seal Has Many For Laugh Month," *Motion Picture News*, December 19, 1925, 1016; "Laugh Month Releases Include 17 Red Seal Short Feature Films," *Exhibitors Herald*, December 25, 1925, 136.

143. Scores are known to exist for "My Bonnie Lies over the Ocean" (1925), "Has Anybody Here Seen Kelly" (1926), and "Tramp, Tramp, Tramp The Boys Are Marching" (1926); information courtesy Daniel Goldmark.

144. Goldmark, "Before Willie," 236–39.

145. Piano score to "My Bonnie Lies over the Ocean," courtesy Daniel Goldmark.

146. Goldmark, "Before Willie," 238.

147. Ibid., 237–38.

148. Fleischer, *Out of the Inkwell*, 37–38.

149. Ibid., 43–44.

150. "Organ Solos: Muth," *Exhibitors Herald*, March 26, 1927, 35.

151. "'Ta-Ra-Ra Boom Der E'—Ko-Ko Song Cartune—Red Seal," *Film Daily*, December 27, 1925, 8.

152. "Buck and Orchestra Head 'Dutch' Show, Partington Creation," *Exhibitors Herald*, April 17, 1926, 54.

153. "Car-Tune at Capitol," ibid., May 15, 1926, 50.

154. "Stages Short Feature with 40 People," ibid., October 31, 1925, 53.

155. "Stages Epilogue with 40 People for Song Car-Tune 'My Bonnie'," *Moving Picture World*, October 17, 1925, 574.

156. Piano score to "My Bonnie Lies over the Ocean," courtesy Daniel Goldmark.

157. "Stages Epilogue with 40 People," 574.

158. "Stages Short Feature with 40 People,"53.

159. "'Ko-Ko' a Presentation Knockout," *Moving Picture World*, May 8, 1926, 183; cited in Sammond, *Birth of an Industry*, 155–57.

CHAPTER 4. COMMUNITY SINGING AND THE "CLASS HOUSE"

1. Erdman, *Blue Vaudeville*, 2–3.

2. Butsch, *Making of American Audiences*, 115–16.

3. William R. Weaver, "Why Not Play the Organs?," *Exhibitors Herald*, July 24, 1926, 42.

4. William R. Weaver, "The Last Word About 'Community Singing,'" ibid., August 21, 1926, 45.

5. Albert F. Brown, "Field Open to Organist with Ideas," ibid., January 29, 1927, 33.

6. "Last Word on Community Singing," ibid., May 14, 1927, 39.

7. "Special Holiday Shows Dominant," ibid., December 25, 1926, 82.

8. Weaver, "Last Word about 'Community Singing,'" 45.

9. Albert F. Brown, "Interest in New Uses of Organ Grows," *Exhibitors Herald*, February 5, 1927, 36; "Last Word on Community Singing," 39–40.

10. "Theatre Men Weigh Organ Solo Values," *Exhibitors Herald*, April 23, 1927, 43.

11. "Last Word on Community Singing," 39.

12. Muri, "Song Slides and Theatre Organists," 13.

13. Weaver, "Why Not Play the Organs?," 42, 46.

14. Weaver, "Last Word about 'Community Singing,'" 45.

15. "Last Word on Community Singing," 39.

16. "Well, Organists, What About It?," *Exhibitors Herald*, October 19, 1926, 54.

17. J. Newton Yates, "After Community Singing—What?," ibid., October 1, 1927, 19; Walter Hirsch, "Steps in Preparing the Organ Solo for the Average House," ibid., August 6, 1927, 18.

18. "Chicago *Oriental*," ibid., July 24, 1926, 43.

19. "Last Word on Community Singing," 39.

20. "'Organ Club' Community Song Fest with Frills," *Exhibitors Herald*, August 28, 1926, 53.

21. "Chicago: Circa 1926," 15.

22. Ibid.

23. Edward Meikel, "Community Sings Passing? Not Yet, Says Organist," *Exhibitors Herald*, November 26, 1927, 25.

24. "Mr. Manager Watch Your Organ Solos," ibid., December 24, 1927.

25. Miller, Miller, and Karp, "Fourth Largest City in America," 23–25.

26. Ibid., 27.

27. Snyder-Grenier, *Brooklyn!*, 185–92.

28. Cinema Treasures, http://cinematreasures.org (accessed on September 29, 2012).

29. "Brooklyn Paramount Theatre," 10.

30. Naylor, *American Picture Palaces*, 136.

31. Ibid., 68–69.

32. Ibid., 136–38.

33. Bloom, *Brooklyn Sees Stars*, 21.

34. The New York City Chapter of the American Guild of Organists, www.nycago.org/Organs/Bkln/html/LIU-Paramount.html (accessed on April 8, 2017).

35. "Zez Confrey's Jazz Orchestra Tops Bill," *Exhibitors Herald*, February 27, 1926, 59.

36. Ruebel, "Ambassador (St. Louis)," *Variety*, October 20, 1926, 69. "Ruebel" was this reviewer's trade press signature.

37. Ibid., 69.

38. "Stuart Barrie, Organ Concert," ibid., November 10, 1926, 16.

39. Ibid., 16.

40. "Organ Solos: Stuart Barrie," *Exhibitors Herald-World*, October 25, 1930, 62.

41. "Organ Solos: Stuart Barrie and Elsie Thompson," ibid., November 22, 1930, 58.

42. Rush, "Rivoli (New York)," *Variety*, August 25, 1926, 24. "Rush" was this reviewer's trade press signature.

43. Hall, *Best Remaining Seats*, 53.

44. "Rivoli," *Variety*, February 17, 1926, 43.

45. Rush, "Rivoli (New York)," 24.

46. "Organ Solos: Henry B. Murtagh," *Exhibitors Herald*, May 14, 1927, 44; September 17, 1927, 42; April 30, 1927, 49; May 21, 1927, 40.

47. Ibid., May 21, 1927, 40.

48. Ibid., March 26, 1927, 35.

49. Loop, "Chicago (Chicago)," *Variety*, April 13, 1927, 25.

50. "New Paramount Jammed at Its Great Premiere," *Exhibitors Herald and Moving Picture World*, December 1, 1928, 46.

51. "Exclusive Showing Rights Offered," *Exhibitors Trade Review*, February 21, 1925, 64.

52. Ibid.

53. Muri, "Song Slides and Theatre Organists," 13.

54. "Organ Solos: Henry Murtagh," *Exhibitors Herald and Moving Picture World*, December 1, 1928, 53.

55. "Organ Solos: Bob West," *Exhibitors Herald-World*, May 11, 1929, 45.

56. Ibid., 45.

57. "Organ Solos: Henry Murtagh," ibid., January 19, 1929, 48.

58. "Organ Solos: Bob West," ibid., May 11, 1929, 45.

59. Nelson. B. Bell, "Behind the Screens," *Washington Post*, August 30, 1930, 8 (clipping from the collection of Thomas Miller).

60. "Organ Solos: Bob West," *Exhibitors Herald-World*, June 29, 1929, 158.

61. Bige, "B'klyn Paramount," *Variety*, January 15, 1930, 53. "Bige" was this reviewer's trade press signature.

62. "Organ Solos: Henry Murtagh," *Exhibitors Herald and Moving Picture World*, December 15, 1928, 50; "Organ Solos: Henry Murtagh," *Exhibitors Herald-World*, January 19, 1929, 48.

63. "Organ Solos: Henry Murtagh," *Exhibitors Herald-World*, February 2, 1929, 53.

64. Hall, *Best Remaining Seats*, 149.

65. "New Paramount Has Gala Opening; Monument to Film Trade and Zukor," *Variety*, November 24, 1926, 8.

66. "New York Paramount," 26.

67. Talbott, "Palace of Splendor," 8.

68. Ibid., 9.

69. "New York Paramount Has Gala Opening," 8.

70. Landon, *Jesse Crawford*, 3–16.

71. Ibid., 20–24.

72. "Chicago *Chicago*," *Exhibitors Herald*, September 4, 1926, 78.

73. "Chicago *Chicago*," ibid., September 11, 1926, 52.

74. "Chicago *Chicago*," ibid., October 23, 1926, 57.

75. Landon, *Jesse Crawford*, 71.

76. "The Lost Organist: An Epilogue to Jesse Crawford, Most Highly Paid Prologuist of the Boom," *New York Times*, April 9, 1939.

77. Ibid.

78. "Organist Giving Extra Song Plug to Screen's Film," *Variety*, August 29, 1928, 20.

79. Hall, *Best Remaining Seats*, 187.

80. "Chicago *McVickers*," *Exhibitors Herald*, June 5, 1926, 55.

81. "Chicago *McVickers*," ibid., September 4, 1926, 78; September 11, 1926, 52.

82. "Chicago *McVickers*," ibid., June 12, 1926, 88; September 11, 1926, 52; Landon, *Jesse Crawford*, 24.

83. "Jesse L. Crawford, 'Organs I Have Played,'" *Variety*, November 24, 1926, 21.

84. Ibid.

85. "Paramount (New York)," *Variety*, December 15, 1926, 20.

86. "Paramount (New York)," ibid., March 23, 1927, 23; February 16, 1927, 22.

87. "Paramount (New York)," ibid., April 27, 1927.

88. "Mrs. Jesse Crawford," ibid., March 9, 1927, 20.

89. "Paramount (New York)," ibid., April 20, 1927, 26.

90. New York City Chapter of the American Guild of Organists, "Paramount Theatre," www.nycago.org/Organs/NYC/html/ParamountTheatre.html (accessed March 2, 2013).

91. "Paramount (New York)," *Variety*, April 6, 1927, 26.

92. "Paramount (New York)," ibid., June 6, 1928, 39.

93. "Paramount," ibid., August 14, 1929, 41.

94. "Paramount," ibid., March 26, 1930, 52.

95. "Organ Solos: Don Isham," *Exhibitors Herald*, August 6, 1927, 49; "New Device Invented for Organists by Anthony," *Exhibitors Herald and Moving Picture World*, October 13, 1928, 45.

96. "Paramount, N.Y.," *Variety*, December 27, 1930, 45.

97. "Paramount (New York)," ibid., June 29, 1927, 28.

98. Skig, "Paramount (New York)," ibid., December 1, 1926, 13. "Skig" was this reviewer's trade press signature.

99. Sid, "Paramount (New York)," ibid., August 22, 1928, 44. "Sid" was this reviewer's trade press signature.

100. "Organ Solos: Henry B. Murtagh," *Exhibitors Herald-World*, March 16, 1929, 53; "Organ Solos: Preston Sellers," ibid., February 25, 1929, 46; "Organ Solos: Kenneth T. Wright," ibid., February 9, 1929, 62.

101. "Organ Solos: Jesse Crawford," ibid., November 9, 1929, 68.

102. Bige, "Film House Reviews: Paramount, B'klyn," *Variety*, November 12, 1930, 53.

103. "Organ Solos: Jesse Crawford," *Exhibitors Herald and Moving Picture World*, December 8, 1928, 56.

104. Sid, "Paramount (New York)," *Variety*, August 22, 1928, 44.

105. "Organ Solos: Jesse Crawford," *Exhibitors Herald-World*, January 12, 1929, 55.

106. "Organ Solos: Jesse Crawford," ibid., March 2, 1929, 47.

107. "Organ Solos: Jesse Crawford," ibid., February 9, 1929, 62.

CHAPTER 5. COMMUNITY SINGING AND LOCAL OUTREACH

1. Levin, *Oriental Theatre*, 3.

2. This case study was previously published in *American Music* under the title "Edward Meikel and Community Singing in a Neighborhood Picture Palace, 1925–1929."

3. Balaban, *Chicago Movie Palaces*, 40, 72.

4. Ibid., 80–81.

5. "Harding," *Variety*, October 21, 1925, 32.

6. "Chicago First Runs," *Exhibitors Herald*, October 24, 1925, 52.

7. "Harding," *Variety*, November 18, 1925, 40.

8. "Harding (Chicago)," ibid., August 18, 1926, 52.

9. "Good Will Show Proper for Xmas," *Exhibitors Herald*, December 17, 1927, 39.

10. "What Is the Value of Your Goodwill in the Community?," ibid., November 5, 1927, 46.

11. "Your Theatre a Community Asset," ibid., December 24, 1927, 12.

12. Hansen, *Babel and Babylon*, 100.

13. Cohen, "Encountering Mass Culture," 14–16.

14. Fones-Wolf, "Sound Comes to the Movies," 8.

15. Parot, "Racial Dilemma," 30.

16. "Harding Publicity Draws Thousands," *Exhibitors Herald*, October 31, 1925, 47.

17. Ibid.

18. Ibid.

19. "Cost Estimated at $2,000,000," ibid., October 31, 1925, 47.

20. "Old Fashioned Movies," *Variety*, March 4, 1925, 35.

21. "Harding," ibid., November 18, 1925, 40.

22. "Harding, Chicago," ibid., December 23, 1925, 33.

23. "'Madame Butterfly' Bit Hits; Paley's Violin Solo Pleases," *Exhibitors Herald*, April 3, 1926, 38.

24. Ibid.

25. "Harding," *Variety*, April 28, 1926, 53.

26. "The Organ Club," ibid., August 25, 1926, 25.

27. "Harding," ibid., November 9, 1927, 26.

28. "Harding," ibid., May 12, 1926, 20.

29. "Organ Club," 25.

30. "Harding," *Variety*, May 12, 1926, 20.

31. Edward Meikel, "Community Sings Passing? Not Yet, Says Organist," *Exhibitors Herald*, November 26, 1927, 25.

32. "Harding," *Variety*, August 18, 1926, 52.

33. Meikel, "Community Sings Passing?," 25.

34. "Organ Club," 25.

35. "Harding," *Variety*, November 9, 1927, 26.

36. Meikel, "Community Sings Passing?," 25.

37. "Organ Solos: Edward Meikels," *Exhibitors Herald*, May 21, 1927, 40. Meikel's name was often misspelled in the trade press, as it is here. Other common misspellings include Miekel and Mickels.

38. Meikel, "Community Sings Passing?," 25.

39. Ibid.

40. "Organ Solos: Edward Mickels," *Exhibitors Herald*, April 2, 1927, 46.

41. "Harding," *Variety*, August 18, 1926, 52.

42. "Organ Solos: Eddie Meikel," *Exhibitors Herald*, October 15, 1927, 58.

43. "Organ Solos: Henri Keates," *Exhibitors Herald-World*, June 7, 1930, 104; "Organ Solos: Preston Sellers," *Exhibitors Herald and Moving Picture World*, October 6, 1928, 52; "Organ Solos: Milton Charles," *Exhibitors Herald*, December 24, 1927, 69.

44. "Organ Solos: Eddie Meikel," *Exhibitors Herald*, October 15, 1927, 58.

45. "Organ Solos: Edward Meikel," ibid. July 2, 1927, 48.

46. "Organ Solos: Ed Meikel," ibid., January 21, 1928, 58.

47. "Organ Solos: Eddie Meikel," *Exhibitors Herald and Moving Picture World*, March 3, 1928, 45.

48. "Organ Solos: Edward Mickels," *Exhibitors Herald*, March 26, 1927, 35.

49. "Organ Solos: Bob West," ibid., August 13, 1927, 40.

50. "Organ Solos: Bill Meeder," *Exhibitors Herald-World*, April 5, 1930, 51; "Organ Solos: Russ Henderson," *Motion Picture Herald*, May 9, 1931, 50.

51. "Organ Solos: Edward Meikels," *Exhibitors Herald*, April 23, 1927, 48.

52. "Organ Solos: Edward Meikel," ibid., October 1, 1927, 41.

53. "Organ Solos: Fred Kinsley," *Exhibitors Herald-World*, April 12, 1930, 67.

54. "Organ Club," 25.

55. Walter Hirsch, "Four Arrangements of Organ Solos," *Exhibitors Herald*, September 3, 1927, 18.

56. Will Whitmore, "Brown Tells 'Herald' Readers How to Use Scrimaphone," ibid., August 6, 1927, 9.

57. "Organ Solos: Adolph Goebel," *Exhibitors Herald-World*, December 7, 1929, 60; "Organ Solos: Preston Sellers," *Exhibitors Herald-World*, September 20, 1930, 61.

58. "Organ Solos: Preston Sellers," *Exhibitors Herald-World*, September 20, 1930, 61.

59. "Harding," *Variety*, August 18, 1926, 52.

60. "Harding," ibid., November 9, 1927, 26.

61. "Organ Solos: Edward Meikel," *Exhibitors Herald*, August 27, 1927, 48.

62. "Organ Solos: Edward Meikel," ibid., July 30, 1927, 34.

63. "Organ Solos: Eddie Meikel," *Exhibitors Herald and Moving Picture World*, November 3, 1928, 48.

64. Nasaw, *Going Out*, 226.

65. "The Tribute an Organist Can Win," *Exhibitors Herald-World*, November 25, 1929, 64.

66. W. S. Russell, "Merchants Boost Meikel Organ Club: Join Paper in Big Tribute to 'Vet' Organist: The 5,000th Performance at the Harding in Chicago Is Occasion for Tieup," *Exhibitors Herald-World*, November 25, 1929, 55–56.

67. A. Raymond Gallo, "Organ Clubs Draw Good Patronage," *Exhibitors Herald and Moving Picture World*, June 2, 1928, 115.

68. Clark Fiers, "Playing the Organ Solo," *Exhibitors Herald*, February 19, 1927, 30.

69. Ibid.

70. Ibid.

71. "Organ Solos: Chauncey Haines," *Exhibitors Herald*, March 17, 1928, 38.

72. Gallo, "Organ Clubs Draw Good Patronage," 115.

73. "E. B. Davis Likes Our Slogan for His Organ Club," *Motion Picture News*, October 26, 1929, 40.

74. "Good Idea," 558.

75. Ibid., 557–58.

76. "Sunday Club Proves Draw at Oriental," *Exhibitors Herald*, August 20, 1927, 33.

77. Ibid., 34.

78. Klenotic, "Like Nickels in a Slot," 26–30.

79. Melnick, *American Showman*, 68–71.

80. "'Kiddie Klub' Sells Tickets," *Exhibitors Herald*, March 26, 1927, 37.

81. Hark, "Theater Man,'" 178–87.

82. Koszarski, *Evening's Entertainment*, 203–8.

83. "Children's Matinees, Builders of Good-Will in the Community," *Film Daily*, March 15, 1925, 16.

84. "Pathe's New Department," *Educational Screen*, October, 1925, 467.

85. "West Coast Co. Proud of Achievements," *Motion Picture News*, January 9, 1926, 163.

86. "'Kiddie Klub' Sells Tickets," 36–37.

87. "Morning Matinee Plan," *Motion Picture News*, July 18, 1925, 311.

88. Harold B. Franklin, "A Good-Will Creator," *Film Daily*, March 15, 1925, 16.

89. Ibid., 16, 50.

90. Lehman, *Colored Cartoon*, 37–38.

91. deCordova, "Ethnography and Exhibition," 97.

92. "Children's Matinees, Builders of Good-Will in the Community," 16. This source spells Harriet Hawley Locher's name as "Lorcher."

93. Headley, *Motion Picture Exhibition in Washington, D.C.*, 114.

94. Irene Juno, "Music for Children's Shows," *Exhibitors Herald*, March 19, 1927, 13.

95. Colman, "War Service," 12.

96. "Plan Pen League Convention Here," *Washington Post*, February 20, 1921, 10.

97. Headley, *Motion Picture Exhibition in Washington, D.C.*, 80.

98. Ibid., 114.

99. Ibid., 80–81.

100. deCordova, "Ethnography and Exhibition," 97; "Gives Free Shows for Children," *Motography*, January 12, 1918, 83–84.

101. "Children's Matinees, Builders of Good-Will in the Community," 16; Headley, *Motion Picture Exhibition in Washington, D.C.*, 114.

102. "Morning Matinee Plan," 311.

103. Ibid.

104. Ibid.

105. Headley, *Motion Picture Exhibition in Washington, D.C.*, 58.

106. "Morning Matinee Plan," 311.

107. Headley, *Motion Picture Exhibition in Washington, D.C.*, 246.

108. "Organ Arrangements," *Variety*, August 13, 1924, 36; "Organist as Feature Writer," *Variety*, November 19, 1924, 33.

109. Irene Juno, "Music in Public Schools a Boon to Theatres," *Exhibitors Herald*, May 14, 1927, 23.

110. Irene Juno, "Music for Children's Shows," ibid., March 19, 1927, 13.

111. Ibid., 51.

112. Ibid., 13, 50.

113. Ibid., 51.

114. "Recess for Songs Found Aid at Children's Matinees," *Motion Picture News*, December 11, 1926, 2272.

115. "How A Novel Idea Turns Junior Matinees into Gold Mines," ibid., March 23, 1929, 897.

116. Ibid.

117. Juno, "Music for Children's Shows," 13.

118. Ibid.

119. Ibid., 50.

120. Ed Dawson, "Competition Adds Organist Jobs," *Motion Picture Herald*, October 17, 1931, 67.

121. "Four Seattle Houses Now Equipped with Sound Devices," ibid., *Motion Picture News*, September 29, 1928, 986.

122. "West Coast to Open Two," ibid., February 25, 1928, 635.

123. "Showmanship at the Organ Consoles of Two Leading Theatres in Northwest," ibid., December 7, 1929, 60.

124. "Community Sing Popular Saturday Mat. Feature," ibid., January 28, 1927, 332.

125. "Organ Solos: Harold Daniels," *Exhibitors Herald and Moving Picture World*, April 28, 1928, 39.

126. Harold Daniels, "Inside Information," ibid., December 22, 1928, 1161.

127. "Organ Solos: Harold Daniels," 39.

128. Daniels, "Inside Information," 1161.

129. Balio, *Grand Design*, 13; Naylor, *American Picture Palaces*, 172.

130. "Kids—Kids—Kids," *Motion Picture News*, November 1, 1930, 125.

131. Paul W. Kunze, "Kiddie Business—And How!," ibid., October 11, 1930, 69.

132. Madaline Woods, "Finds Boosting Kid Patronage Is Good Way to Bring in Adults, Too," ibid., August 2, 1930, 53.

133. Ibid., 53, 72, 74.

134. "Ed. Stone, Organist of North Platte Fox, Gives Us Some Dope," ibid., November 1, 1930, 138.

135. Ibid.

136. Kunze, "Kiddie Business," 70.

137. Ibid., 69.

138. "Maxfield Another to Recognize Possibilities Of Organ," *Motion Picture News*, June 14, 1930, 94.

139. "Bob Soffer Tells Us How He Brings in Kid Business," ibid., August 23, 1930, 62.

140. "Organists' Part Time for W B Kid Matinees," *Variety*, May 27, 1931, 63.

141. "Suggested Programs for Saturday Kiddie Shows," *Motion Picture News*, October 4, 1930, 97.

142. "Push Group Singing Is Wesco Tip," ibid., November 22, 1930, 56.

143. "Plugging Kids' Programs with Special Shows," ibid., October 18, 1930, 55.

144. "Suggested Programs," 97, 99.

145. "Suggested Programs for Saturday Kiddie Shows," *Motion Picture News*, November 1, 1930, 105.

146. "Push Group Singing," 56; "Holidays Offer Flood of Kiddie Show Material," *Motion Picture News*, December 27, 1930, 28.

147. "Plugging Kids' Programs," 55.

148. Ibid., 56.

149. Ibid.

150. Ibid., 94.

151. "Push Group Singing," 57; "Suggested Programs for Saturday Kiddie Shows," *Motion Picture News*, October 4, 1930, 99.

152. "Push Group Singing," 57.

153. "Holidays Offer Flood," 28.

154. Rita McGoldrick, "Educational Subjects," *Film Daily*, May 11, 1924, 13.

155. "Criticism against Hays Is Denounced by Groups," ibid., April 8, 1930, 4; "Rita McGoldrick Discusses Films In Midwest City," *Motion Picture Herald*, March 5, 1932, 35.

156. Rita C. McGoldrick, "Your Public," *Motion Picture Herald*, May 2, 1931, 70.

157. Rita C. McGoldrick, "The Junior Show," ibid., January 2, 1932, 53.

158. Rita C. McGoldrick, "Your Public," ibid., January 30, 1932, 50.

159. Rita C. McGoldrick, "Your Public," ibid., July 18, 1931, 56.

160. Rita C. McGoldrick, "Your Public," ibid., April 25, 1931, 80; August 15, 1931, 22; March 26, 1932, 32.

161. McGoldrick, "Your Public," April 25, 1931, 80; Rita C. McGoldrick, "Your Public," ibid., June 13, 1931, 47.

162. "40 Theatres to Start Junior Show," ibid., May 14, 1932, 49.

163. Rita C. McGoldrick, "The Junior Show," ibid., October 3, 1931, 21–22.

CHAPTER 6. THE ADVENT OF SOUND

1. Koszarski, *Evening's Entertainment*, 90.

2. Crafton, *Talkies*, 111.

3. Ibid., 63–66.

4. Fleischer, *Out of the Inkwell*, 43.

5. Gomery, *Shared Pleasures*, 220; Crafton, *Talkies*, 98.

6. "Five Companies in Pool Seek Deal for Use of Photophone," *Film Daily*, March 4, 1927, 1–2.

7. Crafton, *Talkies*, 104.

8. Crafton, *Talkies*, 101–9.

9. Gomery, *Shared Pleasures*, 219.

10. Ibid., 221.

11. "Moral?," *Variety*, December 11, 1929, 74.

12. "Musicians Open Key Fight on Talkers in Chi; 750 Walk Out; Mgrs. Serve Injunction on Union," *Variety*, September 5, 1928, 16; "Chi Musicians' Walk-Out Strike Settled on Compromise Basis; Minimum of Four Met in Pit," *Variety*, September 12, 1928, 11.

13. Gomery, *Shared Pleasures*, 225.

14. For example from *Variety* "18 N.Y. RKO's Emergency Organists Get Notice," May 22, 1929, 63; "Salary Cuts for Organists in Chi," July 24, 1929, 71; "All Organists Out," December 3, 1930, 65; "18 Organists Dismissed by B&K," April 22, 1931; "Warner Gives Notice to 7 N.J. Organists," May 6, 1931, 66; "Organ Again at Strand," April 2, 1930, 73; "Pit Orchestras Back," April 23, 1930, 72; "Restoring Orchestras," May 14, 1930, 73. "Milwaukee Organists Back at Consoles," *Exhibitors Herald-World*, December 20, 1930, 52; "Organ Returning In Penna. Cities," *Motion Picture Herald*, March 21, 1931, 59.

15. "Publix Having Worries over Texas Organist," *Variety*, November 13, 1929, 42; "Par Orders 15 Wurlitzer Organs; 1st Plans Did Not Call for Them," *Variety*, May 21, 1930, 17.

16. "Publix Orders Organs Back in New Houses," ibid., August 13, 1930, 27.

17. Ed Dawson, "Publix Has Organist Service Station," *Motion Picture Herald*, March 28, 1931, 61.

18. Stanleigh Malotte, "Organist Makes Sound His Ally," *Exhibitors Herald-World*, December 21, 1929, 23.

19. W. S. Russell, "Organist Is Secure in His Position," ibid., June 8, 1929, 48.

20. Albert F. Brown, "Why Be ALARMED!," *Exhibitors Herald*, July 7, 1928, 29–30.

21. "How Portland Views the 'Flesh' Show Idea," *Variety*, August 27, 1930, 4.

22. Eddie Dunstedter, "It's the Personal Touch That the Audience Always Demands," *Exhibitors Herald-World*, March 16, 1929, 67.

23. Brown, "Why Be ALARMED!," 29–30.

24. Russell, "Demand for Organs Optimistic Note," *Exhibitors Herald-World*, May 24, 1930, 48.

25. "Feeling Organists' Return Gives Some 'Flesh' Semblance to Bills," *Variety*, May 14, 1930, 23.

26. Lloyd Hill (Wild Oscar), "Organists Returning As Theatres Reopen And Protect Investments," *Motion Picture Herald*, October 1, 1932, 78.

27. Brown, "Why Be ALARMED!," 29–30.

28. A. Raymond Gallo, "Organists! Do Not Fear Talkies," *Exhibitors Herald*, August 25, 1928, 44.

29. Brown, "Why Be ALARMED!," 29.

30. Louise M. Roesch, "Talkies, Blessing in Disguise," *Exhibitors Herald-World*, July 5, 1930, 48.

31. Ibid., 49.

32. Ibid.

33. "Revival of Interest in Organists by Picture Theatres Noticeable," *Variety*, August 1, 1933, 45.

34. Brown, "Why Be ALARMED!," 30.

35. "Short Subjects: 'The Harmony Club," *Film Daily*, January 12, 1930, 13.

36. The names of the performers are incorrect and absent, respectively, in the *Motion Picture News* review ("Shorts for the Week Show a Wide Range in Entertainment: 'The Harmony Club,'" January 4, 1930, 35).

37. Twelve Screen Songs can be viewed at the following address: www.morgan-ellis.net/films. Other films are also available online.

38. Jake Austen, "Hidey Hidey Hidey Ho," 61.

39. Two Organlogue films can be viewed at the following address: http://www.morgan-ellis.net/films.

40. "Organ Solos: Jesse Crawford," *Motion Picture Herald*, March 7, 1931, 73; "Organ Solos: Dick Leibert," ibid., September 24, 1932, 73.

41. "Talking Shorts: Melody Man," *Variety*, July 11, 1933, 15.

42. "Reviewing the Short Subjects: 'Organlogue-ing the Hits,'" *Film Daily*, December 22, 1933, 15.

43. "Talking Shorts: 'Four Star Broadcast,'" *Variety*, April 18, 1933, 21; "Talking Shorts: Four-Star Organlog," ibid., March 7, 1933, 14; Thomas J. Mathiesen, "Comments on your book," email to author, September 21, 2016.

44. "Talking Shorts: Round the World in Song," *Variety*, January 3, 1933, 19.

45. "Short Subject Reviews: 'Melody Tour,'" *Film Index*, November 10, 1933, 12.

46. "Short Subject Reviews: 'Oriental Fantasy,'" *Film Daily*, July 27, 1933, 6.

47. "Talking Shorts: What's in a Name," *Variety*, October 30, 1934, 16.

48. "Talking Shorts: 'Tongue Twisters,'" ibid., May 9, 1933, 14.

49. Some of the largest theaters, such as the New York Paramount, kept an organist on the payroll until they were permanently shuttered and demolished in the second half of the century. This was the exception, however, and even those organists who kept their jobs were in most cases only required to perform on special occasions.

50. Fleischer, *Out of the Inkwell*, 46–47.

51. In 1929, Weiss issued a handful of shorts under the Biophone label. Some were clearly Fleischer products (for example: "Short Subjects: 'Down in Jungle Town,'" *Film Daily*, October 20, 1929, 10; "Opinions on Pictures: 'My Old Kentucky Home,'" *Motion Picture News*, October 5, 1929, 1264), while others seem to have been knock-offs (for example: "Opinions on Pictures: 'Summer Harmonies,'" *Motion Picture News*, October 5, 1929, 1264).

52. "Organ Solos: Arthur Gutow," *Exhibitors Herald-World*, March 30, 1929, 55.

53. "Sound Act Releases," ibid., November 16, 1929, 54; "Short Features With Sound," ibid., November 16, 1929, 54.

54. "Short Subject Reviews: 'Old Black Joe,'" *Film Daily*, March 10, 1929, 11.

55. "Review of Sound Shorts: 'That Old Gang of Mine,'" ibid., July 5, 1931, 11.

56. Shan, "Talking Shorts: 'Somebody Stole My Gal,'" *Variety*, April 29, 1931, 12. "Shan" was this reviewer's trade press signature.

57. "Paramount, L.A.," ibid., August 11, 1931, 42.

58. "Short Subjects: 'Afraid to Go Home in the Dark,'" *Film Daily*, January 26, 1930, 9; "Sound Shorts: 'The Stein Song,'" ibid., August 3, 1930, 9; "Reviews of Sound Shorts: 'When the Red, Red Robin Comes Bob, Bob, Bobbing Along,'" ibid., March 13, 1932; "Opinions on Pictures: 'Yes, We Have No Bananas,'" *Motion Picture News*, May 24, 1930, 119; "Short Subjects: 'Glow Worm,'" ibid., July 19, 1930, 50.

59. Sid, "Talking Shorts: 'Jungle Festival,'" *Variety*, October 13, 1931, 14.

60. Kauf, "Talking Shorts: 'Please Go 'Way & Let Me Sleep,'" ibid., August 4, 1931, 18. "Kauf" was this reviewer's trade press signature.

61. Rush, "Talking Shorts: 'Let Me Call You Sweetheart,'" ibid., July 26, 1932, 17.

62. "Short Subjects: 'Screen Songs,'" *Film Daily*, May 19, 1929, 9.

63. Sime, "Talking Shorts: 'Daisy Bell,'" *Variety*, May 29, 1929, 14. "Sime" was this reviewer's trade press signature.

64. Sime, "Talking Shorts: 'After the Ball,'" ibid., October 16, 1929, 17. See also Kauf, "Talking Shorts: 'Russian Lullaby,'" ibid., February 23, 1932, 13.

65. Morgan-Ellis, "Nostalgia, Sentiment, and Cynicism," 7.

66. Land, "Talking Shorts: 'This Little Piggie Went to Market,'" *Variety*, June 12, 1934, 19 ("Land" was this reviewer's trade press signature); Sid, "Talking Shorts: 'Ye Olde Melodies,'" ibid., May 8, 1929, 20.

67. "Short Subjects: 'A Hot Time in the Old Town Tonight,'" *Motion Picture News*, July 5, 1930, 42b.

68. "Paramount Offering 80 Sound Shorts," *Exhibitors Herald-World*, June 15, 1929, 126.

69. Lehman, *Colored Cartoon*, 30.

70. Lehman, "Question for Jake Austen," email to author, December 13, 2010.

71. Goldmark, *Tunes for 'Toons*, 84–85.

72. Land, "Talking Shorts: 'I Ain't Got Nobody,'" *Variety*, June 7, 1932, 20.

73. "Reviews of Short Subjects: 'I Ain't Got Nobody,'" *Film Daily*, June 11, 1932, 17.

74. "Reviews of Short Subjects: Shine On Harvest Moon," ibid., June 25, 1932, 4.

75. Abel, "Talking Shorts: 'Romantic Melodies,'" ibid., July 18, 1933, 36.

76. "Sound Shorts: 'Russian Lullaby,'" *Film Daily*, December 27, 1931, 11.

77. Rush, "Talking Shorts: 'Let Me Call You Sweetheart,'" *Variety*, July 26, 1932, 17.

78. "Opinions on Pictures: 'Stein Song,'" *Motion Picture News*, September 6, 1930, 97.

79. Kauf, "Talking Shorts: 'Russian Lullaby,'" *Variety*, February 23, 1932, 13.

80. I acquired copies of the extant Screen Songs from animation historian Jerry Beck in 2008. The remainder of my comments are based on these films.

81. "Reviews of Sound Shorts: 'That Old Gang of Mine,'" *Film Daily*, July 5, 1931, 11.

82. "New Ideas Injected in Paramount Shorts; Big Names and Novelties Bring Favorable Reactions," ibid., November 29, 1931, 8.

EPILOGUE

1. Stan, "Radio Reports: Safeway Square," *Variety*, January 10, 1933, 36. "Stan" was this reviewer's trade press signature.

2. Fox, "Radio Reports: 'Community Sing,'" ibid., July 8, 1936, 32 ("Fox" was this reviewer's trade press signature); Charles M. Pritzker, "Advertiser Must Use Showmanship Tactics," ibid., January 6, 1937, 140.

3. See *Official Song Book of Gillette Original Community Sing*, vol. 1 (1936) and *Gillette's Original "Community Sing" Over CBS Every Sunday Evening: Second Official Song Book* (1937).

4. Shan, "Talking Shorts: 'Community Sing,'" *Variety*, February 17, 1937, 14.

5. Edga, "Radio Reports: 'Come on, Let's Sing,'" ibid., July 8, 1936, 32. "Edga" was this reviewer's trade press signature.

6. "Sing Along With Mitch: What We Gave 'Em Before We'll Give 'Em Once Again,'" ibid., December 31, 1980, 34.

258 NOTES TO EPILOGUE

7. Cook, "Sing Them Again."

8. Wolff, "Theater," 132; Drew, "'Scenes' Dimensions of Karaoke," 66–67.

9. See this tantalizing press release about Columbia's *Community Sing* shorts being "reshot in Spanish for Latin American release": "Plenty of Film Shooting in N.Y." *Variety*, July 22, 1942, 5. See also these references to Screen Songs "breaking through the barrier of language" in the foreign market: "Opinions on Pictures: 'My Old Kentucky Home,'" *Motion Picture News*, October 5, 1929, 1264; "The Latest Sound Shorts Reviewed: 'The Glow Worm,'" *Film Daily*, September 21, 1930, 25.

BIBLIOGRAPHY

PERIODICALS

Trade Journals

Balaban and Katz Magazine
Educational Screen
Exhibitors Herald
Exhibitors Herald and Motography
Exhibitors Herald and Moving Picture World
Exhibitors Herald-World
Exhibitors Trade Review
Film Daily
Motion Picture Herald
Motion Picture News
Motion Picture World
Motography
Moving Picture World
Musical America
Music Trade Review
Presto
Variety

Newspapers

Atlanta Constitution
Baltimore American
Baltimore Catholic Review
Baltimore Evening Sun
Baltimore News
Baltimore Sun
Baltimore Sunday Sun

Boston Globe
Chicago Daily Tribune
Chicago Defender
Los Angeles Times
New York Times
Washington Post

COLLECTIONS

American Theatre Organ Society Archives, Norman, Okla. (accessed in person May 2016)
Archives of the Peabody Institute, 1857–1977, Peabody Institute, Baltimore, Md. (accessed in person May 2015)
Charles Templeton Sheet Music Collection, Mississippi State University, Miss. (accessed digitally January 2017)
Embassy Theatre, Fort Wayne, Ind. (accessed digitally June 2016)
Fox Theatre Historic Collections, Atlanta, Ga. (accessed in person March 2012)
George Eastman House, Rochester, N.Y. (accessed digitally July 2011)
Historic American Sheet Music, Duke University, Durham, N.C. (accessed digitally January 2017)
Indiana Sheet Music, Indiana Historical Society, Indianapolis (accessed digitally January 2017)
IN Harmony: Sheet Music from Indiana, Indiana University, Bloomington (accessed digitally January 2017)
Lester S. Levy Sheet Music Collection, Johns Hopkins University, Baltimore, Md. (accessed digitally January 2017)
MarNan Collection, Minneapolis, Minn. (accessed in person March 2009)
May Garrettson Evans Collection, Peabody Institute, Baltimore, Md. (accessed in person May 2015)
Ohio Theatre, Columbus, Ohio (accessed digitally June 2016)

PRIMARY SOURCES

Addams, Jane. *The Spirit of Youth and the City Streets*. New York: Macmillan, 1909.
Allen, Edward Frank. *Keeping Our Fighters Fit*. New York: Century, 1918.
Balaban, Carrie. *Continuous Performance: The Story of A. J. Balaban*. New York: G. P. Putnam's Sons, 1942.
Beck, Jerry, ed. *Lost Fleischer*. Vols. 3–8. DVD.
Birge, Edward B. "The Music Supervisors National Conference," *Music Supervisors' Journal* 18, no. 4 (1932): 19–21.

Bispham, David. *The David Bispham Song Book*. Philadelphia: John C. Winston, 1920.

Bornschein, Franz C. "Community Singing at Baltimore, MD." *Musician* 20, no. 7 (1915): 436

Bouchard, George Albert. "'Original Organ Novelty.'" *American Organist* 6, no. 4 (1923): 235–37.

Bredin, Elias A. "Community Music: Song Singing or Oratorio." In *Studies in Musical Education History and Aesthetics: Papers and Proceedings of the Music Teachers' National Association at Its Thirty-Ninth Annual Meeting*, 133–41. Vol. 12. Hartford, Conn.: Music Teachers' National Association, 1917.

Breitenfeld, Emil. "Our Friend the Audience." *American Organist* 7, no. 4 (April 1924): 209–12.

Brown, Robert Bertrand. *War Camp Community Service Calls*. New York: War Camp Community Service, 1919.

Brundage, Frances F. *Music in the Camps*. Washington, D.C.: Government Printing Office, 1919.

Buhrman, T. Scott. "New York and the Cinema." In *The Complete Organ Recitalist*, edited by Herbert Westerby, 347–54. London: J. A. Godfrey and Sons, 1927.

Carberry, Frederick W. "'All Ready? Let's Go!': Singing in Rotary." *Rotarian* 27, no. 2 (1925): 25.

"Chicago: Circa 1926." *Theatre Organ* 11, no. 3 (1969): 15.

Clark, Kenneth S., ed. *The Everybody Sing Book*. New York: Paull-Pioneer Music, 1932.

Colman, Edna Mary. "The War Service of the Federation of Women's Clubs of the District of Columbia, as Directed by Mrs. Court F. Wood." Edited by M. L. Williamson. *Social Service Review: A Monthly Summary of Social Service Activities* 5, no. 6 (July 1917): 9–13.

Commission on Training Camp Activities. Washington, D.C.: War Department, 1917.

Community Sing Session: 101 Songs You Love to Sing. New York: Music Publisher's Holding Corporation, 1927.

"Community Singing Conference." *Playground: The World at Play* 11, no. 1 (1917): 238–39.

Community Song Book. New York: Rochester Chamber of Commerce, 1927.

Converse, Frederick S. "The Future of Music in America." In *Proceedings of the Conference of Cities Held in Connection with the Pageant and Masque of St. Louis*, edited by Arthur E. Bostwick, 55. Saint Louis: Pageant Drama Association, 1914.

Conway, Cora. "Community Songs and Singing." *Music Supervisors' Journal* 5, no. 1 (1918): 26–28.

"Critiques of the New Art: Rivoli." *American Organist* 8, no. 12 (1925): 429–30.

Davis, Fay Simmons. "Community Singing: An Ideal Field for the Organist and an Opportunity to Perform a Service to the Community." *American Organist* 12, no. 9 (1929): 559–60.

Davison, Archibald T. "Good Music for Community Singing." *Playground* 16, no. 1 (1922): 455–57, 498–99.

Del Castillo, L. G. "The 'Original Organ Novelty.'" *American Organist* 6, no. 8 (1923): 500–501.

"Down, Down, Down: Shall We Be Monkeys or Professionals; Must We Serve Tabloid Readers; Is There Any Remedy." *American Organist* 10, no. 3 (1927): 65.

Downes, Carrol, and Logan Marshall, eds. *The Community Chorus Book Containing Songs for All.* Philadelphia: John C. Winston, 1918.

Dykema, Peter W. "Community Music and the Spirit of Democracy." *Playground: The World at Play* 10, no. 10 (1917): 368–76.

———. "The Community Music Idea." *Quarterly Journal of the University of North Dakota* 8, no. 4 (1917): 335–46.

———. "More Life in the Open." *School Review* 19, no. 4 (1911): MF8.

———. "Music in Community Life." *Music Supervisors' Journal* 20, no. 4 (1934): 34–35, 73–74.

———. "The Relation of School and Community Music." In *Papers and Proceedings of the Music Teachers' National Association Forty-Second Annual Meeting,* edited by Karl W. Gehrkens, 78–88. Hartford, Conn.: Music Teachers' National Association, 1921.

———. "Report of Committee on Community Songs." *Journal of Proceedings of the Annual Meeting of the Music Supervisors' National Conference* 7 (1914): 103.

———. "Some Essential Passing-Tones: Certain Phases in the Community Music Movement." In *Papers and Proceedings of the Music Teachers' National Association at Its Thirty-Seventh Annual Meeting,* 182–88. Hartford, Conn.: Music Teachers' National Association, 1916.

———. "The Spread of the Community Music Idea." *Annals of the American Academy of Political and Social Science* 67, New Possibilities in Education (1916): 218–23.

Dykema, Peter W., Will Earhart, Hollis Dann, and Osbourse McConathy, eds. *Twice 55 Plus: Community Songs.* Boston: C. C. Birchard, 1919.

18 Songs for Community Singing. Boston: C. C. Birchard, 1913.

Emery-Jones, Edna. "Community Development." *Musical Monitor* 7, no. 4 (1917): 158–59.

Erb, J. Lawrence. "Music for a Better Community." *Musical Quarterly* 12, no. 3 (1926): 441–48.

Feibel, Fred. *The Fred Feibel Master Course in Organ Playing in the Popular Music Style.* Vol. 1. Boston: Boston Music Company, 1957.

———. *The Fred Feibel Master Course in Organ Playing in the Popular Music Style, Volume Two.* Boston: The Boston Music Company, 1959.

Fosdick, Raymond B. *Chronicle of a Generation: An Autobiography.* New York: Harper, 1958.

———. "The Commission on Training Camp Activities." *Proceedings of the Academy of Political Science in the City of New York* 7, no. 4 (February 1918): 163–70.

———. "The War and Navy Departments Commissions on Training Camp Activities." *Annals of the American Academy of Political and Social Science* 79, War Relief Work (1918): 130–42.

Fosdick, Raymond B., and Edward F. Allen. *Keeping Our Fighters Fit for War and After.* New York: Century, 1918.

Freund, John C. "The Musical Alliance." *Music Supervisors' Journal* 4, no. 3 (1918): 22, 24, 26, 28.

Gillette's Original "Community Sing" over CBS Every Sunday Evening: Second Official Song Book. Boston: Gillette Safety Razor, 1937.

"A Good Idea." *American Organist* 12, no. 9 (1929): 557–58.

Gordon, Edgar B. "Community Music." *Music Supervisors' Journal* 3, no. 1 (1916): 22.

Gunczy, Bettina, ed. "The Active Juniors." *National Board of Review Magazine* 6, no. 8 (1931): 11–12.

Hamilton, Wade. "The New Era: Some of the Stepping-Stones Laid Down by the Theater Profession for Those Who Would Follow in the Coming Decade." *American Organist* 10, no. 12 (1927): 321–22.

Harbin, E. O. *Parodology.* Nashville: Cokesbury Press, 1928.

Harris, Charles K. *After the Ball, Forty Years of Melody: An Autobiography.* New York: Frank-Maurice, 1926.

Holman, Genevieve Turner. "Music on the Playground II." *Playground: Community Service* 15, no. 1 (1921): 714–18.

Jenkins, Harry J. "The Saga of Koko and His Bouncing Ball." *Theatre Organ* 11, no. 5 (1969): 6–10.

Jones, Archie N. "Community Singing Goes to War." *Music Educators Journal* 29, no. 1 (1942): 39–42.

Katz, Samuel. "Theatre Management." In *The Story of the Films,* edited by J. P. Kennedy, 263–84. Chicago: A. W. Shaw, 1927.

Let's Sing Community Song Book. New York: Amsco Music Publishing, 1933.

Liberty Song Book. New York: War Camp Community Service, 1918.

Lincoln, Jennette Emeline Carpenter. *The Festival Book.* New York: A. S. Barnes, 1920.

Loew, Marcus. "The Motion Picture and Vaudeville." In *The Story of the Films,* edited by J. P. Kennedy, 285–300. Chicago: A. W. Shaw, 1927.

Low, Henrietta Baker. "Definition of Community Singing." *Musical Monitor* 10, no. 1 (1920): 29.

————. "Rural Life Betterment thru Music: Introductory Remarks by the Chairman." *Journal of Proceedings of the Thirteenth Annual Meeting of the Music Supervisors' National Conference* 13 (1920): 143.

MacKaye, Percy. *The Evergreen Tree.* New York: D. Appleton, 1917.

MacKaye, Percy, and Harry Barnhart. *The Will of Song: A Dramatic Service of Community Singing.* New York: Boni/Liveright, 1919.

Malotte, Stan, Jr. "Stanleigh Malotte: Theatre Organist." *Theatre Organ* 34, no. 3 (1992): 13–15.

Marks, Edward B. *They All Sang: From Tony Pastor to Rudy Vallée.* New York: Viking Press, 1935.

McCutchan, Dean R. G. "Community Music and the Council of Defense." In *Studies in Musical Education History and Aesthetics: Papers and Proceedings of the Music Teachers' National Association at Its Thirty-Ninth Annual Meeting,* 116–24. Vol. 12. Hartford, Conn.: Music Teachers' National Association, 1917.

McNaught, John. "Community Singing." *Journal of Education* 88, no. 3 (July 18, 1918): 467.

Medcalfe, Roy L. "Henry B. Murtagh." *American Organist* 5, no. 19 (October 1922): 450–52.

Meikel, Eddie. *"Adventures in Playing the Organ": The Professional Approach to Organ Instruction.* San Gabriel, Calif.: A. F. S. Publications, 1960.

Melluish, J. G. "Community Singing." In *Papers and Proceedings of the Music Teachers' National Association at Its Thirty-Ninth Annual Meeting,* 142–44. Vol. 12. Studies in Musical Education History and Aesthetics. Hartford, Conn.: Music Teachers' National Association, 1917.

Merson, Theodore. "Some Sorrowful Reflections of a Globe Trotter Who Has Heard Many Novel Novelties." *American Organist* 9, no. 3 (1926): 74–77.

Muri, John. "Silent Movies Weren't Silent." *Theatre Organ* 19, no. 6 (1977): 18–19.

————. "Song Slides and Theatre Organists." *Theatre Organ* 12, no. 4 (1970): 13, 15.

Official Song Book of Gillette Original Community Sing. Vol. 1. Boston: Gillette Safety Razor, 1936.

Owens, Martha Matthews. "Points to Be Considered in Organizing Community Singing." *Journal of Education* 88, no. 3 (1918): 73–75.

"The Paramount." *American Organist* 13, no. 6 (1930): 356.

Pointer, Ray, ed. *Max Fleischer's Ko-Ko Song Car-Tunes.* DVD. Atwater Village, Calif.: Inkwell Images, 2002.

Ridgway, J. A. "Community Singing in Minneapolis Parks." *Playground: Community Service* 15, no. 1 (1921): 257–58.

Rodeheaver's Sociability Songs. Chicago: Rodeheaver, 1928.

Ross, R. W. "'Original Organ Novelty': 'Cataloguing the Old Songs.'" *American Organist* 9, no. 12 (1926): 364.

"The Singing Community at War: A Guide to Wartime Uses of Community Singing." *Music Educators Journal* 29, no. 2 (1942): 15–16.

"Slides." *Reel and Slide* 1, no. 10 (December 1918): 26.

Surette, Thomas W., and Archibald T. Davison. *The Home and Community Song Book*. Boston: E. C. Schirmer Music, 1931.

Talbott, Earl G. "Palace of Splendor Disperses Its Riches." *Marquee* 22, no. 3 (1990): 8–9.

Thomson, Malcolm. "Time to Take Stock: Drifting with the Stream of Popularity and Taking the Easy Way of the Song-Slide Has Not Been Productive of Permanent Good." *American Organist* 12, no. 8 (1929): 489–90.

Tootell, George. "The Cinema Aspect." In *The Complete Organ Recitalist*, edited by Herbert Westerby, 326–28. London: J. A. Godfrey and Sons, 1927.

Tremaine, Charles M. *The History of National Music Week*. New York: National Bureau for the Advancement of Music, 1925.

———. *New York's First Music Week*. New York: National Bureau for the Advancement of Music, 1920.

"War Camp Community Service." *Playground: The World at Play* 11, no. 1 (1917): 481–513.

Warner, Harry M. "Future Developments." In *The Story of the Films*, edited by J. P. Kennedy, 319–35. Chicago: A. W. Shaw, 1927.

Westerby, Herbert. "The Cinema Organ." In *The Complete Organ Recitalist*, edited by Herbert Westerby, 324–25. London: J. A. Godfrey and Sons, 1927.

White, Lew. "The Future Theater Organist: Present Methods Are Excellent for Today but Tomorrow Will Bring a New Demand for Even Cleverer Performers and Finer Musicians and They Who Are Prepared Will Reap a Rich Reward." *American Organist* 11, no. 3 (1928): 106–7.

Whitworth, Reginald. *The Cinema and Theatre Organ: A Comprehensive Description of This Instrument, Its Constituent Parts, and Its Uses*. London: Musical Opinion, 1932.

Widenor, D. Kenneth. "Crawford at the Chicago." *American Organist* 6, no. 11 (1923): 689–92.

Witmark, Isidore, and Isaac Goldberg. *The Story of the House of Witmark: From Ragtime to Swingtime*. New York: L. Furman, 1939.

SECONDARY SOURCES

Abel, Richard. *Americanizing the Movies and "Movie Mad" Audiences, 1910–1914*. Berkeley: University of California Press, 2006.

———. "Reframing the Vaudeville/Moving Picture Debate, with Illustrated Songs." In *The Tenth Muse: Cinema and Other Arts*, edited by Leonardo Quaresima and Laura Vichi, 473–84. Udine, Italy: Forum, 2001.

——. "That Most American of Attractions, the Illustrated Song." In *Sounds of Early Cinema*, edited by Richard Abel and Rick Altman, 143–55. Bloomington: Indiana University Press, 2001.

Ahlquist, Karen, ed. *Chorus and Community*. Urbana: University of Illinois Press, 2006.

Altman, Rick. "Cinema and Popular Song: The Lost Tradition." In *Soundtrack Available: Essays on Film and Popular Music*, edited by Pamela Robertson Wojcik and Arthur Knight, 19–30. Durham, N.C.: Duke University Press, 2001.

——. "The Living Nickelodeon." In *Sounds of Early Cinema*, edited by Richard Abel and Rick Altman, 232–40. Bloomington: Indiana University Press, 2001.

——. *Silent Film Sound*. New York: Columbia University Press, 2004.

Anderson, Gillian B. "The Presentation of Silent Films, or, Music as Anaesthesia." *Journal of Musicology* 5, no. 2 (1987): 257–95.

Anderson, Michael G. "The Wrong Kind of Nickel Madness: Pricing Problems for Pittsburgh Nickelodeons." *Cinema Journal* 5, no. 2 (2002): 71–96.

Austen, Jake. "Hidey Hidey Hidey Ho . . . Boop-Boop-A-Doop!" In *The Cartoon Music Book*, edited by Daniel Goldmark and Yuval Taylor, 61–66. Chicago: A Cappella Books, 2002.

Averill, Gage. *Four Parts, No Waiting: A Social History of American Barbershop Harmony*. New York: Oxford University Press, 2003.

Avery, Susan, Casey Hayes, and Cindy Bell. "Community Choirs: Expressions of Identity through Vocal Performance." In *Community Music Today*, edited by Kari K. Veblen, Stephen J. Messenger, Marissa Silverman, and David J. Elliott, 249–60. Lanham, Md.: Rowan and Littlefield, 2013.

Balaban, David. *The Chicago Movie Palaces of Balaban and Katz*. Charleston, S.C.: Arcadia Publishing, 2006.

Balio, Tino. *Grand Design: Hollywood as a Modern Business Enterprise, 1930–1939*. Vol. 5 of *History of the American Cinema*. Berkeley: University of California Press, 1996.

Balsnes, Anne Haugland. "Choral Singing, Health and Quality of Life: The Story of Diana." *Arts and Health: An International Journal for Research, Policy and Practice* 4, no. 3 (2012): 249–61.

Balsnes, Anne Haugland, and Dag Jansson. "Unfreezing Identities: Exploring Choral Singing in the Workplace." *International Journal of Community Music* 8, no. 2 (2015): 163–78.

Bloom, Ken, ed. *Brooklyn Sees Stars: Theatre and Theatres across the Great Bridge*. Vol. 37. THS Annual. Chicago: Theatre Historical Society of America, 2010.

Bowser, Eileen. *The Transformation of Cinema, 1907–1915*. Vol. 2 of *History of the American Cinema*. Berkeley: University of California Press, 1990.

Bradley, Edwin M. *The First Hollywood Sound Shorts, 1926–1931*. Reprint, Jefferson, N.C.: McFarland, 2009.

Bristow, Nancy K. *Making Men Moral*. New York: New York University Press, 1996.

"Brooklyn Paramount Theatre." *Marquee* 30, no. 3 (1998): 10–18.

Bush, Jeffrey E., and Andrew Krikun. "Community Music in North America: Historical Foundations." In *Community Music Today*, edited by Kari K. Veblen, Stephen J. Messenger, Marissa Silverman, and David J. Elliott, 13–24. Lanham, Md.: Rowan and Littlefield, 2013.

Butsch, Richard. "American Movie Audiences of the 1930s." *International Labor and Working Class History* 59 (2001): 106–20.

———. *The Making of American Audiences: From Stage to Television, 1750–1990.* Cambridge: Cambridge University Press, 2000.

Cabarga, Leslie. *The Fleischer Story.* Rev. ed. New York: DaCapo Press, 1988.

Campbell, Gavin James. "'A Higher Mission Than Merely to Please the Ear': Music and Social Reform in American, 1900–25." *Musical Quarterly* 8, no. 2 (2000): 259–86.

Carbine, Mary. "'The Finest outside the Loop': Motion Picture Exhibition in Chicago's Black Metropolis, 1905–1928." In *Silent Film*, edited by Richard Abel, 234–62. London: Athlone Press, 1996.

Chang, E. Christina. "The Singing Program of World War I: The Crusade for a Singing Army." *Journal of Historical Research in Music Education* 23, no. 1 (2001): 19–45.

Châteauvert, Jean, and André Gaudreault. "The Noises of Spectators, or the Spectator as Additive Spectacle." In *The Sounds of Early Cinema*, edited by Richard Abel and Rick Altman, 183–91. Bloomington: Indiana University Press, 2001.

Chybowski, Julia J. "Developing American Taste: A Cultural History of the Early Twentieth-Century Music Appreciation Movement." Ph.D. diss., University of Wisconsin–Madison, 2007.

"Cinema Treasures." February 8, 2013. http://cinematreasures.org.

Cleary, Sarah. "'Don't Dream It, Be It': The Method in the Madness of *The Rocky Horror Picture Show*." In *Fan Phenomena: The Rocky Horror Picture Show*, edited by Marisa C. Hayes, 108–17. Chicago: Intellect, 2015.

Clift, Stephen. "Singing, Wellbeing, and Health." In *Music, Health, and Wellbeing*, edited by Raymond A. R. MacDonald, Gunter Kreutz, and Laura Mitchell, 113–24. Oxford: Oxford University Press, 2012.

Cohen, Lizabeth. "Encountering Mass Culture at the Grassroots: The Experience of Chicago Workers in the 1920s." *American Quarterly* 41, no. 1 (1989): 6–33.

"Community Sing." In *The Encyclopedia of Old-Time Radio*, 174. Oxford: Oxford University Press, 1998.

Cook, Malcolm. "Animating the Audience: Singalong Films in Britain in the 1920s." In *The Sounds of the Silents in Britain*, edited by Julie Brown and Annette Davison, 222–40. Oxford: Oxford University Press, 2012.

———. "Sing Them Again: Audience Singing in Silent Film." In *Music and Sound in Silent Cinema: From the Nickelodeon to the Artist*, edited by Ruth Barton and Simon Trezise. Routledge Music and Screen Media Series. London: Routledge, forthcoming.

Corbett, Kevin J. "Empty Seats: The Missing History of Movie-Watching." *Journal of Film and Video* 50, no. 4 (1998): 34–48.

Couvares, Francis G. "Hollywood, Main Street, and the Church: Trying to Censor the Movies before the Production Code." In *Movie Censorship and American Culture*, edited by Francis G. Couvares, 129–58. Washington, D.C.: Smithsonian Institution Press, 1996.

Crafton, Donald. *Before Mickey: The Animated Film, 1898–1928.* Chicago: University of Chicago Press, 1993.

———. *The Talkies: American Cinema's Transition to Sound, 1926–1931.* Vol. 4 of *History of the American Cinema.* Berkeley: University of California Press, 1999.

DeBauche, Leslie Midkiff. "Reminiscences of the Past, Conditions of the Present: At the Movies in Milwaukee in 1918." In *American Movie Audiences: From the Turn of the Century to the Early Sound Era*, edited by Melvyn Stokes and Richard Maltby, 129–39. London: BFI Publishing, 1999.

deCordova, Richard. "Ethnography and Exhibition: The Child Audience, the Hays Office and Saturday Matinees." *Camera Obscura* 23, no. 2 (1990): 90–107.

Dial, Donna. "Cartoons in Paradise: How the Fleischer Brothers Moved to Miami and Lost Their Studio." *Florida Historical Quarterly* 78, no. 3 (2000): 309–30.

Disharoon, Richard Alan. "A History of Municipal Music in Baltimore, 1914–1947." Ph.D. diss., University of Maryland, 1980.

Doherty, Thomas. "This Is Where We Came In: The Audible Screen and the Voluble Audience of Early Sound Cinema." In *American Movie Audiences: From the Turn of the Century to the Early Sound Era*, edited by Melvyn Stokes and Richard Maltby, 143–63. London: BFI Publishing, 1999.

Drew, Rob. *Karaoke Knights: An Ethnographic Rhapsody.* Walnut Creek, Calif.: Altamira Press, 2001.

———. "'Scenes' Dimensions of Karaoke in the United States." In *Music Scenes: Local, Translocal and Virtual*, edited by Andy Bennett and Richard A. Peterson, 64–79. Nashville: Vanderbilt University Press, 2004.

Erdman, Andrew L. *Blue Vaudeville: Sex, Morals and the Mass Marketing of Amusement, 1895–1915.* Jefferson, N.C.: McFarland, 2004.

Fleischer, Richard. *Out of the Inkwell: Max Fleischer and the Animation Revolution.* Lexington: University Press of Kentucky, 2005.

Fones-Wolf, Elizabeth. "Sound Comes to the Movies: The Philadelphia Musicians' Struggle against Recorded Music." *Pennsylvania Magazine of History and Biography* 118, nos. 1/2 (1994): 3–31.

Foy, Patricia S. "A Brief Look at the Community Song Movement." *Music Educators Journal* 76, no. 5 (1990): 26–27.

Fuller, Kathryn Helgesen. *At the Picture Show: Small-Town Audiences and the Creation of Movie Fan Culture.* Charlottesville: University of Virginia Press, 2000.

———. "'You Can Have the Strand in Your Own Town': The Marginalization of Small Town Film Exhibition in the Silent Era." *Film History* 6, no. 2 (1994): 166–77.

Garcia, Desirée J. *The Migration of Musical Film: From Ethnic Margins to American Mainstream.* New Brunswick, N.J.: Rutgers University Press, 2014.

Garrett, Charles Hiroshi. "Chinatown, Whose Chinatown? Defining America's Borders with Musical Orientalism." *Journal of the American Musicological Society* 57, no. 1 (2004): 119–74.

Gere, Anne Ruggles. *Intimate Practices: Literacy and Cultural Work in U.S. Women's Clubs, 1880–1920.* Urbana: University of Illinois Press, 1997.

Goff, James R., Jr. *Close Harmony: A History of Southern Gospel.* Chapel Hill: University of North Carolina Press, 2002.

Goldmark, Daniel. "Before Willie: Reconsidering Music and the Animated Cartoon of the 1920s." In *Beyond the Soundtrack: Representing Music in Cinema,* edited by D. Goldmark, L. Kramer, and R. Leppert, 225–45. Berkeley: University of California Press, 2007.

———. "Creating Desire on Tin Pan Alley." *Musical Quarterly* 90, no. 2 (2007): 197–229.

———. *Tunes for 'Toons: Music and the Hollywood Cartoon.* Berkeley: University of California Press, 2005.

Gomery, Douglas. "The Coming of Sound to the American Cinema." Ph.D. diss., University of Wisconsin, 1975.

———. "Film and Business History: The Development of an American Mass Entertainment Industry." *Journal of Contemporary History* 19, no. 1 (1984): 89–103.

———. "A Movie-Going Capital: Washington, D.C., in the History of Movie Presentation." *Washington History* 9, no. 1 (1997): 4–23.

———. "The Movies Become Big Business: Publix Theatres and the Chain Store Strategy." *Cinema Journal* 18, no. 2 (1979): 26–40.

———. *Shared Pleasures: A History of Movie Presentation in the United States.* Madison: University of Wisconsin Press, 1992.

Gorney, Sondra. "On Children's Cinema: America and Britain." *Hollywood Quarterly* 3, no. 1 (1947): 56–62.

Green, Shannon Louise. "'Art for Life's Sake': Music Schools and Activities in U.S. Social Settlement Houses, 1892–1942." Ph.D. diss., University of Wisconsin–Madison, 1998.

Hall, Ben. *The Best Remaining Seats: The Story of the Golden Age of the Movie Palace.* New York: Clarkson N. Potter, 1961.

Hansen, Miriam. *Babel and Babylon: Spectatorship in American Silent Film.* Cambridge, Mass.: Harvard University Press, 1991.

Hanssen, F. Andrew. "Vertical Integration during the Hollywood Studio Era." *Journal of Law and Economics* 53, no. 3 (2010): 519–43.

Hark, Ina Rae. "The 'Theater Man' and 'The Girl in the Box Office': Gender in the Discourse of Motion Picture Theatre Management." *Film History* 6, no. 2 (1994): 178–87.

Headley, Robert K. *Motion Picture Exhibition in Washington, D.C.* Jefferson, N.C.: McFarland, 1999.

Herzog, Amy. "Discordant Visions: The Peculiar Musical Images of the Soundies Jukebox Film." *American Music* 22, no. 1 (2004): 27–39.

Herzog, Charlotte Kopac. "The Motion Picture Theater and Film Exhibition —1896–1932 (Volumes I and II)." Ph.D. diss., Northwestern University, 1980.

Higgins, Lee. *Community Music in Theory and in Practice.* Oxford: Oxford University Press, 2012.

Higgins, Lee, and Lee Willingham. *Engaging in Community Music: An Introduction.* New York: Routledge, 2017.

Howe, Sondra Wieland. *Women Music Educators in the United States: A History.* Lanham, Md.: Scarecrow Press, 2013.

Jones, Janna. "The Downtown Picture Palace: The Significance of Place, Memory, and Cinema." Ph.D. diss., University of South Florida, 1998.

Jowett, Garth S., Ian C. Jarvie, and Kathryn H. Fuller. *Children and the Movies: Media Influence and the Payne Fund Controversy.* Cambridge: Cambridge University Press, 1996.

Kaskowitz, Sheryl. *God Bless America: The Surprising History of an Iconic Song.* Oxford: Oxford University Press, 2013.

Katz, Mark. "Making America More Musical through the Phonograph, 1900–1930." *American Music* 16, no. 4 (1998), 448–76.

Kinerk, Michael D., and Dennis W. Wilhelm. "Dream Palaces: The Motion Picture Playhouse in the Sunshine State." *Journal of Decorative and Propaganda Arts* 23, Florida Theme Issue (1998): 208–37.

King, Lila. *Framing the Cinema: Brenograph Slide Images from the Fox Theatre Collection.* Atlanta: Preservation Maintenance Press, 2000.

Klenotic, Jeffrey F. "'Like Nickels in a Slot': Children of the American Working Classes at the Neighborhood Movie House." *Velvet Light Trap* 48 (2001): 20–33.

Klos, Lloyd E. "The Ted Meyn Story." *Theatre Organ* 14, no. 2 (1972): 7–11.

Koch, Franklin W. "Cooperative Promotional Efforts of the Music Supervisors National Conference and the National Bureau for the Advancement of Music." *Journal of Research in Music Education* 38, no. 4 (1990): 269–81.

Koszarski, Richard. *An Evening's Entertainment: The Age of the Silent Feature Picture, 1915–1928.* Vol. 3 of *History of the American Cinema.* Berkeley: University of California Press, 1994.

———. "Subway Commandos: Hollywood Filmmakers at the Signal Corps Photographic Center." *Film History* 14, nos. 3/4 (2002): 296–315.

Lancaster, Kurt. "When Spectators Become Performers: Contemporary Performance Entertainments Meet the Needs of an 'Unsettled' Audience." *Journal of Popular Culture* 30, no. 4 (1997): 75–88.

Landon, John W. *Behold the Mighty Wurlitzer: The History of the Theatre Pipe Organ.* Westport, Conn.: Greenwood Press, 1983.

———. *Jesse Crawford: Poet of the Organ; Wizard of the Mighty Wurlitzer.* Vestal, N.Y.: Vestal Press, 1974.

Lee, William R. "Music Education and Rural Reform, 1900–1925." *Journal of Research in Music Education* 45, no. 2 (1997): 306–26.

———. "A New Look at a Significant Cultural Moment: The Music Supervisors National Conference 1907–1932." *Journal of Historical Research in Music Education* 28, no. 2 (2007): 93–110.

Lehman, Christopher P. *The Colored Cartoon: Black Representation in American Animated Short Films.* Amherst: University of Massachusetts Press, 2007.

Lethbridge, Stefanie. "History from below: Stanley Holloway's Monologues for the Variety Stage." In *History and Humour: British and American Perspectives*, edited by Barbara Korte and Doris Lechner, 69–86. Wetzlar, Germany: Transcript, 2013.

Levin, Steve, ed. *Oriental Theatre.* Vol. 24. Annual. Chicago: Theatre Historical Society of America, 1994.

Levine, Lawrence W. *Highbrow/Lowbrow: The Emergence of Cultural Hierarchy in America.* Reprint, Cambridge: Harvard University Press, 1990.

Maltby, Richard. "Sticks, Hicks and Flaps: Classical Hollywood's Generic Conception of Its Audiences." In *Identifying Hollywood's Audiences: Cultural Identity and the Movies*, edited by Melvyn Stokes and Richard Maltby, 23–41. London: BFI Publishing, 1999.

Maltin, Leonard. *Of Mice and Magic: A History of American Animated Cartoons.* Rev. Ed. New York: Plume Book, 1987.

Marsh, John L. "Dick Powell: The Indianapolis Years, 1926–1929." *Indiana Magazine of History* 81, no. 4 (1985): 351–77.

Massey, Jonathan. "Organic Architecture and Direct Democracy: Claude Bragdon's Festivals of Song and Light." *Journal of the Society of Architectural Historians* 65, no. 4 (2006): 578–613.

Mathiesen, Thomas. *A Catalogue of Brenograph and Lantern Slides from the Ohio Theatre, Columbus, Ohio.* August 2015. http://fwembassytheatre.org/wp-content/uploads/2016/11/Ohio_Slides_Cat.pdf.

Mathiesen, Thomas, and Penelope Mathiesen. *A Catalogue of Brenograph and Lantern Slides at the Embassy Theatre, Fort Wayne, Indiana.* June 2016. http://fwembassytheatre.org/wp-content/uploads/2016/11/Embassy_Slides_Cat.pdf.

McGuire, Laura M. "A Movie House in Space and Time: Frederick Kiesler's Film Arts Guild Cinema, New York, 1929." *Studies in the Decorative Arts* 14, no. 2 (2007): 45–78.

Melnick, Ross. *American Showman: Samuel 'Roxy' Rothafel and the Birth of the Entertainment Industry*. New York: Columbia University Press, 2012.

——. "Station R-O-X-Y: Roxy and the Radio." *Film History* 17, nos. 2/3 (2005): 217–33.

Melnick, Ross, and Andreas Fuchs. *Cinema Treasures: A New Look at Classic Movie Theaters*. Saint Paul, Minn.: MBI, 2004.

Merritt, Russell. "The Nickelodeon Theater, 1905–1914: Building an Audience for the Movies." In *Exhibition, the Film Reader*, edited by Ina Rae Hark, 21–30. London: Routledge, 2002.

Miller, Karl Hagstrom. *Segregating Sound: Inventing Folk and Pop Music in the Age of Jim Crow*. Durham, N.C.: Duke, 2010.

Miller, Ron, Rita Seiden Miller, and Stephen Karp. "The Fourth Largest City in America—A Sociological History of Brooklyn." In *Brooklyn USA*, edited by Rita Seiden Miller, 3–44. New York: Brooklyn College Press, 1979.

Mooney, Matthew. "'All Join in the Chorus': Sheet Music, Vaudeville, and the Formation of American Cinema, 1904–1914." Ph.D. diss., University of California, Irvine, 2006.

Morgan-Ellis, Esther M. "Edward Meikel and Community Singing in a Neighborhood Picture Palace, 1925–1929." *American Music* 32 (2014): 172–200.

——. "Nostalgia, Sentiment, and Cynicism in Images of 'After the Ball.'" *Magic Lantern Gazette* 23 (2011): 3–8.

——. "Warren Kimsey and Community Singing at Camp Gordon, 1917–1918." *Journal of Historical Research in Music Education*. January 2017. http://journals.sagepub.com/doi/full/10.1177/1536600616677995.

Morrison, Craig. "From Nickelodeon to Picture Palace and Back." *Design Quarterly* 93, Film Spaces (1974): 6–17.

Murray, Michael, and Alexandra Lamont. "Community Music and Social/Health Psychology: Linking Theoretical and Practical Concerns." In *Music, Health, and Wellbeing*, edited by Raymond A. R. MacDonald, Gunter Kreutz, and Laura Mitchell, 76–86. Oxford: Oxford University Press, 2012.

Nasaw, David. *Going Out: The Rise and Fall of Public Amusements*. New York: BasicBooks, 1993.

Naylor, David. *American Picture Palaces: The Architecture of Fantasy*. New York: Van Nostrand Rheinhold, 1981.

Neely, Jack. *The Tennessee Theatre: A Grand Entertainment Palace*. Knoxville: Historic Tennessee Theatre Foundation, 2015.

Newman, Scott A. "Boundless Pleasures: Young Chicagoans, Commercial Amusements, and the Revitalization of Urban Life, 1900–1930." Ph.D. diss., Loyola University, 2004.

Newson, John. "'A Sound Idea': Music for Animated Films." *Quarterly Journal of the Library of Congress* 37, nos. 3/4 (1980): 279–309.

"New York Paramount: Seventy-Fifth Anniversary Tribute." *Marquee* 33, no. 3 (2001): 26–29.

Norton, Kay. *Singing and Wellbeing: Ancient Wisdom, Modern Proof.* New York: Routledge, 2016.

Parker, Alison M. "Mothering the Movies: Women Reformers and Popular Culture." In *Movie Censorship and American Culture,* edited by Francis G. Couvares, 73–96. Washington, D.C.: Smithsonian Institution Press, 1996.

Parot, Joseph. "The Racial Dilemma in Chicago's Polish Neighborhoods, 1920–1970." *Polish American Studies* 32, no. 2 (1975): 27–37.

Pawley, Alisun, and Daniel Müllensiefen. "The Science of Singing Along: A Quantitative Field Study on Sing-Along Behavior in the North of England." *Music Perception* 30, no. 2 (2012): 129–46.

Rosenzweig, Roy. *Eight Hours for What We Will: Workers and Leisure in an Industrial City, 1870–1920.* Cambridge: Cambridge University Press, 1983.

Ross, Steven J. *Working-Class Hollywood: Silent Film and the Shaping of Class in America.* Princeton, N.J.: Princeton University Press, 1998.

Russell, Dave. "Abiding Memories: The Community Singing Movement and English Social Life in the 1920s." *Popular Music* 27, no. 1 (2008): 117–33.

Sammond, Nicholas. *Birth of an Industry: Blackface Minstrelsy and the Rise of American Animation.* Durham, N.C.: Duke University Press, 2015.

———. "'Gentlemen, Please Be Seated': Racial Masquerade and Sadomasochism in 1930s Animation." In *Burnt Cork: Traditions and Legacies of Blackface Minstrelsy,* edited by Stephen Johnson, 164–90. Amherst: University of Massachusetts Press, 2012.

Scherer, Herbert. "Marquee on Main Street: Jack Liebenberg's Movie Theaters: 1928–1941." *Journal of Decorative and Propaganda Arts* 1 (1986): 62–75.

Semmes, Clovis E. *The Regal Theater and Black Culture.* New York: Palgrave Macmillan, 2006.

Slowinska, Maria A. "Consuming Illusion, Illusions of Consumability: American Movie Palaces of the 1920s." *Amerikastudien/American Studies* 50, no. 4 (2005): 575–601.

Snyder-Grenier, Ellen M. *Brooklyn!: An Illustrated History.* Philadelphia: Temple University Press, 1996.

Spurgeon, Alan L. "The Community Music Association in Flint, Michigan, 1917–1920." *Bulletin of Historical Research in Music Education* 16, no. 1 (1994): 29–42.

Strasberg, Andy, Bob Thompson, and Tim Wiles. *Baseball's Greatest Hit: The Story of Take Me out to the Ball Game.* New York: Hal Leonard, 2008.

Streible, Dan. "The Harlem Theater: Black Film Exhibition in Austin, Texas: 1920–1973." In *Black American Cinema,* edited by Manthia Diawara, 221–36. New York: Routledge, 1993.

Stromgren, Richard L. "The Moving Picture World of W. Stephen Bush." *Film History* 2, no. 1 (1988): 13–22.

Suisman, David. *Selling Sounds*. Cambridge: Harvard University Press, 2009.

Valentine, Maggie. *The Show Starts on the Sidewalk: An Architectural History of the Movie Theater*. New Haven, Conn.: Yale University Press, 1994.

Waller, Gregory A. "Imagining and Promoting the Small-Town Theater." *Cinema Journal* 44, no. 3 (2005): 3–19.

Widen, Larry, and Judi Anderson. "Silver Screens: A Pictorial History of Milwaukee's Movie Palaces." *Wisconsin Magazine of History* 90, no. 2 (2006–7): 24–27.

Wolff, Tamsen. "Theater." In *The Oxford Handbook of the American Musical*, edited by Raymond Knapp, Mitchell Morris, and Stacy Wolf, 127–35. Oxford: Oxford University Press, 2011.

Wolner, Edward W. "The City-within-a-City and Skyscraper Patronage in the 1920s." *Journal of Architectural Education* 42, no. 2 (1989): 10–23.

Zarafonetis, Michael James. "The 'Fabulous' Fox Theatre and Atlanta, 1929–1975." Ph.D. diss., Auburn University, 2010.

INDEX